Malawi

Lilongwe ◉

Mozambique

rge

LAKE
CAHORA
Zumbu BASSA

Kanyemba

Songo

Lupata Gorge

a Pools

Tete

◉ Harare

Tambara

Dona Ana Bridge
(longest rail bridge in Africa, 3.7 km)

Mutarara

Sena

Shupanga

Quelimane

Marrompu

Mary Moffat Livingstone's grave

Chinde

Mozambique Channel

Batoka Gorge | 26 July | **55**
Refugees in their own country | 27 July | **56**
Lake Kariba | 4 August | **64**
Fothergills Island | 6 August | **66**
Kariba town | 13 August | **73**
Maputa Gorge | 14 August | **74**
Zumbu Border Mozambique | 17 August | **77**
Andy's fishing camp | 23 August | **83**
Mawaya's Island and lion camp | 25 August | **85**
Cahora Bassa wall | 28 August | **88**
Tete Island camp | 30 August | **90**
Lupata Gorge | 2 September | **93**
Sena Bridge | 4 September | **95**
Mary Livingstone's grave | 9 September | **99**
Paddle into the sea

Zambezi

**The First Solo Journey down
Africa's Mighty River**

Zambezi

The First Solo Journey down Africa's Mighty River

MIKE BOON

CONTENTS

PROLOGUE

I had decided to paddle in a kayak, solo and without formal ongoing support, from the source of the Zambezi to its mouth – a journey of just under 3 000 kilometres. I anticipated it would take three to four months, but time was difficult to gauge accurately as unexpected obstacles were sure to arrive.

I chose to use a Necky Eskia kayak, a design capable of handling both rough white water and flat stretches. It is constructed from Teflon, making it practically unbreakable. It also has a slightly larger storage capacity than most other designs, an essential feature for this trip.

In completing a risk assessment of the journey it became clear that the risks were very high. These escalated dramatically because I would be entirely alone. The situation in 2002 when I embarked on the journey looked like this:

Northwest Zambia

The area was being inundated by refugees fleeing the war in the Democratic Republic of Congo (DRC). Their desperate situation, especially outside of formal refugee camps, posed a danger of theft or assault. Various Congolese anti-government rebel groups were also making use of this relatively safe spot to rest from the fighting in their country. On top of this, well-armed bandits with allegiance to nobody were wandering in and out of Zambia and the DRC.

The Angola/Zambia border area

The area was host to bandits and to civilians displaced by the Angolan civil war. Unita troops fleeing into Zambia after the death of their leader, Jonas Savimbi, could also be encountered.

Angola

Angola's 30-year civil war had only just come to an end. All authorities described the country as extremely dangerous and advised against any travelling outside the capital, Luanda.

In the two months since the death of Jonas Savimbi, many Unita troops had accepted an amnesty and had handed themselves in to be demobbed. However, many others had chosen to splinter into small groups and disappear into the bush.

Savimbi was killed in Moxico Province where the bulk of his remaining troops were likely to be. This is the province through which the Zambezi River flows in Angola. Landmines were an ever-present danger.

No backup (airlift or other) could be expected. Other places on the river were so remote as to render such support most unlikely.

Zimbabwe

Strong anti-white sentiment could be expected, especially in the security forces and amongst the so-called war veterans. The rural population was starving, leading to desperation and crime.

Mozambique

Although the war in Mozambique was over, the country was still littered with anti-personnel mines. The stretch below Cahora Bassa was known to be home to very aggressive crocodiles.

The river

The Zambezi was uncharted in Angola, so there was little knowledge of the whereabouts of big rapids or falls. However, some of the biggest rapids and cataracts in the world could be expected.

In addition to the political and geographic challenges, I had to prepare myself for any number of medical eventualities. Injury and trauma could be caused by assault or by bites from snakes, hippos, crocodiles and other animals. Possible illnesses included malaria, hepatitis, dysentery and infection. I needed to be able to self-administer any number of treatments, such as suturing wounds, setting fractures and carrying out amputations. Snake bites would have to be treated without anti-venom as none could be carried in due to lack of refrigeration.

Being alone meant no help, no matter what the difficulty. Even a relatively simple issue, such as being trapped in the kayak against a boulder or a brush obstacle, could lead to great difficulty and potential death.

The risks were high but, I believed, acceptable. This confidence was based on extensive bush, survival, military, mountaineering and first-aid experience. Also, a fair dose of humility, recognising that I would never be able to fight the river but would need to work with its rhythms and moods.

Source of the mighty Zambezi to Cazombo, Angola

- Arrival at the source
- A close escape
- Into a war zone
- Freezing nights

Just off the simple road from Mwinilunga to Jimbe in northwest Zambia there is an old signboard with an arrow that reads 'The source of the Zambezi River'. A stone's throw from the DRC and barely kilometres from Angola, the overgrown track makes its way through beautiful mopane forests to a dilapidated ruin and a plaque erected in 1964, just after Zambia achieved its independence.

With mounting excitement I leave the Landy and follow the path down the hill. The humidity here is tangible – the forest lush – tangled in lianas and covered with hundreds of yellow and black orb spider webs. It is very quiet here. There before me is a tiny pool of water, and as I make my way uphill from it, I find the spot where the water bubbles up from the very earth.

Here is the source of the mighty Zambezi, a spot no bigger than a dinner plate. The great river does not start

ZAMBIA
INDEPENDENCE MONUMENT
AT SOURCE OF THE GREAT
ZAMBEZI RIVER
4.8 KM →

with modest drips and trickles on mountain tops; she wells up powerfully from the gentle slope of a humble hillside. There is already depth to her – she knows her purpose and her journey before it has even begun.

I gather up some of her precious bounty to take with me to the sea and drink my fill. More wonderful than man's best champagne. Cleaner, fresher and lighter than any imagined elixir. This is a holy, sacred place, and in revered silence I acknowledge her.

Now I wave goodbye to my wife, Annie, who is holding her own bottle of source water, and take the first strokes with my paddle. Rounding a corner, I am suddenly alone with the river. A snake slithers across the water to my kayak and then drifts alongside. It stares at me for several seconds, and then it is gone. I acknowledge the implied message of the dangers that lie ahead for me, then lean forward and paddle.

For the entire year preceding this expedition I had led a deeply emotional and spiritually sapping transformation of a major business organisation. Just eight years after the end of apartheid in South Africa, people continued to struggle with their pain, as they no doubt will for many years to come. I had taken 'healing' into the workplace, recognising that an organisation did not exist in a vacuum – it was an integral part of the society in which it resided. If anger, fear, discrimination, prejudice and even hatred, all related to low trust, exist in society they most certainly will be present in the workplace. I had listened to stories of rape, murder and the awful stripping of human dignity. I had heard first-hand accounts of the most appalling abuse of power, not told by politicians with agendas but by ordinary people in the workplace.

I was quite simply burnt out. I knew at my very core that unless I shed myself of all encumbrances and stripped myself down to the essence of who and what I was, I would die. Death of the spirit is even more terrible than physical death! I never consciously worked this out – I was too exhausted – I simply listened to the first voice of my intuition. I needed to crawl into a cave, naked with my wounds, and heal. This was why I was now on the Zambezi.

Crossed by three quaint, rustic log walkways, the river between the source in Zambia and the Angolan border is narrow, winding,

Opposite, top: Orb spiders are everywhere in the tangled forest. **This page, top:** Annie gently holds her bottle of water drawn at the source. I do the same. We promise to pour these into the Indian Ocean together when I reach the mouth. Both of us feel the crush in our hearts.

and strong flowing. The small rapids are not obstacles – but the overhanging trees jammed across the five-metre wide stream present a significant challenge. Coming around a sharp corner in a fast current to be suddenly brought up against an impenetrable barrier of branches is dangerous and difficult to overcome. Several times I use my panga. Still other occasions have me struggling in deep water alongside my heavy craft.

One such encounter with an overhanging tree has me literally up the creek without a paddle! The fast-flowing stream rounds a sharp corner, sending me straight into a treefall, with my kayak forced into and under the branches. I use my paddle to fend off a branch, but it becomes jammed in a fork in the tree. I struggle with it, but the water forces me forward and deep into the tangled branches. My kayak begins to roll over in the current. To prevent this, and to stop my jammed paddle from bending or, worse still, breaking, I'm forced to let it go. The wash is strong and dangerous, but using both my hands I am able to right the kayak and claw my way free. Now, however, I drift downstream without a paddle and the distance between us grows quickly. I roll over sideways and climb out of the kayak, then begin swimming to the bank. I cannot feel the ground underfoot and the bank is steep, so I have to struggle and flounder upstream in deep water, clinging to brush with one hand while dragging my heavy kayak behind me with the other.

From bitter and tragic experience, I also know that just an instant's doubt or hesitation is what will determine success or failure. In this case, perhaps, life or death.

Losing a paddle in the middle of a big rapid or whirl on a river such as this could cost me my life – my solar plexus tightens with anxiety. My mind is racing. I know that my paddle is jammed in a very awkward place near the centre of the river. I do have a spare paddle, but it's collapsible, so of a less robust design. If I proceed with the spare alone, I'll have no backup unless I construct something myself. I can do this from materials the bush will offer, but this paddle, in turn, will be weaker than the existing spare. I know that the rigours of the enormous river and rapids that lie ahead will test even the most advanced equipment. It's simply too early in the expedition to accept such a loss. Once I realise this, I assess the physical risks and possible approaches to the recovery of the paddle with extreme care. There is only one option, but I decide it is possible. As soon as I have made the decision, I eradicate all other thoughts and emotions. I understand the power of the mind and I know that the faintest negative thought or feeling will instantly convert into hesitant physical action. From bitter and tragic experience, I also know that just an instant's doubt or hesitation is what will determine success or failure. In this case, perhaps, life or death.

The branches onto which I climb are not big enough to singly bear my weight. If they break and I fall through the brush into the current below I could easily become entangled and drown. I spread my weight as evenly as possible between my body, feet, and hands, all resting on different branches, and creep my way out over the river. The paddle is jammed fast, but eventually comes loose and I tightrope myself back to the bank.

Relieved, I give myself a mental pat on the back, climb into my kayak, and only now allow myself the luxury of scanning the water for crocodiles. Then, holding firmly on to my paddle, I take my first strokes, and once again I am on my way.

Periodically I come across fish traps built across the river by villagers. Here, vertical logs are jammed into cracks in rocks and crisscrossed with horizontal sticks forming near watertight dams. In small gaps in these walls, bell-like fish traps are inserted and it is here that fish are taken.

Imperceptibly, kilometre by kilometre, the river widens. Still snaking its way around sharp bends, creating near oxbows, it remains fast and strong. The water is fresh and clear and the bird life wonderful. Very soon the riverine bush is interspersed with three-metre high grass, tough and coarse, with banks that drop sharply into the stream making an exit very difficult.

Rounding a corner I surprise two women having a bath. They are balanced on a tree that stoops low over the water. Awkwardly reaching down for water they almost fall out of the tree in terror as I appear. Naked bodies flee along the bough, but my reassuring calls calm them and they slow down. Quickly drawing wraps around themselves they recover and are able to hold up astonished hands as I sweep by in the fast flow.

A young child sees me and soon 10 or 12 children run, delighted, along the bank trying to keep pace with me. I pass under one of the walkway bridges where three men call down to me. Around the corner a woman does her washing on the bank, and I pull over to explain my journey to the men, who have climbed off the bridge. They listen, astonished, and I prepare to leave, offering a pack of my biscuits to the woman in farewell. I give a final wave and begin to paddle, and a young man calls out with deep sincerity in his voice, 'May God be with you on your journey.' It is a poignant moment, as if he has touched my very soul.

As evening approaches I see a large cloud of smoke and I can hear the crackling roar of a massive bush fire. I'm paddling towards it and it gets louder still. I pass a patch of flaming grass on my left. The heat is intense here, and I see there is another fire further away on my right. The smoke sears my lungs. I'm very alarmed. It's beginning to get dark. I find a spot amongst the mangroves that is mostly surrounded by water, hoping that I'll be safe from the fires. After getting my gear out I slash a three-metre strip in the grass where I can begin a back-firebreak if I need to. The crackling of the flames is very loud. I walk along the narrow point for a better view. Something heavy in the shadows of the darkening tree canopy breaks and runs. Brush cracks

The sound is like a
giant hand ripping
and tearing through
dry reeds.

and water splashes, and with my nerves already wound up by the danger
of the surrounding fires I get a hell of a fright. But then I realise it is a large buck – waterbuck
perhaps. It bounds through the shallow water in the mangroves and is gone.

As darkness sets in, the awful amber glow of the huge fires forms a great encircling ring. The
smoke, acrid and heavy, burns my throat and eyes. I cough and splash water onto my face and breathe
through a wet cloth. The sound is like a giant hand ripping and tearing through dry reeds. Every now
and then a tree bursts into flame, then the inferno quietens down, only to suddenly start afresh in a
new rush of life. But soon I notice that the fire across the river seems to be dying down. The glow is
softer and eventually is almost gone. After a further half-hour, much to my relief, the same happens
on my side of the river.

I sit in the freezing cold and watch to make sure it really has died out. Then I go to sleep, fitfully
waking through the night as I think I hear it restarting.

Bushfires become a constant feature as the days go by, and I learn that they routinely run into
swamps and watercourses that halt their advance. I also discover that they are started purposely by
fishermen and river people when the grass is impenetrable and hinders their access to the river. The
fires burn themselves out on the marshes, so do little damage – but until one knows this, they are a
frightening spectacle. The flames can be seen and the crackling sound of the fire heard from a long
way off.

I lie in my sleeping bag under a flawless, starry sky. The Zambezi river is a few metres from where
I lie – quiet swirling noises come from the water under the overhanging combretum trees, and the
call of a nightjar is not far away. Then comes a magical visit of the silent hunter of the night – an owl
passes overhead in absolute silence, but seeing my head sticking out of the bag, makes a quick turn
for a second assessment and then flies on. An hour or two later another visit – perhaps a different
owl – but this time much more focused, making several turns over my head. The third time he comes
back, in the early hours of the morning, I am awoken by the windy beating of wings and, opening my
eyes, I'm confronted by the owl within two metres of my head, twisting and turning as he assesses me
as a possible meal. It gives me a good idea of how a mouse or rabbit would be feeling under similar
circumstances! I duck my head rapidly into the sleeping bag.

Most days I see no one at all. If I do, it is no more than one or two people or a group of three or
four. It is blessedly quiet.

The river speeds up, running through small rapids that appear in quick succession. I try to snatch
a photograph between two rapids, but the water steepens fast and I don't have time to get the camera

back into its waterproof bag before I'm into the next rapid. In my struggle to keep the camera dry, I strike something that flips the kayak – and that's the end of my camera. It's drenched through. I put it away, cursing, hoping that I'll be able to dry it out later and get it to work. Channels begin to form in the river, and some of the rapids are distinctly challenging.

The water calms and I enjoy the incredible beauty, but soon it quickens again and the roar of the water deepens. I move forward cautiously. My situation is not good for escape, for the river is now bracketed by very thick bush and there are no eddies into which I can turn. Then, as I round a corner, the volume of roaring, tumbling water is suddenly extreme – and perhaps 30 metres ahead of me is the spray and froth at the lip of a drop! Waterfall or rapid? I need to stop quickly. Furiously paddling to the right I try to slow down sufficiently to grab onto some branches. I catch hold, every muscle straining, thorns tearing my arms and hands. With the forward momentum of the kayak I am forced to let go. Another stroke with the paddle and I catch hold again, this time managing to stop. The pressure on the stern of my kayak to push out into the stream and away from the bank is enormous and I struggle to simply hold it from doing so. Then slowly I feel it beginning to move in under my body and towards the bank until it is pointing directly upstream and the pressure on my arms releases somewhat. Now I'm in something of a predicament. Not more than 10 metres away is the lip of the drop. The sound of the tumultuous water is horrific. Under extremely difficult conditions I manage to shove my paddle into the brush on the bank. Then I remove my spray deck, all the while straining with my right arm to

> Then, as I round a corner, the volume of roaring, tumbling water is suddenly extreme – and perhaps 30 metres ahead of me is the spray and froth at the lip of a drop!

keep myself pulled up against the brush and the bank. I drag myself clear of the kayak while holding it with my feet to stop it washing away. I have to burrow into the bush to force a space for myself. Then I manage to contort my body so that I have a hand on the front of the cockpit as well.

I force the kayak upstream centimetre by centimetre, one foot on the kayak and one on the bank in the brush, until I can eventually get hold of it near the bow. Then I let the water take the stern. It washes around in a great arc until the bow is facing back upstream. It is incredibly difficult to hold it. I manage to get my bowline off the handle, where I tuck it away and finally tie the kayak to a branch. Adrenaline is running high. Now I have a good look around me at my situation. The water is running very fast indeed. This can only really be assessed when one is standing still on the bank as opposed to being in the water and part of the stream itself. My kayak is facing upstream as I wanted and seven to 10 metres downstream is a drop. The river channel I am in is about 15 metres wide and I am on an island.

I push and squeeze my way through unbelievably thick and tangled undergrowth. There are great tangles of logs and trees brought down in previous floods, all knitted together by vines and thorns, and I force my way forward until I can see the fall. It is not runnable! Still I search for some break that may give me a chance, but my initial reaction is confirmed. I will be severely injured or die if I go over the drop.

I drag myself back through the bush to my kayak. I have few choices. The fast-flowing river is deep and I cannot touch the bottom of the channel, which precludes me from walking the kayak back upstream. I cannot make my way along the bank using the line to drag the kayak along as the bush is too dense.

The speed of the river now takes on a completely new meaning, for the only way for me to get away from this spot is to paddle across the current. In order to do so I will have to somehow get myself back into the kayak and paddle against the current, gradually edging my way across to the opposite bank where things look a bit friendlier than where I am now. I watch the water for some time, planning my moves. It will be a straight test of strength and fitness, neither of which I can be sure of at this stage of the journey. I reorganise the bowline, leading it from the bow around a thick branch and back to the cockpit, where I will hold it until I am ready to go.

Then I settle myself back into the cockpit and, with one hand, struggle to get the spraydeck on. I have to use the same hand to grip the paddle. One or two deep breaths and I release my grip on the line holding the bow, then get a proper grip on the paddle. The kayak immediately surges backwards and downstream. I cannot paddle properly because my left side is too close to the bank, but using the bank, brush, rock or anything else on the left and the water on the right I paddle like a demon. Initially I continue going backwards and downstream, the terrifying drop just metres behind me. But slowly my forward speed neutralises the downward speed of the current. I paddle for my life; the kayak stays unmoving in the current, but gradually I edge across to the right. Sweat pours from my body, my muscles burn. There is nothing in my mind except my own effort and the place I have to get to. Slowly I move to the right. Then I sense a slight movement of the kayak edging upstream. It's just what I need. Yes! I push harder still and now I see it – I am not just staying abreast of the current but I am moving further from the falls, only slightly, but I'm moving and I'm winning. Then a small eddy and a momentum I use to gain an additional metre or two. Across another forceful current and suddenly I am in relatively gentle calm alongside the opposite bank. An eddy current pushes upstream and I quickly leap out of the kayak and hold it firm in the shallower water against the brush, the tumultuous water dropping off not more than seven or eight metres behind me.

It is a strenuous portage and I fall frequently while struggling knee- and waist-deep in water moving at considerable speed over the tumbled rock. At the base of the falls I pump my cockpit clear of water and climb back in. Not far below the falls I make camp at a spectacular spot. I'm very tired. The ground is sandy and the tree canopy a mixture of mangrove and palms laced together with vines.

I place three candles on the boughs of trees, imbuing each one with special meaning. One for Annie, one for our children, Jess, James and Rory, and one for the light within that I know I need. We are all together here. Two are right above my sitting spot, and one is next to my 'kitchen'. The light flickers and dances around my mosquito net and between the trees. It is magical and so peaceful. I stay here for two nights while I dry my gear and gather my strength. After every effort to repair and dry out my camera has failed I decide to use a little of my satellite phone's precious battery to call Annie. It's wonderful to hear her voice, but we only have seconds. I give her my GPS position, quickly tell her how I'm doing, and get news of family. Then I ask her to try to get a replacement camera to Chavuma in Zambia. She says she will try, and then she's gone.

I watch the falls with great interest. Even here – high up on the Zambezi – the power of the water is very evident. In the rocky pools at the base of the falls I catch a crab and, using it for bait, I'm able to bring in a nice bream for my supper.

When I leave this lovely spot, well-rested and fed, I paddle along a short flat stretch bracketed by the most beautiful riverine forest. Kingfishers of every variety dart across and along the river ahead of me, and I marvel at the beauty. More rapids appear. They are not large, and I enjoy a series of pleasant runs. Now the riverbanks display thick brush behind which lies tall, almost impenetrable reed-like grass. The river slows here and I move forward with great caution, concerned that there might be another drop. Little rapids continue, and after about a kilometre I begin to feel safer and more relaxed. The river takes a sharp turn to the right in the middle of a nicely flowing set of rapids. The water bubbles and swirls noisily around the rocks in its path and the light dances on the ripples and wet boulders.

As I round the corner the river rapidly gathers speed, and in the tumble of protruding boulders I'm unable to cross to the side. Suddenly the reality of the coming river is upon me. Directly ahead of me and almost under my kayak is a small fall, perhaps two metres high. I can't avoid it and so commit to it, paddling hard. But below it is a terrifying gorge, no more than three metres wide. The entire force of the river is confined in this surging pressure sluice. As I drop over the falls, my mind takes in the steep, vertical rock walls on both sides, allowing no escape, and what looks like a dead-end 30 metres ahead of me. Struggling to stabilise after the drop, my kayak's nose emerges, shaking off the boiling water. Ahead lies a steep chute with a big hole at its end; beyond that, an enormous cleft in the rock into which the whole force of the river flows. I catch a glimpse of an exit point to the left – impossible to turn into at this speed.

I approach the chute fast: the speed and power of the water stupendous; the nose of my kayak well down, 30 degrees or more. The water ahead is a frothy, brown, heaving force. Then the nose goes in, and it just keeps going. I seem to be going straight down – the kayak and I – I'm upside down now, well under water – and I need air! I try to roll the kayak upright but to no avail. I am nowhere near the surface, so I kick free – urgently. When I eventually surface, my kayak is on my right and we are both being thrust at phenomenal speed back towards the falls upstream. I try to grab hold of the stern, which is closest to me, but as I touch it the mighty hand of the river takes us and thrusts us down once more. I go down and down. The pressure is enormous. My chest is being squeezed closed.

There is a certain calm acceptance that this is my moment. I simply think, 'Drowned!', as though surprised that this is to be the manner of my passing.

I'm very deep and being whipped and thrown about like a tiny leaf in a tornado. And then I know this is the end. With that recognition come words in my mind, 'I'm going, I'm going'. There is a certain calm acceptance that this is my moment. I simply think, 'Drowned!', as though surprised that this is to be the manner of my passing. Who would have thought? There is no fear. I'm simply there; a strange kind of observer as I am sucked still deeper into the whirlpool, into the very innards of this massive river! I'm very calm. The light becomes bright and gentle. I feel so tranquil and warm, so much at peace. At exactly the moment I know I have reached my end – and as I accept and acknowledge this with my unspoken words, it is as if the river hears, as if it knows. In an instant, I again feel the pressure on my body. Then it releases and I sense that I'm going up. I can feel the froth now. It is lighter, and then – as if spat out by a massive serpent – I break the surface. I seem to hover for a moment and then the river grips me and flings me away and downstream. I look quickly back to make sure that I'm not being sucked in again – but I am free. I am clear of the falls and the powerful grip of the river, moving downstream incredibly fast.

There, where I had been, my kayak is being spun and tossed about like a twig. A piece of equipment floats alongside me, and within a few strokes I grab it and fling it onto the rocky bank. I look warily downriver to other approaching rapids and then swim out as strongly as I can for shore.

When I reach the bank there is no good place to exit the river. The water is deep – steep sided like a canal – right up to the edge. The bank is covered in thick thorn and razor-sharp, hard-leafed undergrowth. I drag myself up and into the scrub where I lie for a few seconds, feeling all squeezed out.

Then, forcing myself to sit up, I draw my feet further away from the water to avoid crocodiles, and I scan it for any equipment or my kayak. I feel utterly exhausted. If I dive in to retrieve anything washing by me at this point I will end up in the next set of rapids so I must make my way quickly upstream. I try going through the bush but it is just too painful and damaging to my body. So I slip into the water and drag myself along against the current by using my hands on brush and rocks. A tree protrudes over the river and I use it to clamber out. The going is a little easier on land here and I make my painful, barefoot way back upstream. My route, forced by the nature of the bush, takes me in an arc first away from the river then back towards it. I am vulnerable to losing equipment or even my kayak at this point because I cannot properly see the water, so I move faster than I would like, cutting my feet and being torn by thorns. I see equipment in the water and walk-trot to the river, dive in and retrieve it, landing back where I had started some 20 metres lower down.

Then back upstream again through the bush. Now I retrieve my paddle, and I'm into the water again, going around and around several times until I feel that I can no more. Crocodiles have also now had time to observe my routine and the danger from that source adds to my nervousness. I see my bag with jacket and track pants go by. I'm too far from the water, barricaded off by spiny bush. It's brightly coloured enough, so I hope to recover it lower downstream.

My kayak has not appeared yet and I catch glimpses of it through the bush still spinning and flipping in the wash. A frightening prospect – to think that I could have still been there myself now, some twenty minutes or so after entering the hole. In order to get closer to the boat I have to detour still further away from the river again to avoid steep rock and thick, spiny bush. Barefoot – over recently burned grass, I've no sooner got myself well away from the river than I see my kayak, nose down and on its side, forlornly washing downstream. If I don't move fast it will hit the next rapids. So, regardless of the potential damage to my feet and the danger of crocodiles, I sprint downhill and jump straight in to retrieve it. Filled with water, it is a difficult, heavy swim, and I only get it to the bank just short of the next rapids.

By now, of course, I am exhausted. Clinging to the brush on the bank with one hand and the kayak with the other, I struggle to get myself, let alone the kayak, onto the bank. The kayak is filled with water and difficult to budge, but I manage to get enough of it onto the bank to ensure it won't wash away. I struggle to stay on my feet, but I must, and I force myself to bail as much water out of the cockpit as possible to make it just a little lighter. Then I drag it further ashore. It only moves a little – but it is better than where it was. I allow myself to collapse now, just folding up like a bundle of debris. I am completely spent but I know I must not let go of my control. I lie there just gasping – forcing myself to breathe properly – slowing down my panting and filling my lungs with precious air, giving myself a moment to recover. Then I drag myself back up and begin emptying the kayak of water.

> I lie there just gasping – forcing myself to breathe properly – slowing down my panting and filling my lungs with precious air, giving myself a moment to recover.

The river claims as her own my glasses, sunglasses and bivouac poles, the fishing rod so carefully chosen by my friend Andy, and a host of other items that had been lashed to the deck. Incredibly, both watertight Pelican cases are still there – containing all my medical and photographic equipment. The camera was already drowned anyway, but the maps are gone, and that is a real loss.

Once I've pumped the hull dry and re-lashed everything that's left, I make my way back upstream on foot to retrieve the final piece of equipment from the rocks where I had thrown it as the river let me go, and to have a good look at the rapid.

What I see is quite terrifying. The stretch of river that had almost taken my life is only 35 to 40 metres long. After the fall the water channels through a three-metre-wide mini gorge before pushing directly into a V-shaped cleft in the rock. The pressure at this point in the river is absolutely stupendous. There is a kind of rocking motion to the river. As the downstream pressure of the river into the V is equalled and then exceeded by the back pressure in the cleft itself, the river blows back upstream under tremendous pressure. At this moment a huge surge forces water both upstream and out of the narrow exit to the side. Where this happens, and on the outside of the gorge exit, there is a whirlpool that spins either fast or slowly depending on the surge. I must have hit the boil at exactly the moment that it blew back upstream. Tons of water flowed over me under enormous pressure, and the force of the water coming from behind took me and my kayak straight down. There I was tossed about underwater until, rising once more, I was caught on a surge going upstream. This is when I must have come up for a split second for the first time and seen my kayak to my right. When I went down the second time I have little idea of where I went. But when I was finally released from the river I had been forced through the narrow exit from the gorge and had come up on the downstream side of the whirlpool. This is where I felt like my body had hovered on the surface for a moment. A moment in which I could have quite easily spun back into the whirlpool, but when the grip of the water flowing out of the whirlpool grasped me I was free.

My death would not have been, could not have been, any great event in a country reeling from 30 years of war.

I stand there, just re-experiencing the power – the awesome deep energy that so easily could have kept me in her grasp – then I raise up both arms for a long silent moment in acknowledgement of the awesome potency, of the revelation of spirit.

As I turn to go, I catch a glimpse of something still caught in the whirling tumble of water. It looks like one of my sandals, but whatever it is the river will definitely be keeping it!

I paddle quietly for a long time. A deep inner quiet. It had been very close! I think just how insignificant a death it would have been. My body would have tumbled around until the river tired of it and then it would have begun floating with the current. What the crocodiles and fish didn't take would have eventually been caught in some brush and there, enveloped in a life vest, the pathetic remains would have stayed. Even if eventually discovered by a local fisherman this would not have been, could not have been, any great event. In a country still reeling from 30 years of war, one more body wouldn't have meant a lot.

A short while later I come across some local fishermen. There are three of them, all dressed in rags, all very thin, visibly showing signs of starvation. They cannot believe their eyes when they see me. First they run, but then my gentle calls or some primal understanding of my vulnerability, and perhaps my desperate need, stops them. I pull over to them, and they cautiously draw closer. I just need to be near other human beings. I sit very still in my kayak, holding on to a branch. When they realise that I am no threat they become curious – peering at my kayak and me. We try different languages and hand signs. When they see, through my gestures, where I have come from and make out what has just happened to me, they are astonished. I am shocked by their appearance for they look like survivors from Auschwitz. Ribs protrude and knees bulge, but still they are deeply concerned about me; bless them.

One young man asks how I will be sleeping and if I have lost my bedding. It is very cold. 'Where is your blanket?' Then he is concerned that I may have lost my food. He is unconvinced when I say that I am all right, that I do have food and that I will be fine. Ignoring this, he reaches behind him into the grass, picks up something dark and furry and says, 'Let me give you a bat, you must eat.' The kindness from these simple fisher folk is humbling. I gently decline the tiny bat, an enormous gesture from people who are starving, so desperate that they are trapping bats for food. They only have two tiny bats between them. There are three of them, let alone the families for whom they are gathering food. I do still have food. Then, after a short time where simple human proximity helps to heal, we wave each other farewell and I carry on.

Lo and behold, just a little way further my eye catches something hooked on a branch and mostly submerged. It is my map and log container. Of course they are all thoroughly wet, but what a bonus to have my maps back.

Taking a pause from paddling, the momentum of the kayak and the current carrying me silently forward, I surprise a young crocodile in the tall grass on the bank. He flings himself into the water. How he knew I was there is a mystery, for he was completely hidden several metres from the water in the tall grass and could not have been able to see or hear me approaching.

I become more cautious of the possibility of military activity, as I began to see terrain that would permit troop movement. I take to not paddling as I come around corners in the hope that I'll be able to see anyone before they see me. Later that afternoon I see a man on the west bank seated on the ground with his back to me, but by the time I see him, he is within a few metres of me and two to three metres higher than me on the bank. Something makes me cautious. Across from him on the east bank I can now hear, but not see, other people. Suddenly there are bursts of gunfire on the east bank. I begin paddling immediately. The man jumps up, reaching for what turns out to be an AK-47 assault rifle, simultaneously shouting to those on the east bank. By now I'm almost directly below him and paddling steadily. I have no other options. In a loud, cheerful voice I call out *'Bom dia! Bom dia!'* (Good morning! Good morning!) with a huge smile on my face and what I hope is a friendly wave. He almost falls into the river, his AK in his right hand as he struggles to bring

Suddenly there are bursts of gunfire on the east bank. I begin paddling immediately. The man jumps up, reaching for what turns out to be an AK-47 assault rifle, simultaneously shouting to those on the east bank.

it to bear on me. The shock and astonishment on his face is vivid. Here is a white man with a bright yellow helmet and kayak almost at his feet. The gunfire continues and green tracers whip both ways across the river. He stays low trying to make sense of it all. Approaching on my left I can see four men, all armed, moving fast towards the river and me. They shout at me but I, with a big smile and cheery calls, continue to shout 'Bon dia' and 'Como está?' (How are you?). Their forward movement slows, their mouths agape in disbelief. This is the critical moment. The wrong move and these poised, battle-hardened men will instantly fire. I keep my hands well above the kayak and call again, this time waving in a manner that must have made them believe they were confronting a lunatic. The kayak is now slowing. Very cautiously, I take a stroke. They shout still more urgently and begin running fast again. I take another stroke. Now very close to a corner, I'm forced to turn, losing sight of the men, who are directly behind me. My back tightens, the hairs on my neck prickling. The momentum carries me around the corner. It is fairly clear that this is a group of anti-government Unita forces. A skirmish has just commenced and it can only be a Fapla (government) patrol that has bumped into them. I am lucky to have arrived amongst the lines of only one side and not to have found myself between the two sets of forces. For some reason I feel it necessary to get maximum distance between us as soon as possible! The crackle and popping of small arms continues for a short while, then all is still but for my breathing.

By the time I begin looking for a spot to camp I have had a long day of reflection and a physically exhausting one too. The cockpit keeps filling with water so I assume, after pumping it dry several times, that there must be a crack or a hole from the pummelling it took at the chute.

This is the critical moment. The wrong move and these poised, battle-hardened men will instantly fire.

When I eventually spot a fisherman's long-deserted spot, marked simply by a small clearing, I decide to stop. I am surrounded by wetland and swamps. I discover that the entire front hatch – with its inner cover and outer hatch still firmly closed – is full of water. Somehow the pressure from those rapids had forced water into the closed and sealed hatch! More importantly though, everything inside is drenched and that includes my sleeping bag. It's almost dark already and I know I'm in for a long, cold, unpleasant night. I quickly take my panga and move up as far away from the river as the water-logged area will allow. I find an area of thick bush and tall grass on a relatively dry spot. I cut away a tunnel-like space and, using the wet groundsheets, fashion something of a home for myself. Then I put on every reasonably dry piece of clothing I can find. The only item that's of any use to me in terms of covering my legs is a light windcheater top. I shove my legs through the arms and tie it as best I can around my waist.

Concerned about hypothermia, I need to get something into my stomach as soon as possible. Shivering and shaking in the dark, I locate a container of freeze-dried food and my gas stove. It is extremely difficult to get it to light. Damp has found its way into almost everything. The lighters I have will not strike. Two sets of different types of matches won't work. The magnesium striker is both too dangerous and difficult to use in the condition in which I find myself. Using this will mean that I have to switch the gas on, simultaneously trying to strike a spark off the magnesium plate. A gas explosion is a strong possibility, even if I could get it right at all. I am racked by shudders in my body from the cold and my hands simply cannot grasp the magnesium plate with sufficient strength. I dig for my last chance; I had put one set of matches and a side strip of a matchbox into an old photographic film container. This, sealed with wax inside several plastic bags, has survived. Finding it while shaking uncontrollably in the dark now becomes the challenge. But at last, success! While waiting for the water to boil, I struggle with the issues of survival. In order to make it through the night and avoid hypothermia, I have to get warm. Perhaps the mosquito net wrapped around my body, even if wet, will trap little pockets of air that my body can warm up. I eat a freeze-dried meal prepared with the now boiling water and then I climb into my tunnel and settle down to sleep. Warmer now with the hot food in my belly, I have a window of opportunity to sleep. I'm very aware that I'll shortly be confronting the greatest moment of danger from hypothermia. This is the reason why the Inuits (Eskimos) only eat cold fish. In extreme conditions, with a weakened body, shock from the sudden drop in temperature after a warm meal is what has killed many an explorer. It gets very cold, and I become concerned about sleep, afraid that I might not wake up if I drift off. So, periodically through the night when I feel myself go completely numb and listless after the constant, uncontrollable shaking, I light the gas stove for a short while. I find that kneeling and bent over forward, tightly curled like an embryo, my hands over my head, I can retain some body heat and protect my head and thighs – both areas where maximum heat loss occurs. I'm quite pleased when the sun comes up!

I do not wait long at my night's campsite. Just before leaving I thank my lucky stars for all the years of survival training, bush craft, military, and mountaineering experience that had helped me make it through the night and the previous day. And what a day it was! I am thoroughly humbled and acknowledge to myself and to God how vulnerable I am. I have been cut down to size very quickly.

The river winds through great arcs, creating near oxbow lakes. Sometimes the water actually washes through the thick bush at the narrowest point of the bow. Mostly it's too thick to penetrate in a kayak, and I paddle the four or five kilometres around the oxbows to arrive back at a spot not 20 metres from where I was an hour or so before. It's frustrating and hard going. My kayak is heavy and I am still getting fit. My lower back is incredibly painful and I know that yesterday's struggle in the water did real damage. Periodically a south wind comes up, blowing into my face and making progress even more difficult. The terrain is flat and primarily wetland, but as I progress, little rises begin to appear.

After an arduous day of flat water paddling, constantly tempered by the great beauty surrounding me, and with the afternoon drawing to a close, I see the first signs of habitation. For many kilometres I had been aware of a prominent hill in the distance and,

I am thoroughly humbled and acknowledge to myself and to God how vulnerable I am. I have been cut down to size very quickly.

Cazombo to Luena and back to Cazombo

- Arrest by Angolan armed forces
- Military flight to Luena
- Interrogation
- Return to Cazombo

On a bend in the river I see what appears to be the remains of an old Portuguese pergola – gracious pillars still standing and a balustrade constructed exactly as if on a villa on the Portuguese coast. Magnificent it must have been, and somehow still is.

But I'm very cautious now, as there will probably be troop concentrations at this spot. I have no idea which forces will be in control, so I plan to just rely on my instincts as events unfold.

Deciding to be overt or clandestine is not an option for me. One or two people have seen me already and have run off into the bush shouting '*Legua! Legua!*' (White man! White man!) in the Luvali language. So I pull the kayak up next to an old dugout I see at the bottom of the slope under the pergola and walk up.

At the top is what must have been a most wonderful building, but more impressive even is the view. Looking north over the sharp bend in the river the magnificence of the breadth of Africa is stupendous. One can only imagine the early Portuguese settlers and travellers sitting on the beautifully formed benches at sunset or making their way down the impressive stairway to the river to take an evening cruise.

But now, dilapidated and sad, the pergola is backed by a number of low, thatched structures (roofs only), and the signs of numerous individual fires and tracks indicate that this was recently a military post. I know it will not be long before I have 'official' company. The word that I'm here will be travelling fast. Anticipating this, I decide to go back down and remove some of the basics from my kayak, leaving the bulk of the overnight gear where it is. With my sleeping bag and groundsheet, a water container, a pot, my little gas stove and some tea, I labour back up the pathway to the top again. Once there, I make a big fuss of shaking out my sleeping bag, while singing Gershwin's 'Summertime' at the top of my voice. I want it to be quite clear to the eyes that I know are watching from somewhere in the bush that I'm not hiding and am no threat. I decide to walk along the track towards where I think the town should be, but after a kilometre or so, and considering the lateness of the hour, decide to wait and do the trip in the morning. Just then I see a man walking towards me in a bright, cheerful Hawaiian-type shirt and a short way behind him a woman, the first woman I have seen for almost two weeks.

I greet loudly from a distance with a big smile. He stops and watches me carefully then, overcoming his initial caution, he approaches. I have to walk the way he's going to get back to the river and so, with some difficulty considering the language challenge, explain what I'm doing and that I will go into Cazombo in the morning. The woman has disappeared.

The fellow and I make our way down to the river's edge – he to look in utter awe at my kayak and I to gather a little more gear for the night. He eventually hops into his dugout and, paddling it with an old polish tin lid, disappears downstream.

Back up at the pergola, I fire up the gas stove and get some water on for tea. Then I hang bits of clothing in prominent places, as if to dry it. I take off my shirt and wander around, wearing only my

shorts, eventually locating an open, flat piece of ground with no grass or cover on it whatsoever. This is where I will head to if I hear troop movements coming my way.

I've just managed to get myself relatively settled with my water beginning to boil, when I hear a big vehicle approaching. I walk casually over to my open piece of ground and stand there stretching, touching my toes, and then looking at the sunset, as if absorbed, with my back towards the approaching soldiers. I sing a little, then sit down and, pulling my left foot up close to my face, begin to probe around under it, as if looking for a splinter or thorn.

By now I can see that the troops have disembarked and are approaching me in an extended line. They are very cautious, squatting periodically on their haunches and just watching. I carry on my farce as if they are not there – as though I have not seen them. I begin to sing again, and now they're close enough for it to be impossible for me not to have noticed them. I look across, as if surprised, and stop singing. As my eyes catch those of a soldier behind a bush about 20 metres away, I fix him with a big smile and, in a very measured movement, wave at him with both hands aloft and shout, *'Bon dia, senhor. Bon dia – Como está?'* (I found out later that I was saying 'Good morning', although it was sunset at the time!) Then, ignoring him, I sweep my eyes across the area where the other troops are partially concealed and say, *'Ah! Paz! Paz de Angola.'* (Peace! Peace in Angola). They don't move. I slowly turn around with my arms away from my body to show them that I have no weapons. Then I just stand, with a big smile on my face, and wait.

Two men break away from the rest and, with weapons poised, approach me. On either flank of their line I can hear others moving – obviously checking to see that I really am alone.

Two men break away from the rest and, with weapons poised, approach me. On either flank of their line I can hear others moving – obviously checking to see that I really am alone. When the two are within a few paces of me – each separated from the other by about 90 degrees – they say something, and one shows me, by turning his finger in a circle, that I'm to turn around. I do so, very slowly and carefully, all the time smiling at them and talking: *'Não problema,'* I say, hoping that I look relaxed. One of them comes over to me and feels my crotch – perhaps looking for a grenade – then he pushes me and gives me a smack. 'Hey, hey! *Não, senhor. Expedição de paz e boa fé,'* I say. (No, sir. Expedition of peace and goodwill). *'Angola paz.'*

The other soldier has now also approached and is about to strike me with his rifle when a loud command is barked from the bush. They stop hassling me and have me stand with my legs apart, while an older man approaches from the bush. This is clearly an officer. He tells two other men to look around my campsite and, while they are doing that, he's also assessing the situation. '*Documentário*,' he commands in a brisk tone, holding out his hand. I cautiously point to the little pile of items that lie alongside the now briskly boiling gas stove. He shows me to go ahead. All four troops have their weapons at their shoulders, poised in the ready position, and are watching me intently. I maintain a cheerful, fairly unconcerned air and, without any fast movements, pick up my passport and step away from the rest of the gear. He takes it from me and in a businesslike fashion pages through it, asking questions I can't understand while he does so.

I try to tell him what I'm doing; that I have travelled from Zambia on the '*Rio* Zambezi' but, try as I might, I can't find a word that he understands to mean 'boat' or 'kayak'. He begins to raise his voice a little in frustration. The troops are now gathering all my gear and beginning to walk toward the bush with it. '*Não, não*,' I say, pointing towards the river and my kayak. But they grab hold of my arms and pull me towards the bush. Just then, I hear someone say in English, 'He does not understand you well.' I stop sharply and, pointing with my head because I can't move my arms, say, '*Inglês. Fala Inglês.*' (English. Speaks English.) The officer says something to the men holding me and they let me go. I point at the few civilians who have gathered 20 or 30 metres away, and try to make it understood that someone there can speak English. The officer, who, I soon learnt, is a colonel, walks over to them, speaking sharply as he approaches. Fearfully, a young man raises his hand – and I have a translator! His name is Pedro Mutonilo. His English is not perfect, but it is an enormous help.

Now I'm able to explain myself and get them to understand that I have a kayak. We walk back towards the river. I keep pointing

The troops are now gathering all my gear and beginning to walk toward the bush with it. '*Nau, nau*,' I say, pointing towards the river and my kayak.

Opposite: An extremely dangerous young man.
Below, left: Car park in Cazombo.

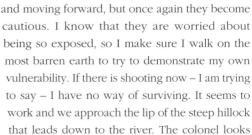

and moving forward, but once again they become cautious. I know that they are worried about being so exposed, so I make sure I walk on the most barren earth to try to demonstrate my own vulnerability. If there is shooting now – I am trying to say – I have no way of surviving. It seems to work and we approach the lip of the steep hillock that leads down to the river. The colonel looks at the river as if expecting to see a great ship and, when he doesn't, looks from me to the translator, Pedro, and barks for an explanation. I keep trying to creep forward, pointing down at the water's edge and, eventually, he seems to understand. 'Ah, *barco, barco,*' he says, dispatching some men to run down to look. I cannot believe my own stupidity at not knowing the word used for kayak or canoe in Portuguese.

Shouts come up from below and soon the colonel, several troops, and I are inspecting my humble craft. They are fascinated. But the colonel, aware of the disappearing light, gives an order, and my kayak is hoisted onto the shoulders of some troops and taken up to the pergola. They all swear and complain at its weight.

Now I'm told that I should accompany them to the town and join them all in 'the Boma' where I will have a 'much more comfortable night'. This is not a suggestion. But the tone has changed dramatically. Seeing my bright yellow kayak with its flags and expedition description adorning it has definitely eased their concerns. My gear is again gathered up and loaded onto the vehicle and my kayak, too. The vehicle is a Russian GAZ – a powerful looking vehicle with enormous rugged and torn tyres.

The colonel signals for me to join him up front. It is not difficult to see the irony of the situation: an ex-South African Airborne officer who, many years before had seen combat against these forces here in Angola, seated between a Fapla colonel of a similar age and an NCO in the cab of a Russian truck with 20 or so troops on the back with my kayak.

Cazombo town looks like a place directly out of the old Wild West. One wide street, a small church (pretty much untouched) and a few buildings all shot to hell but having had basic repairs to make them liveable. There are not many civilians around. Little groups of troops stand here and there but clearly everyone in town knows about me by now.

We stop outside the administrator's home (electricity, satellite dish, TV) and wait. The colonel comes out, accompanied by a policeman, the *Comandante* of Police, I'm told. He is formally handed my passport by the colonel. Off to one side I'm trying to make conversation with the troops and civilians when a junior officer

comes over and tells them quite clearly not to talk to me. He then gesticulates, forcefully and aggressively, for me to get onto the GAZ. I climb onto the back with the remaining troops, with whom I have already developed some rapport. There even seems to be some pride from them that they are the ones that have brought in this strange prize. It strikes me how lucky I had been that it had been the colonel, and not a junior officer like this one, who had been with the troops when I was arrested. If that had not been the case, I would, at the very least, have sustained a severe beating. My own military experience told the same story. The young men would very quickly and easily, for little reason, take a life.

Now it is quite dark. I'm taken off again by the police for questioning. In a little room with no windows, I stand waiting. The police *comandante* comes in and sits down at the table, a candle in the centre of it casting weird shadows all around. I try to talk to him but he indicates silence. He says something to the two guards and one goes outside, returning a little later with a chair. I'm told to sit down, and do so with considerable relief. The *comandante* looks at me and studies the picture in my passport in great detail. Then he begins to ask questions. This is what I had tried to tell him earlier: I can speak very little Portuguese and he speaks no English at all. '*Senhor fala Inglês*,' I say, pointing at the door. '*Não falou Portuguêse*,' I emphasise, pointing at myself. He turns to the guards and a quick exchange takes place between the three of them.

One guard leaves again, soon returning with Pedro, my translator, who looks quite terrified. By now I have managed to begin interacting with the *comandante* on a fairly reasonable level by drawing maps and pictures for him, using my hands and what little Portuguese I can muster. Pedro, however, can take us to a different level. It is about 23h00. I'm exhausted from a long and strenuous day's paddle, and now the psychological weariness is kicking in as well. The same questions, over and over: Who sent you? What is your mission? Do you know where you are? Do you know there is a war here? Why are you here? Who do you work for? I try, as patiently as possible, to answer each question without signs of irritation, but it becomes more and more clear that he just does not buy that I would be mad enough to do something like this alone in a war zone. He certainly can't understand that I don't work for anyone. Have you ever been to Angola before? Why? What is your purpose? Why? What is your mission? Who sent you? On and on.

Fusion of African ancestry with Roman Catholicism.

Cazombo town looks like a place directly out of the old Wild West. One wide street, a small church (pretty much untouched) and a few buildings all shot to hell but having had basic repairs to make them liveable.

I decide I will have to break this cycle somehow. Telling him that this is simply a self-funded adventure, to travel from the source of the Zambezi to the mouth, solo and unsupported, is not working. So, very carefully, I now act as though as I have just understood something. 'Oh, what work do I do?' I say to him. 'I am a writer. I write books and articles for magazines and newspapers.'

'Ah! *Journalista!*' he exclaims.

'No, a writer. I work freelance. I am travelling through Angola to see what has happened to the birds, wildlife and the people now that the war is ending.' But still he wants to know who I work for. It's quite clear that he can't understand that people can simply work for themselves. So now I recite the names of every publication I have ever heard of in my life.

'Ah, Geographic,' he says, nodding. I support this by telling him to look at the equipment and he would see a bird book as evidence. 'But why a GPS?' he asks.

Okay, at least we're getting somewhere now, and he's slowly beginning to let up on the questions.

Eventually he says, through Pedro of course, that it's late and that he will consult with his superiors in the morning. I ask for my passport, and he politely but firmly tells me that he will be keeping it. '*Não problema,*' he says. I'm not sure that I agree, but he's certainly more relaxed now, and I'm not going to push it.

At the only building in which lights are still showing, we stop. The *comandante* straightens his uniform and beret and taps politely on the door. The guards stay well back in the shadows. We wait some minutes but eventually the door opens and the colonel is standing there. He glances at me and then steps outside. A brief exchange occurs between the two men. The colonel seems to relax – nodding his head. Then he comes over to me and tugs at my T-shirt in an apparent effort to make me look a little neater. He goes back inside. We wait. Pedro now has a chance to whisper to me that this is the residence of the administrator, a 'big man'. He's practically quivering in his shoes. But he also says that the *comandante* is satisfied with my story and that there will be no problem. I think that I will wait and see. The colonel reappears and calls us in.

The administrator turns out to be a fairly short, round man. He's dressed in smart flannel trousers and an open-necked shirt. His crocodile skin shoes shine brilliantly. I shake his hand. His name is Alfredo Muque. There are two other men present. One, a lieutenant colonel, is the second in command of the forces in this area. He has a big moustache and slightly blurred eyes. When he brings his gaze to bear, it feels as though he's looking right through me. He never smiles, remaining formal and poised at all times. The other is a man by the name of Venacio Mugundengu, a recently appointed administrator from another district. He is a tall, gangly man with a slight stoop and a friendly smile. I like him immediately. The colonel who had been with the troops when I was brought in, and who had met us at the door, also stays. I now discover that his name is Nicolau and that he is the *comandante* of all the forces in this, the most easterly panhandle of Angola. I am in the very best company!

I soon find out that Administrator Alfredo has responsibility for six districts. Each of these is responsible to the regional headquarters that is based here in Cazombo. He is the region's most senior administrator. Venacio has just arrived from a place called Luena for a briefing, as he is being posted to a sub-district that has recently been 'liberated'. Several other districts are no-go areas and are still purely military zones. I have, of course, discovered this myself on the river! Administrator Alfredo is very polite. He offers me a chair and then tells Pedro, who is standing, awkward and fearful near the door, to sit next to me. The *comandante* excuses himself and disappears.

The building we're in is an old colonial residence. Very basic: corrugated iron shutters on the windows, no running water, but clean, warm, and quite comfortable. In the room are two tables drawn together around which we all sit with the administrator presiding at the head. The mandatory picture of President dos Santos hangs on the wall over an old dresser filled with normal household items – cups, plates, some crocheted tea doilies and a gaudy tray cloth.

Everyone is curious. The administrator asks me to tell my story. They are particularly interested in why I'm doing it. He also keeps emphasising that much of the area is still very dangerous – too dangerous to travel through. I joke and smile, saying that I guess I'm crazy. They all laugh and agree. Alfredo seems quite keen that I should get a good impression of order and control. I tentatively ask for an idea of what is going on in the area, and he obliges. His brief sketch of the situation reveals that Unita troops have been coming in since the end of March and handing in their weapons. Although some remain cautious and stay in the bush, the inflow is increasing each day. He tells me that some 2 000 Unita soldiers have come into Cazombo town alone over the preceding weeks.

In the middle of all this, a woman arrives with food for me. To me, it is an absolute feast: spaghetti with a sprinkling of mince on top. I'm given a bread roll that is pure bliss to eat, and am even able to spread margarine on it. It's a little embarrassing being the only one with food, so I offer to share it. They all decline, but Pedro looks starving. Alfredo sees this, and soon Pedro has some too.

I mention the skirmish of a few days before. 'Yes,' Alfredo acknowledges. There are still skirmishes taking place, but not many as everyone is realising that peace really has come to Angola this time. I say that I certainly hope so; that war is pointless and such a waste. Everyone nods in agreement.

The administrator's task is enormous. He has little infrastructure and very little or no appropriate equipment. So, to keep the troops from both sides active, he sets tasks for them. Road construction is what they are focusing on now, but so much else needs to be done.

By now I can barely keep my eyes open. As politely as I can, I ask if I could be given a place to sleep. I'm shown a little cubicle with corrugated iron nailed over the window. Once I have been to the toilet and return to the room, most of the others have left. No sooner am I in my room than I hear the key turn in my door-lock. They are all being very polite but they are clearly still taking no chances with me.

He also keeps emphasising that much of the area is still very dangerous – too dangerous to travel through. I joke and smile, saying that I guess I'm crazy. They all laugh and agree.

The morning brings with it a beautiful day. Through the cracks in the shutters, I can see little groups of people beginning to gather on the streets, mostly troops and police at this early hour. I knock on the door and am allowed out. I go out to the veranda and watch the little settlement awaken. The people watch me too.

A good wash, clean hair and wonderful breakfast with Administrator Alfredo – bread, cheese, an egg and coffee – hot milky coffee! A great start to a new day. After making arrangements and getting permission to walk about the area, I get cheeky and ask if Alfredo perhaps has a camera I could use. I explain what had happened to my own camera in 'the hole'. He is cautious but agrees, so using my own film, and accompanied by Pedro and a 'photo guard', I'm able to get a number of photos on my walk. Each time I point the camera at what, to the guard, appears sensitive, he says, 'Não, não,' and stops me taking the shots.

A fine old Catholic church stands untouched at the entrance to the village – witness to the turmoil that has reigned around it for so many years. A view from the bell tower shows the bare skeleton of what was once a thriving agricultural area. Rice was once grown and exported from here. Apparently the original entrepreneur – whose ribbed vehicles now stand destroyed and rusting neatly in a row where they were left 30 years before – is still alive and living in Portugal.

A soldier comes running over to us to tell us to return to the administrator's residence. There, Colonel Nicolau tells me that I will be going somewhere else for further interviews. My heart sinks and I am alarmed, but I smile politely and try, to no avail, to get more information. Midday brings with it a Russian Antanov 32 transport plane from Luena in Moxico Province, onto which my tiny craft and I are loaded. A troop escort especially for me and a few civilians all clamber on board. The limited cargo consists of dried fish caught in the Zambezi. The aircraft carries its own spare fuel drums, spare wheels and a crew of four Ukrainian airmen. 'Time, time, time, Mike!' barks the colonel as I snap my last picture, remove the film and hand the camera to *Comandante* Alfredo's guard to return it to him. He hustles me aboard, politely, in military fashion. Seated next to Colonel Nicolau, I have an interesting journey, the first part of which gives me a wonderful view of the next few kilometres of the Zambezi River, which I hope I will still have a chance to paddle.

Glancing up every now and again and looking back down towards the ramp gives a most fascinating picture. There sits my bright yellow kayak and in the seats facing it on either side, men in camouflage uniforms. There are also two women: one very, very thin (I can't help wondering about AIDS or starvation). The other has a tiny baby. There is also my old friend from the night before, Venacio – the newly appointed administrator. He tells me that it was decided that he cannot yet take up his post as it is still too dangerous. However he expects to be back in a few weeks time once the military has properly secured the area.

Arriving at Luena, a busy military centre, my kayak is unloaded off the ramp along with a few medical patients and, of course, the bales of dried fish. Everywhere there is handshaking, embracing, and delight as old comrades see one another again. Of course, the expat aircrew are also curious about me and come over to say hello now that they have a chance and are outside a combat zone. They think I'm quite mad and say so – but are very friendly at the same time. A bright yellow kayak on the side of a runway with a lone white man surrounded by troops makes an interesting spectacle in a military base in Africa.

Waving goodbye to Venacio I am yet again loaded onto a Russian military vehicle and driven out past a large gathering of interested troops. From the back of the vehicle I have a good view of a typical military airfield. Six or seven Russian choppers sit neatly outside a hangar and everything

looks disciplined and ordered. The perimeter of the airbase shows signs of heavy fighting and bombing, with buildings partially collapsed and bullet-riddled. The odd high explosive hit from RPG rocket launchers or mortars – or perhaps even tanks and bombers – is in clear evidence on buildings close to the airfield.

Luena itself is just a five-minute drive from the airport. Quite a large centre and the capital of Moxico Province, it shows lots of signs of recovery. Everywhere there are people cleaning up the roads and sidewalks – slashing long grass and filling up the potholes and bomb craters. Buildings are in the process of being repaired and many have already been repainted. I am taken directly to the military general headquarters where I'm treated once again politely but firmly. Each province has a military general and head of police who work very closely together with political administrators. Obviously, in areas of martial law the administrators are absent, but as soon as reconstruction begins they arrive and all structures thereafter report to them.

While waiting, a constant flow of interested officers and NCOs come over to where I'm seated on my kayak to look at it and me, and to ask for more information. One of these is a sergeant by the name of Joaquim Pinto. His *nom de guerre* is Pausada, which means 'the calm one'. He can speak some English and I quickly latch onto him and tell Colonel Nicolau that he is a translator. Nicolau tells Pausada to go off and get permission to stay with us, and soon he's back, looking very pleased with himself. He instantly becomes quite the celebrity and the resident expert on my expedition.

Nicolau disappears and Pausada takes me into a mess where I'm given a meal of rice topped with a fried egg and a small piece of boiled meat. Pausada talks with obvious admiration of '*Ponte Negro*' who is, I discover, Colonel Nicolau. Many men take a *nom de guerre* in war, and this is his. Shortly after I've finished my meal, I'm summoned. The General Officer commanding Moxico Province has arrived. His name is General Nzumbi. Seated in the waiting area outside his comfortable office are Colonel Nicolau and a second colonel by the name of Mukondu whom, I soon discover, is the adjutant and can speak a little English. Everyone sits nervously outside the door, and it's amusing to me to see, from a different angle now, the military command structure at work. My interview is formal, fairly brief, and to the point: 'Could you please explain the purpose of your expedition?

Top: Luena, Angola.
Middle: The railway concourse was unveiled in 1972. It was burned out in 1975 and has been shot to pieces ever since.
Above: The once proud Luena Theatre.

Do you know where you are? Do you know it is very dangerous?' The general tests this a few times and then says that he has no problem with me continuing, but that the Angolan authorities cannot be held responsible for my safety. I will spend the night in Luena and fly back to Cazombo, all going well, the next day. Dismissed, with appropriate military salutes all round and a handshake for me, I am on my way. The Angolan army arranges for Colonel Nicolau and me to stay at the local hotel. The hotel, called the Horizontale, is basic but comfortable. A flush toilet makes up for the fact that there is a shared washroom at the end of the hall, no hot water, and no lights in my room. Pretty soon, an NCO runs in and asks for my passport for the general. Two hours later it's returned to me with a letter from the general and permission to go!

The Angolan military here appears to be a very organised, reasonably disciplined machine. The headquarters of the area is clean and tidy, the vehicles parked in a good military fashion. Weapons are kept in good order and uniforms, boots etc. are neat and well polished. All of this is good, considering that it is the discipline of the armed forces that will determine the eventual order of the countryside while civil rule is being re-established.

I have ample time now to ask Pausada for more information on what is going on. He tells me that, as soon as peace was declared, the name of the Angolan armed forces changed from Fapla (which was the military wing of the MPLA political movement) to FAA – Forces de Armada de Angola. This was done specifically to incorporate Unita into a brand new military machine. Several senior Unita officers had been given command posts in the new army to demonstrate its neutrality. The message was clear: FAA belonged to the whole of Angola, not to a single political grouping. Clearly, the Angolans had learned some important lessons from the failure of peace back in 1998.

I muse on my own involvement in the post-hostility amalgamation of armed forces in South Africa, in which I facilitated. I wish these Angolans well in their efforts for peace.

That night I have dinner in the mess. Rice and boiled meat. Junior officers and NCOs share the same mess and I'm quietly told by Pausada, at my request, which of the various individuals are ex-Unita. It's good to see that integration is actually underway and that no antipathy between the former rivals is evident. If anything, there is relief.

Back in my room I'm soon fast asleep. I awake to sounds of stirring in the room next to me. An officer arrives on a motorcycle and waves up at me as I stand at my first-floor window. Soon Colonel Nicolau knocks on my door and introduces his pretty young wife, Anna. Both are concerned for my comfort and have come to check that I have slept well. He goes off with Anna and the adjutant to check on flight arrangements. Watching the activity on the road outside the hotel makes it very clear just what a massive industry the job of development and reconstruction is. There is lots of military activity, but also vehicles and representatives from UNICEF, the World Food Programme, Médecins sans Frontières, Grupo Consultor de Minas (landmine lifting engineers), Save the Children, and other humanitarian agencies.

At the general headquarters I see a brigadier (ex-Unita, Pausada tells me), in serious conversation with several other officers. He is a tough, hard looking man with a sharp eye and skin like leather. He is white, perhaps Portuguese, and upon inquiry I am told he is Angolan. Outside the HQ, pulled up to the kerb, a Russian Jeep idles with the driver behind the wheel. This man is ex-Fapla. His hair is flecked with grey, though he looks quite young. He is also white. Does any of this matter? Only insofar as Africans are Africans, black or white, and civil war tears all people apart.

Pausada, my helpful sergeant, makes some observations. The problem with finding work outside the army, he says, is that unless you have family in positions of power your qualifications do not really help. 'It is all about who you know , not what you know.' And the reason for all the fighting in Angola, he assures me, is because of diamonds and oil, nothing else. 'Angola is a wealthy country, yet the people are poor. It is the powerful people who want the wealth who cause the war.'

The days pass by and each day I am told that the aircraft will come 'maybe tomorrow'. I wait and explore Luena.

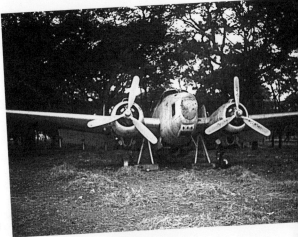

A bustling street market. Fabric wraps, caps, cigarettes, belts, shoes, and belts with little mirrors on them. The constant delight on people's faces as they see me and call, 'Chick Norr, Chick Norr.' If I wasn't Chuck Norris then I must be his brother, comes the constant banter. To them, a man with a beard and the same colouring as Chuck Norris meant that it just had to be him.

There are river fish of all kinds – dried black and stacked a metre high; tiny fingerlings and large bream. The pressure on the river as a source of food is enormous. Buck (not yet gutted and bloating in the sun), meat, chicken, biscuits and World Food Programme emergency food ration packs (stamped 'Not for Sale'), all for sale among the moneychangers and the traders.

In one short five-minute period I see three people, each with one leg missing – mines – and many other people on crutches.

At the old central hospital, I walk through the dilapidated corridors past broken window panes and dirty walls. Even with no doctors and no medicines the nurses do what they can. Conditions are bad but people just keep going. Outside I look at the hospital walls sprayed with bullet holes and marvel at the resilience of humanity. A government doctor is now visiting here once a week.

Top: An old Portuguese-era aircraft.
Above: Exploring Luena.

Until three months before, Unita was making nightly raids on the government forces in town and would periodically mortar or shell the town by day. When Unita had occupied the town several years before, a similar situation had occurred but the other way around. The civilian population just carried on around this.

As I walk the streets of Luena two choppers approach, both are Russian MI-8s – one of them armed with rocket pods. They fly directly over me and disappear into the west. Déjà vu! Twenty-five years ago here in Angola, I would not have been standing watching them impassively as I do now.

I walk over to the Médecins sans Frontières 'hospital'. Inside I am confronted by a series of tents that are hospital wards, each one large enough for probably 60 patients. The system works from left to right: those on the left are new arrivals and in a desperate state

'Angola is a wealthy country, yet the people are poor. It is the powerful people who want the wealth who cause the war.'

of malnutrition or disease. As the patients improve, they are moved up to the right, through the tent wards until they are fully rehabilitated and ready to return to their homes. I walk into the first ward, where the doctor is busy with a patient. She is a girl of about eight years old, in an advanced stage of starvation. Her eyes huge in her head, her skeletal legs and pronounced knees lie over to one side. The rest of her body is propped up slightly on cushions. Nothing moves except her eyes as I enter. She looks at me in total silence. I smile at her, but I am shocked and I hope she doesn't see it in my expression. The doctor walks over to me and says, sadly, 'There is little hope for this little one, but still we will try.' I look around the rest of the ward. It looks like a scene from Auschwitz. My God, I think, what have these people done to deserve this? It is soon clear that almost all of these people come from areas previously held by Unita. Because of the war there has been no way for them to plant crops. Even when they have, some or other army has simply taken the food. Here they lie now, the women, the children, the innocent. These are the real victims of war. And if this war has been about power and greed, this is the real cost of owning the diamond mines and oil fields.

The forlorn old Portuguese graveyard is in the process of being cleaned up. The area has been cleared of weeds and neatly raked. The mausoleum standing in the centre is damaged by mortar fire but is still imposing. Cleaning up the graves of their previous colonial oppressors shows amazing forgiveness for an era now past by a people tired of conflict.

The old Portuguese park still has railings around it, but whatever was between the horizontal bars is all gone. A swimming pool is still intact but empty. An old Portuguese bomber – a few shrapnel holes in it – stands on the corner of the park, just where the Portuguese put it.

A young hooker follows along behind me smiling and calling out, 'Como está?' She is pretty. What else is there for women to do? Only the soldiers have money.

The wide, attractively laid-out main boulevard past the station: a central pedestrian walkway set out with trees and park benches. Roads on either side with tall evenly spaced trees. Even now with its battle scars it is attractive. Many of the benches bear the scars of bullets and shrapnel – clearly they were good places for troops to take cover. The trees are all scarred by signs of war but they still stand. Alongside them are long lines of railway cars – some derailed and opened like cans from direct hits.

The station itself, opened in 1972, was clearly a very busy place back then. The buildings are extensive and there is still a lot of rolling stock standing on the tracks, a mixture of open wagons, closed cars, and two or three passenger coaches. Now because there is no running water in city taps or waterborne sewage the entire area is used as a latrine for the town residents.

After six long days in Luena, a plane at last is coming from Luanda that will proceed to Cazombo.

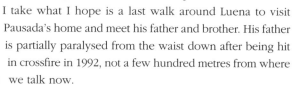

I take what I hope is a last walk around Luena to visit Pausada's home and meet his father and brother. His father is partially paralysed from the waist down after being hit in crossfire in 1992, not a few hundred metres from where we talk now.

The Antonov 32 taking us to Cazombo is crewed by five Moldavians who have only been in the country for two weeks. I am invited to sit up front in the cockpit next to the navigator. He sits behind the co-pilot, who is flying the aircraft on this leg. The engineer sits directly in front of me between the captain and the co-pilot. A box of ration packs is stuffed in behind the captain's seat.

Above and below: Luena, Angola.

These are all ex-Soviets in a Russian aircraft, and I sit with them in the cockpit! How silly the world can be. I find out from Colonel Nicolau that Colonel Mukondu has been in the military for 28 years – six of those at the academy in Petrograd, Russia, between 1983 and 1989. Colonel Nicolau has been in for 30. Both of them would have been in the military from the early 1970s. They, in the course of their careers, would have crossed paths and fought with or against Portuguese, South Africans, Russians, East Germans, American CIA operatives, Cubans and, of course, other Angolans. Sounds familiar!

I ask Nicolau about his *nom de guerre*, *Ponte Negro*. He laughs, with a touch of irony and forcefulness in his voice. 'I am lead nigger,' he says. 'The first black man in front of soldiers.' I sense the racial undertones and understand his aggressive tone. As a boy he was raised under the oppressive Portuguese colonial rule. *Ponte Negro* – it is a good name.

Cazombo is a very busy place when we arrive back. It looks like there are around one and a half companies of FAA in barracks close to the airfield. Most come out to watch the aircraft and to see what is going on. I remember doing exactly the same at forward military airfields when I was in uniform many years before. All the cargo from Luena is unloaded, and the space is filled with cargo from Cazombo: American rice coming in, Unita weapons going out to Luanda. I count around 160 AK-47s, 40 other assault rifles, several Russian light machine guns, three field mortars, and an RPG-7 rocket launcher. The weapons are in appalling condition and I am amazed that this is what Unita was using. I can't help wondering if the real weapons are still hidden in caches somewhere 'just in case' Unita once again decides to go back to the bush. Somehow, I don't really think so this time, as they did five years before.

While foodstuffs are being unloaded, troops have come to within a few metres of the aircraft. One man is seen to slip something inside his shirt. A brief scuffle occurs between the sergeant major and the soldier. The troops begin to shout and wave their arms. The mood becomes tense. The item is found on the man and torn away from him. He is cuffed by an NCO and walks away, cowed. The troops growl, their mood suddenly hostile and aggressive. The aircrew is nervous and get back into the plane. Goods off, passengers begin embarking, but there are too many, and one man, without the necessary authority in his possession, is told to get off. Once again, the troops shout and gesticulate. Then, when the man tries forcefully to re-enter the aircraft, some of the troops surge forward to assist him. Colonel Nicolau runs at them, shouting, his eyes blazing, swinging his arms. The men scatter but, from a safe distance, jeer and taunt. The flight crew start one engine even though the loading is still underway. When a second attempt is made by this desperate man to board supported by several other troops a fight breaks out. The pilot, clearly afraid of the unfolding situation, begins taxiing away with the ramp still down. Some goods fall off the back. Nicolau stands tensely near me. I murmur that the situation is not good. 'Problema, Mike, *problema*,' he says.

I know that what these men need is a killer-dose of discipline. My own experience of combat troops suddenly faced with inactivity is not dissimilar. They begin to get up to all sorts of no-good. But the blatant disregard of rank and discipline here is very disturbing.

Nicolau tells the NCOs to move the men away, which they do with difficulty. Then, seated on the piles of rations – mostly rice – we wait for transport to arrive. I watch my kayak and gear like a hawk, greatly concerned that I could lose more precious equipment. The faithful old GAZ trucks arrive. Colonel Nicolau decides to move me out first, so my yellow *barco* is loaded up with some troops. I say my farewells to Nicolau and he embraces me warmly. 'Good journey, Mike,' he says, concentrating on each word. He grasps my shoulder firmly and looks deep into my eyes. I nod and smile, but I'm sad to be leaving him. I have got to know him quite well over the past week and I like his inner strength and warmth.

'Goodbye, Nicolau,' I say. 'Look after yourself.' The GAZ begins to move and Nicolau turns away to deal with an officer, while shouting an instruction to someone further away. I watch him for as long as I can while the vehicle bumps away from the airfield. My thoughts are on him and the incident I've just witnessed. Back in Luena, the discipline was clear. Here, at the front, in an operational base, it shows signs of slipping. With Nicolau back here in person, I hope it improves, but it really is a delicate and dangerous situation that so easily could spin out of control.

My kayak being loaded onto a Soviet-era aircraft.

We go to Administrator Alfredo's office to get final clearance. He greets me warmly and says that I must spend the night as it is already late. I protest, saying that I really must get going as I have lost a whole week on the water. Considering what I have just seen at the airfield I really want to be away from here as quickly as possible. If I leave this afternoon, I tell him, I could still get in one or two hours of paddling. As for permission, the letter I have from General Nzumbi does the trick, and I am clear to go. During my discussion with Administrator Alfredo it is revealed that in the week that I was in Luena, another 200-odd Unita combatants had come in from the bush and given themselves up. This information tallied with the weapons I saw at the airfield. Peace really does seem to be coming to Angola.

The lieutenant colonel I had met a week before is tasked with returning me to the river. A few other curious young officers come along. As we drive out of Cazombo on our way back to the river, soldiers wave and smile. Clearly, I am no longer a bogeyman here!

The lieutenant colonel takes a few pictures of my *barco* being carried from the GAZ down the slope to the water. Then he poses next to it with me. He will have an interesting story to tell his family, just as I will.

I quickly prepare my gear as they all watch with great interest. I have my primary slashing knife around my neck. The lieutenant colonel turns to the others and says '*Commando*' as he watches me quickly rig myself and slip my second dagger into its sheath at the back of my neck. He, of course, doesn't realise how ironic his comment is.

Handshakes all around – into my *barco* and away I go. I paddle slightly upstream from there, then a turn with the current and a fast 'fly past' in farewell. Once again, after a seven-day interlude, I'm alone with the river.

As we drive out of Cazombo on our way back to the river, soldiers wave and smile. Clearly, I am no longer a bogeyman here!

Cazombo to Caripande and the border with Zambia

- Back on the river
- Battling my demons
- Crocodile encounter
- Missionary hospitality and a visit from an old friend

The bridge into Cazombo – built in 1954 – is destroyed. It looks quite beautiful from the water. As my camera is damaged, I do a quick sketch of it and plan to finish it later. It will be a big job to reconstruct the entire infrastructure in Angola; a massive task just to get roads serviceable again. With the number of landmines that have been laid in Angola over 30 years, I think I'll wait a while before venturing here in a vehicle or on foot.

I paddle well and the current is strong – so I manage 12 kilometres in an hour and a half. The terrain here is different to that north of Cazombo. Here, there are ridges and trees running right down

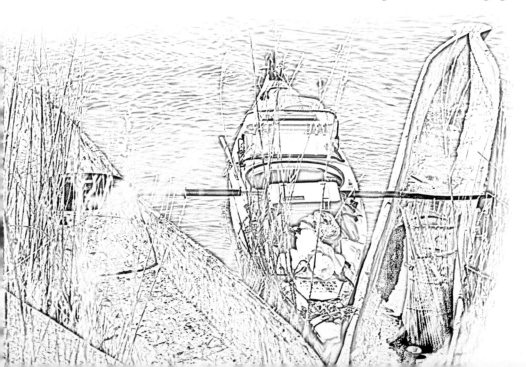

to the water, whereas north of Cazombo it is low wetland. I see quite a few fishermen on this stretch; about six or seven of them. I stop and make camp in a beautiful spot under some trees, and I am very happy to be back in the bush. The moon is out, the night beautiful, and I am a lucky man to be here.

I pass only two rapids through the next day; they are very small and not far from where I camped. The rest of the route is flat water although it is mostly flowing quite fast. I see two sets of troops in different places, to whom I wave and call greetings. In one case I find them a little too curious and concerned, so I shout across that I'm from Colonel Nicolau '*Ponte Negro*' in Cazombo, en route to Zambia. That gets their attention and they just wave me on. There are many more fishermen here than in the north. I see probably 10 people on the river in three different family settlements during the day. My back, which has been taking strain with all the days of paddling, is really a problem now. Even though I have been dosing myself with anti-inflammatory tablets and keep stopping to stretch, the pain is becoming excruciating. I try hard to put it out of my mind.

In certain places, particularly eddies, there is lots of fish activity and I frequently see the big reddish tails of tiger fish. One crocodile, surprised on the bank, leaps into the water, but it does not appear to be a major crocodile area.

After eight hours of paddling, sundown catches me near a place called Lumbala Kaquenque, and I pull off in the bush short of where the village once stood. Yet again I am careful of this point

My back, which has been taking strain with all the days of paddling, is really a problem now.

being a likely place for troops to be and I don't know what side they will be from. I make my way through the abandoned diamond workings alongside the river and brew up my traditional cup of tea.

The next morning I leave my camp early and I'm able to whip past Lumbala without being detained or hassled. I run into a group of troops, mostly naked and washing themselves on the bank, but they belong to the Angolan Army and all they do is wave. One runs along shouting '*Bon viagem*' (Have a good journey). I guess Colonel *Ponte Negro's* message has got here. Just past Lumbala I find the remains of the old pont; sunk, but just below the surface and visible at low water. Whoever blew it up made sure it would never be used again – it is opened up like a can on the deck and the sides.

It turns out to be a day of great variety. In some places I see the most wonderful bird sights imaginable. These include encounters with woolly-necked storks (what majestic, beautiful birds!), and colonies of white-fronted bee-eaters. Neither of these were present north of this area and Cazombo. In fact, the past two days have seemed a veritable paradise of birds. Apart from the storks and bee-eaters, I've seen brown-fronted herons, cormorants, kingfishers of several kinds, lilac-breasted rollers, fish eagles, bateleur eagles, Ross's louries, hadedas, and green-backed herons.

At 12°21'39S there is a small rapid that marks the start of a completely new geography. I use the change as an opportunity to stop and stretch my aching back. I stand on the bank and look around. How beautiful it is. Up to this point the river is cutting through clay. Now suddenly, just after the rapid, it passes over beautiful white sand. The banks are gentler, the grass quite different, and the trees are now interspersed with little hillocks and grasslands. It is spectacularly beautiful. At an abandoned mining village, called Cambila, I decide to have a break and to explore. Perhaps a walk will help loosen up the spasms in my back. I do so somewhat gingerly for fear of landmines but, tying my *barco* up on a sandy bank and with panga in hand, off I go. Several hundred metres from the river there are two wattle and daub dwellings, which have been abandoned for a long time.

Inside one of these I find a little dugout – clearly a toy for some child. This truly was a labour of love for it must have taken considerable time for the father to carve. Yet, in the hurry to run from advancing soldiers, this and a few other items were left behind. There they lie now – rusty and rotten – a monument to a foolish war.

Just beyond the dwelling is the old Portuguese road from Lumbala Kaquenque. Although covered in grass the gravel foundation is in good condition, and one run with a grader and a good check for mines will make it like new.

I see soldiers' tracks on the road – about five men going north towards Lumbala. I use their tracks as a clear route to avoid landmines and walk north for about two kilometres. There appears to be no other building standing, but there are clear signs of old open-cast mining. Suddenly, through the grass a few hundred metres ahead of me and coming towards me, is a soldier. He is alone and looks quite relaxed. When he sees me he unslings his rifle from his shoulder.

When close enough to greet, I do so, and what a pleasant, cheerful fellow I meet. His name is Petrov and he is on 'patrol'. Camouflage pants, green T-shirt hanging out, slip-slops, an AKM with one magazine, and an enormous smile. I tell him that I've seen signs of elephant and he confirms a herd of six in the area. I am very excited, relieved to know that at least some game has survived the 30 years of war. There are signs of many other animals here, too, and I take a real liking to the place. I have a good chat with Petrov and he says that there is no trouble in this area at all. His very appearance demonstrates this, and it's good to know.

While walking back to my kayak I muse on how much untruth there is in the world. During the dark days of apartheid, South African Defence Force soldiers were often in battle against the MPLA, which was reinforced with Cuban troops and East German and Russian Special Forces troops and officers. The Soviet presence was clear but continually denied in order to position all South Africans as racist apartheid soldiers. But after travelling in two Antonov 32 aircraft (both flown by ex-Soviets), meeting with Colonel Mukondu (who spent six

> There appears to be no other building standing, but there are clear signs of old open-cast mining. Suddenly, through the grass a few hundred metres ahead of me and coming towards me, is a soldier.

years at the military academy in Petrograd), being delivered to the river in a Russian GAZ and, meeting an ordinary soldier bearing the name Petrov, the Soviet influence is difficult to deny. I don't even need to raise my own experience of battle against Cubans to make the point.

The confluence between the Luena and Zambezi rivers is one of God's most special places.

None of this matters now, of course, but the lesson is clear: political propaganda on all sides, be it in war or peace, needs to be viewed with considerable scepticism. What, for example, are the real truths between the USA and Al Qaeda and international terrorism? I myself crossed paths with the CIA in Angola in 1975. They were there to provide weapons and advisory support to Unita against the Marxist government. Perhaps, one day, other young people will be paddling down a river reflecting on how they too were fed lies by some or other government or religious order or powerful lobby group.

The confluence between the Luena and Zambezi rivers is one of God's most special places. I paddle right into the middle of the junction, turn around and, drifting backwards, drink in the enormous beauty. It is all so quiet, so beautiful and so special. It will not be long before people begin re-inhabiting this area and tour operators begin running the river. But I have had a moment in paradise.

I love the bush so much. I am drawn to it – it is my friend. I paddle along thinking of ways to somehow rescue this little piece of Africa from destruction and poor development. It would make the most magnificent game reserve; a soul-retreat in a country desperate for peace.

The afternoon is filled with spectacularly beautiful vistas, and although weary and in pain, I enjoy it thoroughly. This is a very, very beautiful country and, because of my timing, I have seen it in all its glory. May God grant it lasting peace.

I awake to a heavy wind blowing in from the south and south-east. If it stays like this I'll be paddling into it the whole day. Inwardly, I groan.

I launch my kayak but I feel depressed. This is potentially my last day in Angola. I'm not sure what my feelings are. All tangled up inside me are the stresses of the journey and the close calls with the water and with military forces. So much life intertwined with death, and so much of the buried past being dragged into the present.

When I started the journey I had been in burnout for a long time. My emotions were dull, my life just happened by rote. I got up in the morning and did what I had to do through discipline alone. There was no longer any passion, no fire, inside. It took enormous effort to create passion when I needed to and when my work demanded it. I was always tired and irritable. I was simply not a very nice person any more. I knew that I was dying inside; I knew that I did not have long before I would slide finally into a dark place from which I would probably never return. A place where I would exist, but not truly live.

The effort of forcing the time and space for this river trip was enormous. Everything conspired against me going. Like crooked hands clawing at my very soul, holding me back, I felt the pressures to not go dragging at me. I had to find a wilfulness – even an unpleasant forcefulness – to break myself free of my 'responsibilities', my 'duty', and my lethargy. Ringing constantly in my head at the time were Aquinas's words: 'You cannot give what you have not got'. I needed to give so much, but I was so empty, so depleted. I just had to go.

Here I am now and, through the constant challenge of a different kind of life, one that is constantly close to death, I am beginning to shrug off death of the spirit.

The people I have met and known begin to fuse in my mind. Colonel Nicolau, with his untidy, big, black moustache, so similar to my first commanding officer when I arrived at 1 Parachute Battalion as a young second lieutenant, Commandant Eve Olchers. One was my mentor and respected leader – the other, the enemy. Now I didn't really know or care who was who. They were both just men. Good men – men that I came to respect and like and admire.

The soldiers I had known, the things I had seen and experienced, all became one. Who was the enemy, who the friend? The young white soldier whose head I felt like ripping off as he fooled around with a black enemy soldier's finger, severed at the knuckle, stuck up his nose. The speed at which the young Angolans dipped into aggression and began to hit me. The older man's intervention. Were we not all the same in the end, universally connected to both the darkness and the light? The constant struggle within us all between the two, especially when we are young.

I am weary. The river goes on and on and I need some respite. But the wind blows directly into my face and gives me no quarter. Then, a slight turn, and I seek shelter in the lee of the ridge. The water here is calm and I hug the reed bank and tree line to stay in the lee for as long as possible. I catch my breath and look around at this beautiful place. On my right, across the rippled water, is an eddy, behind which the reeds bend and sway in the wind. Ahead and on the left, the steep clay bank, rising out of the water for 40 metres, dark and pitted with holes dug by pied kingfishers. Directly left of me, the black-brown boughs of trees growing out of and hanging over the grey-green water. Light green leaves sparkle in the sunlight. It is very beautiful, but I am so tired. For some reason I think of crocodiles, noting that I haven't seen any for a long time. I wonder if there are any here at all. My eyes scan the water – nothing in front, and behind … I look over my left shoulder, and instantly my innards freeze. Coming at me, and less than three metres away, is an enormous crocodile! Only the tiniest of ripples belie his stealthy, reptilian forward movement, his yellow-green eyes and protruding teeth utterly terrifying. Instinctively I swing my paddle at him, shouting, splashing water over his eyes. He doesn't even blink. An incredible terror grips me and I am at a loss as to what to do. He holds me in his steady, awful gaze. I try to keep my paddle pointed at him to protect myself should he launch at me now. But in order to move away from him I have to paddle forward. If I move, I will expose the side of my torso to his terrifying jaws. There is a moment in which a strange kind of stand-off occurs – a moment of total exposure – but I have no choice. If I stay he will kill me. I quickly move my paddle for a stroke then point it back at him. I try not to take my eyes off him at any time. I do it again and move a little further from him. Without any visible movement he closes the gap again. My kayak has now moved so that he lies almost directly behind me. I do the only thing I can and begin paddling as hard and fast as I can without showing any sign that he may perceive as panic. Then my kayak begins moving really fast. I struggle not to slow down to look back as everything in me is telling me to do. But once I am 20 or so metres away I turn the kayak slightly so that I can look back at where he was. He has followed me a short way but is clearly letting me go. It is quite clear: this is his turf and his medium. If he wanted to, seated as close to the water as I am, he could have had me out of my kayak in an instant. If I hadn't looked around and seen him, I'm sure he would have. But, I guess, at 46, I would make a rather stringy, distasteful meal – thank goodness! He drifts around behind me and then disappears beneath the water for good. For a while I paddle quite fast!

On and on the wind blows. On and on the river flows. To keep myself going, I count the strokes of my paddle. I practise multiples, emphasising the multiple each time my counting passes it by: one, two, three, four, five, *six*, seven, eight, nine, 10, 11, *12*, I go. Up to 100, then gently paddle for eight strokes and start again: one, two, three, four … On and on it goes. I recite values from Boy Scout days, still so embedded in me and part of my makeup: trusty, loyal, helpful, brotherly, courteous, kind, smiling, clean in thought, word and deed. One value, one stroke. Over and over I repeat the rhyme. The word 'obedient' should follow 'kind'. I force myself to debate why I am not comfortable with obedience. My body screams; my mind is tangled and struggling. I was obedient and went to the army because the State conscripted me. I was obedient when told to apologise for trying to arrange for a member of the then banned ANC to talk to our debating society at high school, and was arrested for doing so. I didn't even understand what the ANC was; that's why we wanted to hear from them! Ghandi's civil disobedience, Mandela's refusal to acknowledge an apartheid court, Martin Luther King's disobedience in the face of white supremacy. I struggle and struggle, and leave out the word 'obedient'. There are times when one must disobey.

I hit the wall after paddling about 50 kilometres. Everything just shuts down. No energy, nothing. I can hardly lift the paddle. I try to force myself to recover, to move through this awful place. I sit bent forward in my craft, utterly exhausted. I am totally vulnerable now. Even a small croc would be able to take me. I am spent, but deep inside I continue to fight. Slowly, slowly, I claw myself forward and out of this awful hole. I become able to lift the paddle again. Everything in me is screaming to stop. Each movement is an agony; a battle rages in my head: 'Shut down, shut down,' one voice cries.

'No – carry on. Push. Push.'

'Stop. Stop!' The awful clamour continues in my brain.

But gradually my strength returns. I take a gentle stroke and rest. Then another and rest again. But now I can feel I am breaking free. Another stroke and another. My body adjusts and I slowly find my second wind. Now on a new plane I begin to push my body still harder until once again I am covering good distance.

There in the distance I see a protruding hill. This is only the second such feature along the whole Angolan stretch of the river. The first one was at Cazombo. My map tells me that this ridge

> I hit the wall after paddling about 50 kilometres. Everything just shuts down. No energy, nothing. I can hardly lift the paddle. I try to force myself to recover, to move through this awful place.

marks the border with Zambia and the location of Chavuma Falls. The vegetation and terrain change dramatically as the border gets closer. Palm trees are suddenly everywhere, and the trees begin to thin out. The tall, big-girthed trees of further north are far behind. The war in that part of Angola at least saved the big trees.

The sunset comes and goes and darkness takes hold. I see the flickering fires of the village of Caripande marking the Angolan side of the border. In the darkness I approach a barrage or dyke that forms the first rapid in a very long way. I run several rapids in the dark but, knowing that Chavuma Falls lie ahead, my nerves are stretched to the limit. Eventually I decide that Chavuma will have to wait until morning and I pull into the bush for the night, totally exhausted.

Because my camera was destroyed in the rapids in Angola, Annie had arranged to get one to the missionaries at Chavuma for me. Always keen for an adventure, my lifelong friend Andy had undertaken to deliver it. However, he was pressed for time and would only be there for a few hours before he had to leave for Livingstone, Zambia, a 21-hour drive on appalling roads. From there he would fly back to Johannesburg. I would be lucky to catch him at all!

In the morning I paddle through some pleasant, gentle rapids and, 40 minutes later, I see someone standing on a vehicle with a small crowd gathered. As I approach I'm ecstatic to see that it's Andy, accompanied by another friend, GG. I'm very excited and pleased to see them, and Andy is clearly relieved to see me! He and GG tell me that, at Annie's urging, the missionaries have been keeping an eye out for me for some days, and that they are keen to have me stop over for a shower and a rest if I want to. I certainly do!

Now I realise how tired I really am. Yesterday was extremely tough physically ... I am thoroughly exhausted but have difficulty shutting down my mind.

We load the kayak onto the vehicle and drive up the hill to Chavuma Mission, where I meet Jeanette Young and June Speichisger – two of the mission staff, who warmly welcome me and make sure that I am alright. They allocate me a little guest cottage where Andy and GG had spent the previous night. I have a wonderful shower, something to eat, and then quickly have the chance to sort out the passport formalities. That being done, I take a quick look at Chavuma Falls, then begin sorting out gear, getting rid of certain things now that I am out of a war zone. All too quickly two hours have gone past, and it's time for Andy and GG to get on the road. It's been really wonderful to see Andy. True friendship is not something that comes easily and we have known each other and shared so much over the past 36 years. A lot of love exists here and I am so sad to see him go. Both of us have tears in our eyes as the vehicle drives away.

Now I realise how tired I really am. Yesterday was extremely tough physically, and the other days before that were full of their own challenges, not to mention the particular stresses of being in a war zone for part of the time. I am thoroughly exhausted but have difficulty shutting down my mind.

That afternoon I spend cleaning, repairing and preparing gear and, after a short nap, I am visited by Ray and Ruth Williams, who kindly invite me to their home for supper. Ray and Ruth are a wonderful couple; both of them missionaries, medical doctors and 'refugees' from the DRC. They now run the mission hospital at Chavuma. They had lived in the DRC since the Belgian colonial days of the '50s and '60s and had been through all manner of conflicts there over the past 40 years. However, in the final incident they lost their house and their car, and Ray very nearly lost his life when he was arrested by Kabila's forces for being a spy. Ray simply points, with a wry smile, that it at least got them to Chavuma – pure luxury compared to their previous world.

The missionaries and their families are the most peaceful, loving, kind and hospitable people one could ever hope to meet. Several of the families have been there a few generations and all of them are totally committed to their work and to the Zambian people. I decide at their bidding to spend a further day resting and have the opportunity, with them, to explore philosophical and spiritual questions. This is very important to me, as my journey throughout has been underpinned by the search for greater meaning.

For the missionaries, there is also a terrible and tragic side to living in so remote and wild a place. One of their friends and colleagues had not long before been on the Kabompo River – a tributary of the Zambezi that I would still need to pass not far south of Chavuma – when a terrible tragedy occurred. The missionary colleague, together with a friend of his and the missionary's 14-year-old son, were travelling down the river close to the town called Zambezi where the Kabompo joins the Zambezi River. Their boat overturned in some rapids. The two adults swam to one side and the son to the other. Realising this, the son shouted that he was coming over and dived back in. But the adults shouted at him to go back for fear of crocodiles. He turned around and had just regained the bank when a large crocodile shot out of the water and dragged him back under the water. He reappeared after a while in the middle of the river – screaming desperately for help – and then disappeared under the water again. His father, who was very blind without his glasses, which had been lost in the accident, had to be physically restrained by his friend from jumping into the river. The terrible agony of this moment for him is almost impossible to imagine. There was nothing that could be done. No part of the boy's body was ever recovered.

A short while before I arrived in Chavuma, two local youngsters had been on the banks of the massive water. I had unknowingly met Andy at the exact spot. One was taken by a crocodile. The other was simultaneously knocked into the water and, in his terror, was drowned.

Another missionary family suffered the loss of a child to a bite from a black mamba.

These sad snippets represent just a tiny illustration of the difficulties and tragedies that are constantly there for people who live on the river.

The evening before leaving Chavuma, I have dinner again with Ray and Ruth, and we are joined a little later by Jeanette. Earlier in the day, Ruth had handled an emergency at the hospital in which a baby was born with considerable difficulty. Ray is clearly proud of the way Ruth handled it, yet here she is now, a gracious hostess, and still somehow managing to bake me a loaf of bread and make me sandwiches for my journey the next day!

For the missionaries, there is also a terrible and tragic side to living in so remote and wild a place.

Chavuma Mission to Kanja

- Western Zambia and the Barotse flood plains
- *Mekoro* and fisherfolk
- Bird paradise
- The Lozi people
- I meet a *sangoma*

The river from Chavuma Falls south towards Chinyingi has once again changed its mantle. Now the banks are sandy – sometimes levy-like, sometimes extending in long, beautiful beaches. The trees are sparser, but the grasses appear more palatable than those north of the Angolan border, and there are many more people here. I must have passed between 30 and 40 dugouts in the first 35 kilometres that I travelled. Most of the people speak English and all are friendly, smiley and curious.

I see two big crocodiles – both splashing off the bank as I approach. A short distance away is a group of children, fishing and playing near the water. Life is dangerous here and I feel great concern for the kids.

This evening while I am making my supper, two women – one with a baby on her back and firewood on her head – chance upon my camp. One of them, whose name is Ruth, giggles at the fright she gets when she sees me and then in good English has a conversation with me. She is curious and says, 'OK, I'll see you in the morning,' as she leaves. I hope she is not too early!

I have a bad night's sleep and wake up feeling terrible – nauseous and with muscular pain everywhere. I only get going at 11h00, climbing into my kayak just as Ruth arrives with her little boy – he looks about five or six years old. We have a quick chat and she wants to know when I will be returning upriver as she and her husband want me to stay at their home then. I'm afraid I have to disappoint her, but she is so cheerful and sweet, she adds considerably to what turns out to be a lovely day.

As I paddle, the gentle sounds of cowbells and marimbas being played in the riverine forest verge reach my ears, joining the call of birds and the splash of a crocodile to make a symphony more wonderful than any. I go to the bank, intending to explore the source of the marimbas but the playing stops and I cannot find them. I pick up a purple-blue feather from a Ross's Lourie, intending to carry it as a gift for Annie. Perhaps this is why I was drawn to the bank. A short distance further on a drummer practises his rhythm in the forest – staccato rolls and taps – slowly building to a powerful swaying beat.

This part of the river is characterised by beautiful sandy beaches. Sometimes there are three-metre-high sandstone, cliff-like banks on one side of the river, topped with lush vegetation and oozing sparkling water.

At Chinyingi there is a pont, as well as a most spectacular pedestrian bridge. This is the first proper bridge across the Zambezi since I entered Angola in the north. It was erected in 1975 by an Italian missionary who did all the high and

The gentle sounds of cowbells and marimbas being played in the riverine forest verge reach my ears, joining the call of birds and the splash of a crocodile to make a symphony more wonderful than any.

Below, left: The first vehicle pont since the source, Chinyingi.
Below, right: The suspension bridge at Chinyingi.

dangerous cable work himself. It carries people from the mission, which lies on the west bank, across to the east, and all manner of traffic can be seen: women with loads on their heads, a young boy on a bicycle, and young children. All 30 or so metres above the crocodile-infested Zambezi. Not far from the bridge a group of young girls are washing and run giggling and laughing to cover themselves when I appear.

The evening's campsite is next to a well-worn pathway running alongside the river. Beyond the sparse tree-line lies beautiful open grassland, and cattle are being herded towards the north. The dust in the setting sun gives a gentle glow and surrounds the lowing cattle as they walk past a distant tree.

The town of Zambezi boasts a pedestrian pont. It is simply a very long *mokoro* seating six passengers and paddled by one man. There is also a vehicle pont and, of course, a water pump station. Electricity cables cross the river – the first I have seen since the river source. The urbanisation disturbs me. It intrudes on my silent reverie. It looks foreign to the river, and even though the people are friendly and curious, I don't want to be there and I do not stop.

Downstream of the town my protective feelings for the river emerge and I am saddened and disgusted to see plastic bags and even a surgical glove hooked on branches overhanging the water.

Urbanised humanity has now definitely touched the river, and it is not pretty.

Bird life here is also sparse, though I see falcons at a distance, a grey cuckoo hawk and a gymnogene. It seems strange that I have not encountered one fish eagle since re-entering Zambia. As the distance grows between me and Zambezi town, so too does the bird life. I begin to see marabou and white storks, hadedas, fork-tailed drongos and bulbuls.

People are very relaxed about the water here – standing right in it while bathing or washing clothes. My enquiries tell me that crocodiles are not a big danger here, but to be particularly careful of both crocs and hippo downstream of Chitokoloki.

The pollution, though not extreme, has disturbed me. I think a lot about humanity and our interaction with the environment, the natural world and each other. The ancient law of custodianship, so carefully nurtured by all primal peoples, is all but lost. In our pursuit of progress we destroy so much. Not only the obvious environment with our pollution and our chainsaws, but also aspects of our humanity: the understanding of our interdependence, the loss of our very meaning. We move so easily from living to existing.

The ancient peoples understood all of this so well. The San and KhoiKhoi, the North American Indians, the aboriginal Australians, and so many others all understood that everything was interconnected, that we are all part of one organism. They knew that when we destroyed or caused damage, we were doing this to our own bodies. And we are doing it right now with our deforestation and pollution and our holes in the ozone. The industrialised, apparently civilised, First World is the prime culprit. Refusal by some governments to sign agreements such as the Kyoto Protocol to limit emissions because it would 'cost too much', is akin to saying that it costs too much to live.

Refusal by some governments to sign agreements such as the Kyoto Protocol to limit emissions because it would 'cost too much', is akin to saying that it costs too much to live.

I come across a pretty school set well back from the river bank – white walls with the rafters in light blue. This little settlement is called Gatshana, and everyone can speak English to this point. However, 10 kilometres further on and suddenly English doesn't work. Somehow I like that.

At a village called Kakongi (14°04'S) the river becomes very shallow, flowing over a great sandstone plate. There are small, low-water rapids here and children wade three quarters of the way across the river, stopping just short of the deeper channel on the western side. Looking down through the clear water, wonderful shapes are visible in the sandstone; little caves and cracks and surfaces that make the riverbed look like a huge sponge.

This area (between Mayengu and Lukulu) is well populated and people can at least be heard, if not seen, most of the time. There is a big reduction in the English speakers now, but there is always someone who can converse. As evening approaches, I see groups of large dugouts moving upstream. I happen to be close to an overnight stop for travellers going from Lukulu to Zambezi.

Many of them say they left at as early as six o'clock, which means they've been paddling upstream for eleven hours. The goods are a mixture of fish, other food such as maize meal, and people. When I ask one man what he bought in Lukulu he points at the back of his dugout near his feet. There, amidst his other acquisitions, lies a lovely soft-coated Labrador-type dog – his head resting peacefully on the gunwale. I'm not quick enough for a photo and the light is beginning to fade, but what a lovely memory is embedded in my mind.

The other three dugouts in his group are being poled by his three sons – the youngest about 10 years old! The trains of vessels make me think of camel trains in a desert – this is somehow just as romantic. The people – some drivers, some passengers, some family – all making their way like so many generations before them. One train has nine dugouts in it, all heavily laden. Sadly, this area also shows signs of considerable deforestation. Slash-and-burn is happening all along the banks, the trees being cut down for firewood and replaced with cassava.

As evening approaches, two groups pass me while I am washing on the bank. They are going towards Lukulu. One driver calls out, concerned, 'Are you alone? Are you sleeping here? Come, I will wait for you; we can camp together.' His is a concern echoed constantly by the river people: 'It is safer to be together, so come with us.' I'm sure they think it very strange that I choose to be alone.

Having explained that I have already travelled from the source and that I am going to Mozambique, one fellow calls out, 'For what purpose do you make this journey, sah?' Yes, for what purpose indeed? Somewhere I know the answer is unfolding in the journey itself!

One fellow, his dugout loaded with sweet potatoes, is on his way to Lukulu to trade. He expects to sell his load for K500 000 ($125) over four days, buy his own provisions and head back home. With two days to get to Lukulu and three days back, this is a nine-day trip. Talk about popping down to the shops! I chat to people as I pass them by. A dugout can be bought for K100 000 ($25) and takes four men a week to make. Of course, the problem nowadays is finding big enough trees, so the boat carvers travel up the Zambezi where forests can still provide material. In my mind's eye,

I see Angolan forests pristine and magnificent, which will soon be traded away as well.

I join Vaskus Rakambo for a while as he poles along. He is a boat builder and he has two dugouts tied together that he is taking to Lukulu to sell. When I ask, 'How much?' he says they would be $50 each for me. They are large, he explains, and have taken a lot of work to carve.

There is a market in Lukulu – a town very reminiscent of Zambezi but prettier and friendlier. The 'harbour' with its hodgepodge of dugouts, big, small, straight and bent, is a colourful spot where vegetables and fish are readily available. Lukulu is also the place where, for the first time, people begin to get concerned about hippos. At the harbour where I passed the first of two vehicle ferries (one driven by a Mariner 25), several people call out to be aware of hippos.

Sure enough, some 15 kilometres further south – hippos – a pod of three. They display unusual behaviour, and are very wary, staying under water for long periods of time and only coming up to blow and disappear again. They are unwelcome here: the hippos desperate to survive; the farmers trying to protect their crops. It's all about survival. Each species challenged by the same immutable laws. Be it here or in a city, the constant is survival.

The countryside changes quickly. North of Lukulu one sees the commencement of acacia, fever trees and palms. From Lukulu and south one enters the start of what was once called the Barotse floodplain – the home of the Lozi people. The river begins to break up into little channels and beaches fringed with reeds that become rolling dunes in places. The countryside is understandably flat with relatively low, gentle sandy banks to the river itself.

Top and above: The 'port' of Lukulu.
Below: Fishermen visiting my sleeping ledge cut in a sandbank.

This area also boasts fish eagles, bateleur eagles and gymnogenes. I spot white-crowned and blacksmith plovers, reed cormorants, green-backed herons (who have kept me company right from the source), darters and grey-headed gulls. I am intrigued by the African skimmers – short-legged birds with distinctly large red beaks – which look so squat and disproportionate on land but become quite spectacular in flight. Angular and purposeful, they fly along the surface of the water, skimming with their lower mandibles.

The water shimmers like a mirror, and the upside-down reflections as the skimmers whip by make for a surreal picture. I see pied kingfishers, somewhat scarce in these parts, wagtails, blue-cheeked bee-eaters, forktailed drongos,

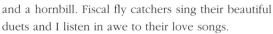

and a hornbill. Fiscal fly catchers sing their beautiful duets and I listen in awe to their love songs.

I am in bird paradise!

Gradually the riverine bush becomes sparser, eventually disappearing almost completely. The countryside is dry and harsh. Where bush does exist, it offers little shelter, but as the evening approaches I see in the distance a lone acacia tree. Surrounded by spiky inhospitable bush, it plays host to a gymnogene, which watches me curiously as I begin to make my way across the water to the tree. I don't wish to disturb her, so look around for another camp spot, but have no choice. Mind-messaging to her, I apologise and begin to make my way back upstream to the tree. Soon she flies away and I cut my way through the fierce thorns and make a bed for myself.

I start of with a heavy south to southeast wind blowing, and most of the time I'm going directly into it. Somehow, beyond the hard work that it is, it's exhilarating to have the fresh gusts directly in my face. The chop at least allows me to see that I am moving. Around a corner, and for the first time, it looks like I can use my sail, for there is a stretch of river running westwards. Up it goes and what fun! Part of the excitement, I'm sure, is because I am not paddling, and I make good progress for a short while. Unfortunately, I do not have another occasion to use the sail, but through this wonderful, varied day, I see so much and love it.

At a spot where the locals shout, 'Cross over, there's a hippo!' I dutifully do so – and run right into our friendly hippo, who has now also crossed over. I am hugging the reed bank and he is in it and then under me! Both of us get quite a start but mine is doubly so, for within metres a very large crocodile slithers off the bank and there are holes and passages in the reeds that look quite ominous. This would not have been a good place to get tipped into the river by a hippo.

In my kayak, I creep up on pygmy kingfishers, who always elude my camera, and watch one enter its clay hole in the bank. There I wait for a photograph but eventually must go on, disappointed. The floodplain opens up fully now – flat and endless. Channels run in many directions and it's sometimes difficult to choose which one to take. Evening comes; ordinary, somewhat overcast and bland. Yet it is calm and the water is still. Every now and again my rudder scrapes on a sandbar, making the only sound other than my paddles.

I muse on life. This river is a wonderful metaphor for life itself. Mostly, it isn't hugely spectacular, and not every moment of the big picture is filled with beauty and delight. But the small things are, and the small things are always there. Just like this 'ordinary' evening. It becomes wonderful as I watch the skimmers play across the still surface. White crowned plovers strut startled along a reed-broken beach. Pied kingfishers try and try to catch their evening meal and francolin set up their evening din. From somewhere across the watery plains comes the sounds of marimbas and, because I watch so intently, the very ripples take on a magic movement of their own. Slowly the evening begins to bloom and I marvel at its unending beauty. No camera can capture this moment. The beauty is there, if only we choose to see it.

Suddenly the sun is gone and the light goes fast. I am caught somewhat short by my own reverie, my intense enjoyment of this splendour. In the floodplains, finding a suitable camp spot is not so easy, and now darkness chases me too. I see the white of sand through some reeds and pull up next to it. It is steep and the other side is marshy and wet, but it will do. Using my panga, I cut a shelf for my bed and another to sit and cook on. Mountaineering experience comes in handy here!

I prepare my meal, and in the windless, dark night I'm surprised to hear people paddling along the reeds. A lantern appears, set at the front of the dugout, and then the hunters. They are armed with a trident-like spear – one man paddling, the other intently watching the water. They pass me by and I watch and hear the plunging harpoon every now and again. I hope they are lucky. Just below me and to my left, five or six metres away, I can hear a heavy body moving in the reeds. It eventually goes away. All night the fishermen work the river.

In the morning I receive a visit from last night's fishermen. With smiling, open faces they tell me their names – Kyombo Chisapa and Chinyemba Ndikola – and I find out they live on an island not far from here. They have worked 14 hours for their humble catch, yet they offer some to me. Chinyemba asks if I perhaps have a novel for him to read; not hooks, nor line, nor matches, but a novel! Sadly, I cannot help. Handshakes, and then with good wishes they are gone.

I come across an old commercial fishing lodge. There are three visitors camped in the run-down ruin:

> Slowly the evening begins to bloom and I marvel at its unending beauty. No camera can capture this moment. The beauty is there, if only we choose to see it.

a Zambian couple from Kitwe and their friend. They have a motor boat and, using *rapalas*, have caught seven large bream and a tiger fish in the couple of hours they've been fishing. The humble people like Kyombo and Chinyemba are up for hours at night hoping for just one fish that size.

Still I travel through the depths of the magnificent Barotse floodplains. There are many channels but I become philosophical: if the water is flowing in, it must come out somewhere. There are many fishing people along the banks, living in simple grass shelters. Friendly people, all. 'How far?' is the opening question, which is my cue to tell them of my journey. Many believe the kayak must have an engine for such a journey and are quite disbelieving when I jokingly slap my biceps and say, 'Yes – two engines!'

Periodically – mostly to amuse the locals – I haul up my sail. Laughter and excited astonishment follows. One fellow, seeing it flapping above me while I paddle asks, 'For what purpose is that, sah?' It says everything about how little the sail helps with prevailing winds from east and south, as well as the British heritage in the language!

I see my first motorised transport on the river (besides the motorboat of the three from Kitwe) – a heavily laden ferry going upstream. Designed to carry no more than 10, it's crammed with at least 20 people, and driven by a tiny outboard engine. To my surprise, seated in the middle, is a young white woman. I wonder what she is doing here, alone and so far from civilisation, and then I catch myself, for no doubt she is thinking exactly the same of me.

For weeks now, I have suffered very badly from muscle spasm in my lower back, but today it is so crippling I try everything from stopping and stretching to painkillers. But when it decides to go into spasm it simply does. I am forced to stop every 20 minutes or so to try and stretch it out. Eventually, I rig up a contraption that holds my Leatherman multi-tool in exactly the right spot on my back, and I press my back into the pain and, in agony, refuse to stop.

Along the way I hear marimbas again and this time I am able to see them from the bank. I stop and play around with the four young men, who are really great musicians. The resonators are all calabashes and the deep bass a truly massive one. Musicians are the same the world over. Once they get into jamming they go somewhere into music heaven. The looks on their faces tells it all.

Early evening camp and a visit from Justin who offers me fish. Here the people do not say, 'Give me … ,' as one gets in so many urban areas around the world, but, 'What can I give you?'

The stars are spectacular and after macaroni and powdered cheese with little bits of biltong broken up into it, I am a very satisfied soul.

A very physical day. Heavy wind, mostly directly onto my nose – but great. Something broke through in me today; an old inner power. At first the effort was enormous and then – a decision deep inside – to enjoy the physical pressure and to revel in it. Suddenly the movement of muscle and fibre is joyous in itself. The power in my body emerges. I go through the inner debate – 'Stop, have a break,' 'No, don't. Keep pushing.' On and on, but suddenly, no more debate – I hit the point where struggle turns into pleasure.

The beauty of this place is awesome. The mood of it shifts and changes. Heavy wind sends big waves breaking over the bow, and then the evening falls calm, the water a mirror. And the birds – skimmers, so magnificent in flight, and there the grey-headed gulls, the herons and egrets. But the light! Oh the splendour of it all. Water and sky all one but for a thin sliver of land.

A hippo greets my cold camp spot with his grunts. It is very cold and there is no shelter, but the air is crisp and the stars dazzling. I talk to my children, their voices distant on the satellite phone, and I love them so very much. I talk to Christine and I talk to my old childhood friend and military comrade, Mark, who happens to be there.

My sleep is disturbed by sounds out there and voices within. The red sun sees in the day, so calm. Early travellers pass by; overloaded *mekoro* and people with their questions. Why? Why do you do this journey, sir? So many answers I can give them, but which one is the truth? Do I run, or do I seek? Do I explore or retreat? Do I travel the river because it's there or seek something that eludes me, something within myself? And last night's conversation with my family and friends – I feel so strongly I should be there with them. My children grow and I am not there. I love so much yet feel so unable to show it – to do things that are supposed to be done. But what is supposed to be done?

For a while I find myself pausing. Lost in thought, disorganised, I cannot pack the kayak. I put on my paddling shorts the wrong way around, then I catch myself and sit down to write. I have a headache and my spirits are low. I would have so loved a 'normal' family life. A place with Sunday lunches and fireside chats. A place where I could

Something broke through in me today; an old inner power. At first the effort was enormous and then – a decision deep inside – to enjoy the physical pressure and to revel in it.

Below: The first and only motorised ferry I see on the Barotse Floodplains.

just be, feeling settled and safe. Yet not there – not here! I pace within. What is 'normal'? Is it mundane conformity? If so, what sacrifices, huge sacrifices, are made to stand outside of the norm?

I don't know if I should struggle anymore. Do I just accept myself or do I explore still further, perhaps in therapy or in any way I can? I am restless, unsatisfied, unfulfilled. I love my family – I want to be with them but I know I cannot truly and fully be. Did the war do this? Did my youth and childhood preordain this?

I leave late. I have been writing and my gear is wet from the heavy dew. I paddle aimlessly. The channels come and go – a decision at each one. Like life. Yet all of them stay connected to the great river.

By early afternoon I have settled down a bit. The countryside is still floodplain but then I round a corner and I am greeted by birds – hundreds, no, maybe thousands of them. Grey-headed gulls all sitting on a beach where gulls should be, but this one is a very long way from the ocean. It lifts my spirits. I watch them dance and play in the air. How is it that they never collide? It's wonderful to see. Then a flock of African skimmers arrive and put the gulls in a panic. Some settle on an island with cormorants. This is truly beautiful.

The wind stays throughout the day. I round another sharp turn in the river. Trees and a western-style building. It is a school I am told and, yes – there just beyond it – another group of trees, exotic eucalyptus, and more buildings. Africa has such magnificent indigenous trees, but where settlers have been we find exotics!

The little children at the school are at break when I arrive. They are tiny and very excited to see me and, of course, my most unusual boat. I smile and chat, then wave goodbye. For several hours I paddle and then, there in the distance, a ridge begins to emerge. It has trees on it! I am quite excited but the river slowly turns away. But not too much further, real land! A proper bank of clay and soil with ordinary grass on it. I feel like a castaway seeing land after months at sea. Soon – proper Barotse homesteads – no longer the reed structures of the floodplains. Pretty, ordered homesteads and cattle. Lots of cattle.

Here there are many more people and I feel as though I have really arrived in Barotseland.

The famous Lozi (Barotse) people who live in this western province of Zambia are led by a traditional monarchy. The king's title is *Lithunga*. He is the traditional leader of the Lozi, but is also the senior government official for the province. Each year as the floodwaters over the plains begin to rise, the Lithunga signals that it is time for the people to leave. He does so in a ceremony called *Kuomboka*.

Besides symbolising the Lithunga's historical role, the *Kuomboka* also gives open recognition to the interdependence of the Lozi people and the river. Without the annual flood, the grass and crops could not sustain the following year's needs.

Here I am at Nalolo, the Queen's palace. She is, of course, not in residence here now because of the time of the year. But soon, as the waters subside, she will return.

Very soon, the river turns away once more and back into the reeds and marshes I go. But the evening is calm and beautiful: the sunset pink and orange. I only just find a bank in time and yet again carve myself a ledge on which I construct a bed, just metres from the water. At 19h00 and again at 20h00 I look up as arranged with my children and find the Southern Cross. My eyes find it and my heart extends across time and space, and in this way I convey my love to my children. They are doing the same thing on their holiday in Mozambique and, just for an instant, we are joined.

Dawn gently unfolds. The first predawn travellers are hippos on their way downstream after a night of feeding close to the humans. Then a lone dugout – two paddlers, two passengers. The pink silvery light deepens and at 06h35 – rush hour! Gulls, herons, whistling ducks, kingfishers, cormorants. A great cacophony of sounds and movement. Each flock has meaning and travels with purpose, generally westwards. Every now and again a lone heron or gull flies across the traffic or directly into it. With my things packed away, I paddle out slowly into the river.

Top and above: The nets have been out all night, but the catch is small.

I stop for lunch on a little sandbank, and have just finished when two dugouts pass by going south. I join them for the afternoon. It's a family group going to Senanga to trade. They will be selling fish and, most importantly, buying a new net. The matriarch sits perched on her pile of hand-woven grass mats all ready for the market. Two of her sons paddle for her. The bigger one is called Oliver. The old man leads in the other dugout. Two others paddle with him and one young man stays seated. His name is Brand, and I discover that he has pulled a back muscle and is in considerable discomfort. He asks for painkillers and I am able to give him some. I hope it helps and he is very thankful. I need to slow down for them to keep up and decide to do so. They are steady and pretty soon I discover other important things. They know the river well, of course, and suddenly turn off into a little channel. I am unsure and ask them which is the way to Senanga. They point and call for me to follow. Four times through the afternoon this occurs and in so doing we cut great loops off our journey. These channels are the start of oxbow lakes, but unless you know them they would be overlooked.

I decide to treat myself, so I tuck in behind them and no longer concern myself with navigation. It becomes a wonderful, mentally relaxed afternoon. Every now and then the group stops to chat to people going the other way or on the bank. But, more than anything, they enjoy the astonishment that greets our little flotilla's arrival at each homestead. They take ownership of me and keep repeating my journey to those on the bank and laugh uproariously at people's reactions.

The back end of Oliver's dugout is broken and patched – with clay! If you don't have hot glue or Bostik, make a plan. It works well and whereas the other canoe needs bailing periodically, this one remains dry all afternoon. Mum seems quite happy with that.

We see Senanga from a distance. There is a ridge of land and on it nestles a pretty little village amongst some lovely trees. Well-sited, overlooking the Barotse floodplains, is an impressive stone church. Then there is what looks like a boat club – boasting a river cruiser and beautiful lawns. We enter the town on

The back end of Oliver's dugout is broken and patched – with clay! If you don't have hot glue or Bostik, make a plan.

the river as the sun dips below the horizon. My friends make for the bank and I offer farewells and keep going. I only have 15 minutes or so of light left and find a spot just south of the village. I cut away some branches of a bush and set my bed up there. Then a cup of tea and some supper – a good day indeed.

The stars are magnificent. One very bright one in the west stands out. I don't know its name – but it is beautiful and I appreciate it. I don't forget my evening 'star call' for Jess and James. As I look at the Southern Cross I give each of them in turn my full, focused energy. I love them dearly. I decide that the Southern Cross works very well, for I can identify a star for each of us. Annie, Rory, me, Jess, James and Chris – the four of the cross and the two pointers. Perfect. I really miss Annie.

In the morning I decide to walk in to Senanga to stretch my legs and visit the village. The leg bit is almost instantly a problem for I have not used them much for weeks. I feel a shin splint coming on within a few hundred metres and I have a blister from the sandals within a kilometre. Past the prison with lovely vegetable gardens (and lots of free labour), past the Zambian Police with a disused amphibious vehicle rusting out front, past the Halaal meat suppliers, and into town I go. It is quite

a colourful place with a tar road and a busy market behind all the
formal, fairly deserted shops. This is where the fish that Oliver's family
were bringing in yesterday end up. There are fish everywhere – all
different sizes and types and fresh or dried.

I wander around enjoying the sights then make my way towards
the 'boat club' and church. The former turns out to be the Senanga
Safari Lodge, with comfortable accommodation and fishing safaris on
offer. I am approached by two young men wanting to sell me 'some
stuff'. I decline but wonder what their 'stuff' is. On the way back I
buy a loaf of bread and drink a Coke – not sure that I like the taste
now, but it is icy cold and enjoyable. On the way back to my kayak I
decide to nibble at the bread. Passing the police station again, I make
the mistake of having too close a look at the amphibious vehicle. Its
tracks are off. It is clearly disused, but to the
police it is a problem that I look. I am called
over, so into the station I go.

They begin with the customary stern
questioning. Passport? What am I doing here?
Why was I looking at the 'tank'? Why have I
not reported my presence to the police?

After an initial display of irritation I catch
myself and say, 'I am sorry, I was just looking
– it is clearly old – and this is a democracy.'
One of the inspectors laughs and says, 'Yes, we
are told it is a democracy.' Understanding that
they too are curious about me, I regale them
with stories from the trip and close encounters
of the Boon kind, relating my name to the

place in town I discovered called Boon's Restaurant and Nightclub.
It looked like a brothel to me, and once again we laugh. As I leave
them with promises to be a good boy, I buy a second Coke. By the
time I reach my kayak, two-and-a-half hours after leaving it, my bread
is practically history. Wonder where it went? Yummy!

I only begin to paddle at midday but have had an enjoyable
morning. After an hour or so I pass by a ferry point. It is transporting
vehicles and goods as I approach. It's situated at the prettiest Lozi
village one can imagine. A magnificent, huge tree protrudes steadfast
and tall on the banks of the great river. Like a grandfather caring
for his clan, it is positioned central to the village, with neat rows of
huts extending left and right. The huts are not perfectly uniform in
shape or distance from each other, so each expresses its well-crafted
individuality. The roofs of some are very steep, some less so, but all
display the distinctive Lozi top-knot on the coarse grey-brown thatching.
Each knot (or, more accurately, tie) is identical in style and design,

Opposite, bottom left: I find a
restaurant that bears my name.
Opposite, bottom right: The
Senanga Fish Market.
This page, above: Senanga Safari
Lodge tourist launch versus the
traditional river craft!

and it is this that so neatly declares the connectedness of the whole. Three or four much smaller trees bracket the old grandfather and, with the huts tucked in beneath the trees, the whole village takes on the form of a giant hut. Little hedges grow here and there amongst the dwellings – all neatly trimmed. In the foreground is the dark blue of the river and a thin line of the freshest green reeds at the water's edge. Beyond all this, the light blue of a flawless sky makes for perfect symmetry. I sit still and quiet in my kayak and drink in its beauty and its wholeness.

But, sadly, because of its very beauty, the damage done by man is even more painful to see: patches where even the riverine, difficult-to-burn shrubs and trees are all gone. Only the stumps remain.

I carry on downstream but, having heard drums for some way, decide to investigate. It is a *sangoma* – a traditional healer and diviner. She is performing a ceremony to sort out a case of witchcraft. Her name, I discover, is Dr Gertrude Monde Kufanga. She is dressed completely in white and I watch as she turns to a large white cloth and meditates. There is an axe-like instrument hooked over the top corner. On a platform in front of this is an assortment of tools. The skin of a genet forms the base and on that is an enamel cup filled with water. I see matches as well, and one spent match is floating in the water.

All the people involved are lined up. She splashes them with water using her ox-tail wand and then gets them to wash their hands and faces in the water she has prepared. It is very serious business indeed, and the men on trial are clearly afraid. She sends them to an adjacent courtyard. The gathered tribes-people sing and chant. The drummers change periodically but never miss a beat. A dancer steps out every now and again. It is a shoulder shake, much like the Xhosa Xhensa of South Africa.

I feel completely at ease here. I am so African. The textures and rhythms of the place touch me – cracked clay walls on a hut, lined faces that sing ancient rhymes, the smooth beauty of youth, the regal walk of the sangoma – and the cowering respect and fear of the accused.

Back at the kayak I reflect on responses and reactions to my arrival. Children that flee in terror; adults with hands quickly raised to mouths in surprise. '*Legua, Legua!*' goes the call (White man, white man). Fear, surprise, respect. Yet, here I am, rough, bearded, barefoot and alone. All along the river goes that call as I paddle: '*Legua, Legua*'. Although I understand why, it still jars and disturbs. What has the white man done to deserve such recognition?

For 21 years, between 1843 and 1864, Sebitoane of the Kololo tribe occupied the Lozi lands – Barotseland as it was then known. After his occupation, parts of the Kololo language remained. The white man occupied Zambia for 60-odd years. After they left, what remained was a language – and respect, fear, contempt and admiration. But lots of fear. Generations later, the call still goes out, '*Legua, Legua,*' and people are not sure whether to run and hide or greet and welcome.

The afternoon turns to evening; mirror-like the waters flow. The beauty palpable. The silence complete. I drift, unwilling to disturb this time. I pass people on the banks, mostly women in ones and twos. They bathe gently at this quiet and peaceful time.

I have paddled enough to give myself momentum and, in silence, move along the reed bank. A woman stands looking at the water. Her body, silhouetted sideways against the western sky, tall and glistening wet. Youthful beauty, pronounced by the old woman who stands bent and fully clothed not far behind. Both are surprised by my appearance. The old lady quickly holds up a hand and greets. The younger one, with a little scream, flees for a wrap to cover her nakedness. Here in this place, the naked body is right. Its feminine beauty reflects only the beauty of the great natural garden surrounding it. The moment etches itself in my mind.

Approaching darkness forces a reluctant halt for I do not want the wonder of this time to end. As I land some men across the river who are herding cattle see me. 'Legua!' – I hear the word called from one to the other. A man on my side of the river acts as though he has not seen me and walks hastily away. I want to reassure him, so call out. I have to do so several times for he bluffs that he hasn't heard me. I can see that his decision is whether to run or to turn. He turns; I smile and wave.

Tools of the traditional healer.

The night is pitch black and silent. I prepare my food and write my notes. At around 21h00 I hear a strange sound from across the river. It is what the Zulu people call an *ngungu*, a drum with a velum through which a reed is passed. By wetting one's hands and drawing them along the reed one at a time, the velum begins to hum. Doing this rhythmically, following one hand with the other, an almost constant drone begins to sound. It is an ancient sound – one that I love – but I also know that it is probably being sounded because I am here. The men will have gathered and will be singing or chanting quietly along with the *ngungu*.

The pace changes – it is faster, more urgent. It stops and starts a few times. Then, with a slow draw on the reed, it shudders and is quiet. There is some danger for me now, but I am glad I have heard this here. It's like a door has opened and I have stepped into a tribal world that is still in place and functioning. It is African and so am I. I love being here. I am very keen to bring Annie and the children and perhaps a few close friends back here.

I awake to be greeted by the green-backed heron, Burchell's coucal, fiscal flycatcher, grey lourie, spurwing goose, lilac-breasted roller, little bee-eater, and lots of LBJs. The sounds of fish eagles calling close by bring me great joy.

Kanja town is just a dot on a map and I soon pass it and the hippos that keep it company. It is, however, the place that marks the start of acacia veld. Sioma Mission and its falls lie ahead.

It's like a door has opened and I have stepped into a tribal world that is still in place and functioning. It is African and so am I.

Sioma to Mutemwa, heading for Caprivi

- Sioma Falls
- Peasant hospitality
- Military encounters and transformation
- Mutemwa Lodge

The river widens enormously and breaks into channels once again. I pass by a few hippo snorting and burbling, and enjoy the villages that I pass. Then I begin to hear the roar of rapids. My heart picks up and I breathe faster. I sit up straight but using my binoculars I'm still unable to see them. I paddle closer, and then cross left to right across a very wide stretch of river. A man shouts urgently at me from the bank. I know he is trying to warn me. I feel a little twinge in my solar plexus and let the nerves play themselves through. I paddle hard. There is a person on the bank. 'Not far – *big* rapids!'

The roar gets louder. I pass another man in a dugout going upstream. He says, 'If you go there you will … put yourself in much problem.' I try to find out which side to portage – it seems to be the right-hand side.

Several women are standing at the start of what looks like a small set of rapids. They are feeling under rocks and in the reed roots. To my surprise they are catching little fish by hand as the fish tangle themselves in the weedy undergrowth

under the banks and rocks. I'm cautioned again here, so I get out and recce ahead on foot. These are small rapids and I'm assured that there are still only small ones further downstream. But the roar is enormous. They point in its direction and I understand that that is where it is bad, not here.

If these are Sioma Falls, they really are not much to talk of. I am helped down the rocky but gentle rapid by a young man and I'm on my way again. Within 40 metres I see some young boys in a dugout near a little channel going off to the left, towards the sound of big water. Using hand signals I try to ask if I can get through that way and if it will take me closer to the big water that I would like to see. They appear to be a little afraid of me and do not really understand, so I take my chances and go off that way anyway. I notice that they cautiously follow in their dugout – a good sign, I think, for they wouldn't be doing so if they were likely to run into trouble.

The stream gets very narrow – just wider than my kayak and now is overgrown with reeds as well. It is getting late and I don't want to be stuck in overgrown rapids with little water in them and certainly nowhere to sleep when night falls. At a sharp turn to the right – away from the sound – I decide to stop and again recce on foot. Taking my camera I walk towards the sound. Then – absolute amazement, delight and joy!

The sun is just catching the top of a truly magnificent waterfall. The water below heaves and boils angrily over enormous boulders. It is absolutely awe-inspiring. I run this way and that, trying to use the last light for photography. Now I notice that the boys have followed. I try to call them over but they are afraid. Eventually, however, one of them – Bonifa – responds. I get him to stand on a rock to try and give the rapids some perspective. I show him how to take a picture of me. Hope it works. By now the other three – who are all around 10 or 12 years old – have realised I won't hurt them and they join my gambolling as well.

The falls are absolutely beautiful – the power of the water unnerving.

I can stay no longer and we make our way back to my kayak. I ask them if there is a way to get my kayak so that I can put in close to the falls we were at. They seem to understand and soon I have four boys helping me as we push, shove and struggle with the kayak along the tiniest, rockiest stream. But when we get to where it reaches the big water my concern rockets, for there is a steep drop

> The sun is just catching the top of a truly magnificent waterfall. The water below heaves and boils angrily over enormous boulders. It is absolutely awe-inspiring.

One tiny corner of Sioma Falls.

and it is straight into turbulent water. Bonifa, however, his confidence high now, assures me that they are strong boys and that we will manage. I decide to do it so we go ahead. With some difficulty we manage to get the kayak down to the main river but then it's still not done. The water running by, frothing and surging, is not going to allow me to easily get into the kayak and pull the spray deck over before I am jetting downstream. But with three of the boys straining to hold the kayak, I sit in the kayak, get organised, thank them, and then tell them to let go. One moment I am still, then the turning current catches me and I am gone. I shout goodbye and thanks again.

It's a fantastic ride. There is an eddy in the middle of the river so I paddle into it and turn facing upstream so that I can wave at the boys. Looking around I see the reason for the eddy – there is a second drop of falls pushing water in at a sharp angle from my right and after that I realise there is still another, and another after that. It is pure beauty. I play a little in the powerful water, skidding across this way and that, paddling upstream, surfing the surges and running back to eddies. It's fantastic! A powerful thrust catches me from the side and I almost go over. The beauty of the place is spectacular. I don't want to leave the eddy I am in. I just drink and drink in the joy of the moment: the surging water under me; the sheets of white water dropping vertically down towards me off to my right. Directly ahead of me, as I look upstream, are enormous rapids beneath yet another fall. To the right of these two falls is a buttress on which there is a tree and, at the base, the prettiest little white sand beach.

Amongst the tangled broken basalt and sandstone, the beach is gentle and inviting. Paddling constantly upstream in the eddy, I wonder if I could get there and so, using every current and surge to my favour, I begin the crossing. Happily, I make it. It is almost dark now. I spring out of my kayak and dig for my satellite phone. I want to share this beauty and excitement with Annie. I wish she were here. I get through and tell her in a tumble of words where I am. On a buttress in the middle of Sioma Falls, on a little beach at the base, I make sure she knows that I love her.

I am in one of God's most magnificent places on earth and I am humbled.

Hoping that this could work as a spot to spend the night, I quickly explore. Yes! Not just a 'will do' spot – a magnificent one. The tree is enormous, with huge tangled protruding roots and two great trunks. Soon I have ferried my gear up high, tied my boat to a rock and lifted it well clear of the water. I am excited, happy, joyous and now tired. I make myself a welcome cup of tea and macaroni and cheese – with my 'Boons Special recipe' bits of biltong thrown in, and I am a very satisfied boy. Last of the biltong, I'm afraid!

The sound of the water all around me is, in a way, quite frightening and my imagination takes flight. After all, I am completely surrounded by powerful torrential water, and I periodically hear and feel the thump of enormous boulders being moved by the torrent. But I am in a good place for a rest;

it is safe and I will wake to more beauty tomorrow. I feel a little of what Livingstone must have felt when he first saw Victoria Falls. He too slept on an island – the one that now bears his name at the lip of the falls. I am on a buttress in the falls themselves. I feel a connection with the great man, across 150 years.

I awaken to the first sounds of birds and a gently lightening sky. I lie still and watch as the sunbirds flutter in the low, scrubby branches over my head. The light now throwing across the rocks and water is amber and pink. Spray, caught in the rising sun, carves rainbows over the powerful rushing water. The ancient tree trunks alongside which I lie create a window through which I get a little glimpse of another part of Eden.

I am soon running around exploring, taking photographs and enjoying the great variety of this place. Little bird tracks in the sand alongside those of otter. Tiny flowers amidst tumbled rocks. Ferns with drops of moisture hang over beds of moss.

It's already late before I make myself some breakfast, after which I take to my kayak and play in this very varied water. Later, as I sit on the rocks, an otter appears, swimming effortlessly in the currents. A good look at me and my kayak and he is gone to find another fishing spot.

Exploring the geology of this spot is quite fascinating for it is easy to see how this area was formed from the visible evidence that abounds. A vast bed of sand, aeolian (windblown) in origin, originally covered the

> Spray, caught in the rising sun, carves rainbows over the powerful rushing water. The ancient tree trunks alongside which I lie create a window through which I get a little glimpse of another part of Eden.

Opposite, top: My three helpful little friends.
Opposite, bottom: A set of rapids at Sioma.
Below: The rapidly dropping water levels expose incredible sand sculptures.

I am in one of God's most magnificent places on earth and I am humbled.

entire Barotseland. Periodically, volcanic basalt dykes or cracks appeared, through which massive volumes of molten rock oozed out to the earth's surface. This very hard basalt rock created a reservoir effect, backing up the river and slowing its downward erosion of the sandy base over which it flows.

I saw the first of these dykes in Angola at 12°21'39S, where it formed only a gentle rapid. The flora, however, changed immediately. Here, at Sioma, I am at the second dyke – a massive one. It is this that has created the magnificent falls. As the lava flowed over the sands, it baked it hard. In some instances the sandstone glistens like glass and is embedded with small blobs of larva. In other places the clear layering of the sandstone is visible over which the lava then flowed. It's a perfect spot for a geology lesson.

Above the falls, the Zambezi, trapped by the dyke, backs up into something resembling a lake – a wide, gently flowing expanse with numerous channels and islands. Below the falls the river has cut a shallow but impressive gorge. The water is tumultuous at this point and drives through the twisting valley at speed. Enormous waves at the end of smooth but powerful entry washes.

I find it difficult to leave my wonderful island; a little piece of paradise in which I had been privileged to linger. Fascinated by the geology, I scramble around taking my last few photos and ensuring I have my 'treasure' for my loved ones. Then, a final check of the coming rapids, and away I go.

The first rapid is, as I anticipated, no problem; and, as the angle widens, I can see more of the falls. What a sight! They just seem to go on and on. They must be at least a kilometre wide with eight drops of water, not the five I initially thought.

But just ahead of me is my next rapid, which looks a lot bigger than I had thought, so I decide to recce first. It is very big and has me worried. I walk along the tumbled basalt and sandstone and then climb right up to look further downstream. Still more rapids and very steep sides to the gorge. What to do? Firstly, I drink in the splendour of the place, wondering how I can show my family and friends this spectacular place. Then I put my mind to the task at hand. The first challenge is the big rapid. Below it, however, a further three channels push water into the same area, creating whirls, undertows and boils that are clearly visible. After my experience in Angola, my concern is high. If I really struggle with my kayak, I can probably drag it over the rock on the side and then contend with the currents. But no. I know that if I do this, I'll be doing it all the way to Livingstone. I watch the river for a long time. The terrifying

water penetrates the deepest recesses of my urge to live. I know that at this place I could die. For a moment I'm tempted to honour Annie's wish that should I confront extreme danger, and have the chance to, I will call her and, at the very least, say goodbye. I wrestle with this thought. I don't want to frighten her, yet I know the danger here is extreme. I choose not to call – suppose I make it through but the phone is damaged and I can't tell her I'm OK?

Taking a big breath, I untie my kayak, have a last look at the line I will have to take and prepare to go. I allow myself to be pushed back upstream by the eddy immediately above the rapid. Then, with a feeling akin to my first freefall parachute dive, I lean forward and paddle hard. The paddles bite into the water and the current now has me. This time, however, I'm on a good line and in control! I had thought I might be able to run along the side of the main run but within seconds it's clear that this is impossible. Straight down the centre I go, pointing my nose directly at the first enormous wave. Over that one, down the other side and into a wall of water that gives meaning to the term 'stopper'. My kayak is completely engulfed. Water breaks right over me but, still upright, I come out the other side. Down again and up at 45°. My kayak is five metres long and these waves are even longer than that.

The terrifying water penetrates the deepest recesses of my urge to live. I know that at this place I could die.

Total concentration. Caught suddenly by a side current and wave that hit like a punch from the right, I almost go over, but hold it and now I can see I'm emerging into the smaller waves. I let rip with a bellow of excitement but soon am working hard in the flatter water swirls and currents. The next rapid comes soon, within 50 metres; only a little smaller than the first. I'm now really confident. Still another follows and at this one are some women getting water. Once through the bigger waves and feeling quite cocky now, I glance over at them, wave and hit the 'flat' water currents – and over I go! My immediate reaction is to laugh at myself. Serves you right, I think to myself. But I have a problem. The next rapid is coming fast and, try as I might, I can neither right the kayak nor swim it to the side; the current is way too strong. So, swimming it around so that it points downstream – even though upside down – I take a firm hold of the grabline and swim the next one. Fortunately, it isn't too big but the currents, swirls, undertows and sidewashes below the rapid are quite unbelievable. Being in the water I can now feel the tugging on my body and I tighten my grip! But ahead of me now I can see an extremely threatening situation. The water, flowing at considerable speed, runs into a protruding cliff. The water splitting to the right immediately enters a further set of severe rapids, while that going to the left plunges into a massive whirlpool. In the centre of the whirlpool I can see enormous tree trunks tumbling about like twigs.

I work desperately to get myself and my heavy kayak to travel almost directly to the point where the water boils and splits. But I'm too far left and, no matter what I do, I will go the way of the whirlpool. So rather than fight it, I turn and swim directly with the circling current, and only once I have sufficient momentum do I begin to gradually swim across the concentric circular lines of the wash toward the outside. Eventually I make it to the side. I glance over at the centre of the whirlpool, watching the debris and logs for a few seconds. Then I right and bale out my kayak and chastise myself yet again, though still chuckling, at being such a cocky git!

A lone figure appears above me a few hundred metres away, peering down into the water. Whoever it is, is clearly trying to see where I am or if I have drowned. I shout and wave and I can see visible relief in the body language. He comes over my way. He's an old man, grey-bearded and river-wise. He looks at my kayak and me and shakes his head in disbelief. I climb up closer to him and shake his big strong hand – surprising in an old man. He's carrying a barbed spear so, after discussing my escapade, I ask if he uses his spear for fishing. 'No,' he says, 'for crocodile.' I ask where he hunts his crocodiles and he points at the water and says, 'Many crocodiles here.' Well, I think, I chose a great place for a swim. Interested, though, I ask him if he hunts them for food. No, comes the answer – he doesn't eat them but he kills them wherever he can and, of course, uses the spear as protection as well. We discuss what the water looks like further downstream – but in the broken communication I'm not sure that I really understand. 'Five minutes,' he says – but whether that means another fall in five minutes or no more rapids in five minutes, or whatever, I can't make out. In my kayak I decide I will be particularly careful – and definitely so for the next five minutes!

Leaving this spot is not so easy. The circular wash pushes upstream sometimes, then downstream at other times, and the appearance of the whirlpools in the centre of each are very uninviting. I get myself out of it, then through a few more rapids, and in five minutes am in flat water. So this was what the old man meant. What a great run it's been!

The gorge here, though low compared to the Batoka Gorge at the Victoria Falls, is still impressive. The river is narrow but must be deep considering the volume of water that enters it. For a long way the undercurrents and sidewashes make paddling difficult and one must concentrate constantly. But it is beautiful in all its rugged tumble of rock and a completely different run to that which lies just above

Sioma Falls. It occurs to me that were it not for Victoria Falls, the Sioma Falls would be the ones that people from around the world would be coming to see. They are absolutely magnificent.

There are several hunting camps or lodges towards the end of the gorge. Power lines cross the river here again and, as the pattern repeats itself, the river shows signs of bad deforestation. Remaining relatively narrow now at about 150 metres wide, the banks are adorned with acacia and mopane veld. The first real rapid after Sioma Falls Gorge lies at 16°49'00S and is a simple run compared to those further upstream.

The river moves from beautiful gorge to wonderful tree-lined banks and, almost immediately, to deforestation. Not just by the local villagers but through timber concessions granted to mills. Foreign companies, here to harvest the hardwoods, strip the forests bare. It is tragic to see. In and out of beautiful forests, in and out of treeless scrub I travel.

Then acacias – lots of them – and I camp amongst their impaling branches. An old man sees me and comes over to greet and bid me a good night. Be careful of hyenas, I am warned, they are very hungry and very dangerous at the moment. I sleep soundly under my mosquito net – no hungry night-time visitors.

I awaken and prepare my cup of tea. Beside the river in my reverie, my mind takes me to another time and space. It is as if one blinks for just a little too long, and years and years fly by. One moment our children are little, pudgy-handed, curious innocents. The next, they are grown and they are gone. One look in the mirror dispels the myth that we are still 21 years old ourselves. Yet inside – that inability to comprehend how fleeting it all is for us.

I close my eyes and see my daughter Jess on a swing. Little hands clasped around the chains. Feet well clear of the ground – her face is rounded, her hair just catching the sun is golden. She takes in everything. Curious she asks never-ending questions and has firm opinions on what she wants and does not want. Her voice is like music. Its child's resonance lilting, gentle and pure. She searches for words and mispronounces others. I watch her as she beats our coffee table with a mug, as she hangs on to our dog Benji's longhaired coat. Ever patient with her he stands still or walks very slowly so that she doesn't fall.

Suddenly she is at the door and ready for school. Pigtailed hair, satchel on back. Her moment of fear – her moving on. The many days of school, and soon they are over and she is standing there – a woman.

Yes, one blinks and the years are gone. Here in the same bush not far from where I sit next to this great river, I walk forward with extreme caution. My face covered with five days of beard, camouflaged and filthy, I am 22 years old. My rifle is poised and I watch for tracks and signs. Two others with me. Herby on my right and behind. Something feels wrong. I hold up my hand and the others quickly go down on their haunches. Alone I creep quietly forward a few paces. My eyes search through every tree, track and shrub. In a bush – tucked well underneath and facing away from me – is an enemy soldier, his boots protruding slightly on my side. I look quickly for others and at the same time hold my hand out, thumb pointing down. Enemy! I point at the bush and sign for Herby to cover me. The others I show to scan around us. Silently I move forward. Rifle now on the ground, pistol in hand. Then I'm on him! Hand over his mouth. Barrel to his temple. He struggles but quickly relents. I show him to be totally silent; finger pressed to my lips, barrel directly in his face. He understands. I have thrown his AK to one side and I now check him for hand weapons and grenades. I drag him out of the bush by one foot. He moans and then I see the blood on his legs. A glance at Herby. A quick thumbs up from him – all clear. I call him over for help. He takes the weapons, I take the man. We pull back as silently as when we arrived.

I walk through the bush now and I am quiet. Thirty-five days of beard on my face, camera in hand. Instinctively, I watch for tracks and find myself carefully anti-tracking my own spoor. I stand tall and stop periodically, just looking at the bush. I am 46 years old. In an instant. I walk to where the map tells me the road must be. In the middle of the dusty, potholed road, I remember. Battle groups and shelling. Now it is so quiet, so peaceful. Something catches in my heart.

I lie next to the river and I close my eyes. My son Jamie is in nappies still. He crawls around, curious and stubborn and tough, and I love him so. He wears his tiny Zulu *ubeshu* and *isinene* (traditional clothing) and he dances now; tiny-tyke feet kicking like his dad – a serious expression and then delight. Suddenly it's high school – rugby, skateboards, friends. I love him so much. In an instant the years are gone.

It occurs to me that were it not for Victoria Falls, the Sioma Falls would be the ones that people from around the world would be coming to see. They are absolutely magnificent.

Opposite: A pestle and mortar are so much a part of rural life.
Top: Beauty at every turn.
Above: Wire and wood truck complete with steering wheel – this child's only toy.

I lie next to the river. The helicopter gunship opens up and the air is filled with sound. Military vehicles, soldiers – Zambian Army, come to support Swapo. We try to tell them to get out of the way, that we have no quarrel with them. The days pass frenetically, adrenaline-filled, somehow fast and tiresomely slow.

I lie next to the river. It is evening and we are well hidden. The sun is descending gently in the west. Not far away is a homestead, I guess, for coming our way is an old man. He stops every now and then to look at the sunset and the river. He picks up the odd piece of firewood and throws it onto a path. He is very close now. We lie quite still, hoping he will stick to his path. He stops again; another look at the river. He looks around, sees something in the bush and walks off the path directly towards us. Almost standing on one of my men he suddenly sees, and in an instant we are on him. Knives drawn, pistol in face, he lies beneath us.

He is terrified, rigid with fear and makes no sound or struggle. I show him to be silent. I draw a knife across my throat to show what will happen if he shouts. He understands. I tell base I have him and, as I know the operation is nearly over, ask what to do. 'Kill him,' comes the terse response.

'Negative – out.' My men look long at me. After a while I give the old man a piece of army biscuit and a capful of water. The river is so close, yet completely inaccessible. Our tracks so easily seen; our tongues swollen, we cannot drink.

It is dark now. We leave. The old man comes too. He understands to do everything I do. I crouch, he crouches. I walk fast or slow, so does he. We walk a long way. When I know he is too far away from his village to get there before our next assault begins in the morning, I tell him to go. The moon is bright now. He does not leave. I gesticulate again, 'Go! Go!' There is fear in his face, then real terror. He thinks he is about to be shot. He steps back a few paces then he turns and walks a few paces, fast. He stops and turns. He looks directly at me and slowly nods his head once. Then he turns and is gone in the darkness.

I walk through the bush next to the same river, 24 years later – a mere instant in time. The deforestation disturbs me. I take a picture of one of the many burnt stumps of ancient trees. I look across at my peaceful camp and hear the sound of voices drift across the river. The knock of a paddle on a dugout catches my attention and I watch as the old man I saw yesterday crosses for a visit. He is very friendly and wants to check if I slept well, and has brought me a fish. I look at him with deep emotion weighing in my heart. I give him some hooks and fishing line.

I miss my children so much it hurts. I miss my family here next to the river. I feel like I am being rent apart inside as my youth at last fuses with my present. My journey within is as trying as the journey on the outside.

It is already 12h30 before I start paddling but even then I have a delay as the local headman has paddled over to have a discussion with me. He is looking for investors and partners to develop the area. Lodges, game reserves, tourism – he says his people are poor and they have to find another way.

I think it might be possible to reach Mutemwa Lodge today, although I have left it very late. I sent a small box with supplies to Mutemwa before I left South Africa, and I'm keen to collect them. My supply of batteries, in particular, is running low.

I paddle hard across the lake-like water – past hippo pods which, in their deep voices, burble and blow their disapproval of my presence. I travel back into Eden as the afternoon progresses. A beautiful little side channel lures me west. It feels strange now to be on a river only 10 metres wide after the huge one I have paddled on for so many days. Yet it was much smaller than this, of course, when I started. The sun is setting directly behind me. All is quiet.

I don't stop but paddle into the darkness, soon regaining the main river. There is a warning grumble from hippos to my right, so I switch on my torch to show them where I am. Not much further along I see the flickering light of a fire through the bush. I have been struggling in the darkness to find an exit point through the thick undergrowth alongside the river. I approach the area of the fire, hoping that there will be a break in the trees where *mekoro* land. I find no clear break but a great tree that has fallen out across the water and provides a support for me to hold onto while I get out of my kayak. It is difficult in the dark. Once up on the bank I can see the glow of the fire and hear muffled laughter. I move towards it. There is nowhere to sleep right where I am anyway and I want to see who is there. It is not easy as the bush and grass is thick. I get myself well and truly hooked to a 'wait-a-bit' bush and then chastise myself for sneaking about in the dark. There is no need, but old instincts prevail. I switch on my

I feel like I am being rent apart inside as my youth at last fuses with my present. My journey within is as trying as the journey on the outside.

torch to unhook the painful thorns from my skin. Now that I have made myself known – and free of the bush – I walk over towards the fire and greet everyone.

It is a group of five men who, once their astonishment has abated, soon suggest that I should join them for the night. I decide that I will and they tell me where their *mekoro* are tied up. After moving my kayak, I join them with my gear. They watch everything I do with the greatest interest and I guess I do the same to them.

They are a group of brothers. Susiku Leambo is the eldest and is sitting quietly playing a small hand-carved guitar, which he himself made from a single piece of wood. He is very thin. The picking is typically African – lilting, repetitive and perfect for this time and place. Another brother sits at the fireside.

The other three are lying in their bed. They ask a lot of questions. They, too, are travellers and have already been travelling for four days.

They are *mokoro* carvers and all nine *mekoro* at the riverbank are being taken downstream for sale. Their entire trip will take 21 days because, after selling the *mekoro*, they will walk back to their village. Once home, they will spend two months carving out new *mekoro*

which, once again, will do this trip. The only time of the year they do not do this is during planting season – August and September – but right after that, back to the routine they go. The trees they fell to make their *mekoro* are *mukusi* (teak), *musauli* (copperwood), *mungongo* (maketi), *mwande* (pod mahogany) and *milombi* – all hardwoods that take a very, very long time to grow. They expect to get K200 000 ($50) for a large *mokoro* and K100 000 ($25) to K150 000 ($38) for the smaller ones.

I quietly do some calculations. They will get, at best, approximately US$320 for the *mekoro* they have with them now. They spend three months either planting or harvesting their meagre crops. This means that they can only fit in three such *mokoro* cutting, carving and selling cycles per year. Total income for the five brothers is, therefore, $960 for the year. In other words, each brother will earn at best $192 a year, or 59 US cents a day. With this, each person will have to feed and clothe a family, build houses, pay for school uniforms, books and medicines, look after elderly parents and ultimately, pay for funerals.

Eventually Susiku and his brother are also ready for bed, when they seem to suddenly realise that they have not seen me eat and that maybe I do not have food. They offer me food. I decline, saying I have already eaten, but they seem concerned. Even so, we all prepare to sleep; me in my sleeping bag and they on a grass mat – all five of them in a row under one blanket. It is cold but the fire has been built up and they sleep downwind to catch the warmth. They lie in bed, joking and chuckling at one another's comments, and then all is quiet and there are just the flickering flames over our still forms.

In the morning the brothers are all cold and they sit huddled close to the fire to warm up. A little carved stool is set in the circle for me and I join them. Susiko leaves the fire and goes down to the *mokoro*, returning with an old enamel cup. He gives it to me, saying, 'Here is something for you to eat.' The cup is full of shelled ground nuts. They are so poor, yet they give me something of what they have. I am deeply appreciative.

We all leave our camp together – figures magical in the low morning mist. With upper bodies protruding and *mekoro* only partially visible in the sunlit moisture, it appears that they are floating on air. We all wave goodbye – they to continue on this side of the river – me to cross over and begin the search for Mutemwa.

I paddle across and soon see the lodge tucked into the trees on the bank. A young man, who I later find out is Howard Johnson, calls over his brother, Gavin, and they both greet me warmly. A big man with an even bigger smile, Gavin and his wife, Penny, own and run this wonderful spot called Mutemwa, meaning 'big forest, the place of trees' in the Lozi language. Penny is away with their

They are so poor, yet they give me something of what they have. I am deeply appreciative.

two small children for a few weeks, but Gavin insists on sitting me down and giving me a real feast of a breakfast. Having been alone and in the bush for some time now, I feel a little awkward at the magnificent table. My clothes are faded, my hair long and untidy, but they welcome me and press me to stay a few days and relax. Over the next hours we sit chatting, swapping stories, and getting to know one another. Gavin is a retired Springbok rugby player who represented South Africa on many occasions. His gentleness and love of the bush is unequalled.

There is a large crocodile skull on the wall adjacent to the lodge's pub and lounge. It has a neat bullet hole in it, so I ask for the story.

A crocodile had killed several local people but had evaded the angry hunters who always sought him out after such an attack. Time passed by with no further attacks and people began to think that he had moved on or died. On a very hot night at a village not far from Gavin's place, several people were struggling to sleep in the heat inside their huts. Searching for a cooler spot, one man decided to go outside to escape the heat and hopefully, in the breeze, the mosquitoes. He lay down on his mat, tossed a blanket over himself, sighed with relief in the gentle breeze, and went to sleep.

Making its massive lizard-like way across the land 40 metres from the water, came a 4.5-metre crocodile. Pausing periodically, it moved closer and then – crushing jaws closed over the man's sleeping form. The scream muffled by the blanket was not heard. The man, struggling desperately in terror, shook himself partially free. But the crocodile tossed him around once or twice and gained a better hold. Lumbering with the man now dragging between his legs, the crocodile slithered down the bank into the water. Held under water until there was no more movement the crocodile then gripped onto a limb and, twisting around and around like a propeller, ripped it from the man's body. He was totally consumed.

The villagers were terrified. Crocodiles do not behave in this way, and witchcraft and sorcery were beginning to be blamed. So now a massive hunt was put in place. Eventually, with the help of rangers from Sioma Ngwenya Game Reserve, it was shot. The stomach contents of the crocodile left no doubt that he was the culprit. The head was removed and left on an ant heap where soon it was baking white in the sun.

This terrifying trophy now sits quietly off to one side in Mutemwa camp: a gentle reminder to guests that the beauty and tranquillity that is seen across the most serene of waters hides within it a savageness that must be respected.

Howard is very keen to join me for a few kilometres on the river, so when I leave, he paddles along as far as another lodge called Zambelozi, a short distance downstream.

This terrifying trophy now sits quietly off to one side: a gentle reminder that the beauty and tranquillity across the waters hides within it a savageness that must be respected.

Caprivi to Victoria Falls

- A strange piece of land
- The camp of the low budget spoon
- Quiet nights and family

A series of gentle rapids and ever-increasing signs of motor vehicles and buildings begin to alert me to the approaching border towns. I have an exciting run through a large set of rapids and soon see Katima Zambia coming up on my right. Just over the border lies the town of Katima Mulilo, Namibia, but I can't see it yet. Then a ferry and, just downriver of that, a new bridge under construction. I find myself somehow anxious and perhaps overly cautious. I keep asking fishermen if we are in Namibia yet.

Then Sesheke, Zambia, on my left and Katima Mulilo on my right. A million thoughts go through my head. So many young South African men, national servicemen and men on three-month military camps, spent time here on the Caprivi Strip. The strange and foolish Caprivi Strip. I pass an old bunker, still sandbagged. I have a picture of former South African Prime Minister PW Botha in my head when he visited here in the late '70s peering across the river at Sesheke – at 'them'. Back then the river was the dividing line between so much. The propaganda machine was so powerful that every thing across the river in Zambia became '*die vyand*' (the enemy), and '*die Kommunis*'.

The Caprivi was created simply because Germany, then in possession of 'South West Africa', wanted access to the Zambezi river. In 1890 the British and German governments brought the Caprivi strip into existence – a strange strip of land some 30 kilometres wide and 400 kilometres long. Strategically it was very important to South Africa during the 1970s and '80s when hundreds of thousands of young South Africans, mostly white, did time 'on the border'. The border extended all the way from here on the Zambezi through Owamboland and the Kaokoveld to the Atlantic Ocean.

So here I sit once again after so many years. In Namibia, under the stars, and alone with the echoes of earlier times. Of course, the Caprivi has not only seen military action with South Africans. In the 1890s the Germans practically annihilated the Herero, who retreated east into the Caprivi. Those who could, fled into Botswana, where a population of them has remained ever since. In 1914 the first action, if one can call it that, of the First World War occurred on the Caprivi at a place called Shuckmansburg, which was the administrative centre for the German colonial government in Caprivi at the time. The first action of the South African bush war also occurred in Caprivi. Here, too, the first member of the South African Armed Forces to lose his life in action since the Korean War was killed – Lieutenant Fred Zielie – in 1974, just 18 months before I arrived here as a soldier for my first bush tour of duty.

I sit quietly under the trees next to the river. So many things running through my head simultaneously: Connie van Wyk – dead, Frans van Zyl – dead, Poggie – so terribly wounded, Pete – blind, Kriek – with only one leg. In my head, I hear the sounds of contact. So loud – so fast. So busy. I see the choppers landing, the walking wounded. Holding their own drips. Limp forms – busy medics. Slung in a groundsheet a casualty is carried by four others. But here I am now in the silence. The bush. The crickets and the frogs. Somewhere far off a dog barks. I sit physically still for a long time, but my mind is back in another time.

Morning greets me with a spectacular sunrise, the amber fireball reflected in the still water. Sounds of a *mokoro* across the river in Zambia. I get up and wave. A cheery 'Good morning' call across to me. I glance at my calloused hands for a moment and then prepare to leave.

The border posts at Katima, Sesheke and Kazangula are all very proper and ordered. Sometimes it is quick, sometimes so tiresomely slow and difficult to get through the border. Thank goodness I don't need to go there.

The irony is that not more than one kilometre out of Katima the people cross back and forth in their dugouts; colonial boundaries ignored, as they always have been. Sport fishermen come up in motor boats, this time fishing for tigerfish. Six or seven boats. You can hear them coming from a very long way off, an intrusive presence in this quiet place. I watch Namibia as I paddle. My thoughts run present to past to present. Philosophy to practicality. Beauty to savagery. I find a spot, catch a 'tiger' for supper, and prepare for the night.

I wake up early after a restless night. It is predawn but there is light beginning to show in the eastern sky. I read a little of my writing on Namibia. My spirits are low. It is difficult to get going. Once in the boat I paddle listlessly, consciously trying to lift myself. I focus on paddling, so lethargic, I'm slipping down, down into the awful hole. I count my paddle stokes. Like counting paces in the bush. I give myself a target – I will not stop until 25° easterly. I struggle inside. Everything is screaming 'Stop!' but I force myself on. My mind screams, 'Stop, stop!' but the thoughts keep tumbling through.

A white man in the road. He sits rocking amongst the broken corpses. There is a leg lying a few paces from him. It's not his. I approach the remains of the bakkie. Probing here and there for other mines, but each footstep is taken with a body braced and a heart that's sick. There are lots of bodies, I begin to realise – three, four, seven, about 11 in all. The front of the bakkie is almost completely gone. Bits of flesh and clothing cling to jagged edges.

There are only three of us. We are operational Pathfinders, not medics. So many casualties. We do what we can. With an awful shock I realise the white man is not white. He is a black man with practically every bit of his skin seared and burned from his body. Shreds of scorched skin hang off of his back and behind his thighs. He has no hair or eyebrows. His lips are burnt back in an awful grimace. I try to help him to lie down but don't know where to touch him. His flesh is soft – there is little blood. He stares vacantly. He flops onto his side and then his back, moaning. I try to reassure him but don't even know what language to use. We are not equipped for this at all. We rip up bits of clothing to use as dressings. We work from person to person, but soon have nothing to work with at all.

Then – horrific discovery. There is another vehicle about 200 metres away. Another mine. As many casualties again. I soon realise that most of those are dead. Still, I pick my way between torsos and limbs and check for life. Much later an armoured troop arrives – our guys. I am worried; I cannot talk to them on the radio and am carrying an AK. I'm not sure that they know we are here. The light is poor now, darkness is coming fast. I stand in the middle of the track, my rifle in the bush on the right. My hands and legs are spread-eagled and I am not armed, but still the mighty cannons swing around to point at me.

The sun goes fast. Choppers. We run back and forth with the casualties. Then the one who is so badly burned – incredibly, he is still conscious. I run over. There are three men, one on his feet and two about to lift his arms. 'Stop! Stop!' I shout. But too late. As I get there, they lift. A big chunk of cooked flesh peels off in one man's hands. He retches and pukes, dropping the man. I shout for more men. Now, with six of us, we slide our hands under his body. I feel pieces of his back coming off. The others are battling to keep focused on the task – it's almost too much. Eventually we get him into the Puma – the flight engineer swearing at us, 'This one's finished; what the hell did you bring him for?'

'That's it!' I shout. 'Get out of here!'

The Puma begins to pick up revs. Someone shouts that the Alouette is there for the three of us.

Thank shit! It picks us up and we are gone.

The Caprivi at this spot is flat, flat, flat. Not even a bush protrudes above the marsh of low grass and reeds. The water – with flecks of brown foam floating on the surface – looks dirty. It reflects the way I feel. I'm really down. There is no sign of life here. No birds, hippos, crocodiles. Nothing.

I stop on a sandbar to write and then begin paddling again. I go through an awful place. There is a long stretch with nothing. Then I round a corner and there is a man and his *mokoro*. Behind him is the neatest, prettiest village. He greets and questions and listens. Then with such care in his voice he says, 'It is a dangerous journey. I hope you reach your destination safely.' Just like the chopper all those years ago, he seems to have arrived to pick me up.

I feel better. My spirits are on the way up. I marvel at the human mind. My body gains energy and power and I paddle well. I pass pretty Lozi homesteads; the huts neatly in a row along the river. There are pleasant shade trees and mango trees at each dwelling. But the people here are different. They do not readily ask me questions or even greet me – even when I greet them. They are exposed to the speedboats and sport fishermen and they keep their distance from me. But then one of the fishing boats pulls over to check where I'm going. It's a middle-aged couple and they are both concerned and interested.

Much later, many kilometres further on, just before last light, the same couple motor up to me again and offer me something to drink. The woman asks, 'What are you going to eat tonight?' She's not just curious, she's concerned. The light is going fast. I am forced to be as brief as possible or I will be benighted here in this swampy tangle of reed channels. They're very kind and try to help me with where I might find a dry spot to sleep. I bid them a quick farewell and paddle fast towards a channel and some trees. As I round a corner there is a lodge. Oh dear! I paddle across, above some small rapids, towards the lodge which I cannot avoid. It's just too late to go much further. A man is standing on a powerboat casting with a fly rod. I pause to try not to disturb his cast, all the while paddling upstream and say, 'I'm sorry I didn't mean to get in the way, but I wonder if I could disturb you for a moment?' No response. He just carries on casting. I paddle over to the people at the lodge, three of whom are watching the man in the boat. I greet them. They do not respond and act a little disgusted. I greet again, loudly, and this time ask who is the owner of the lodge. A woman casts her hand in the direction of the fly fisherman, in an offhand fashion, as if I should know. 'That's him over there.'

I paddle back to the man. 'Excuse me interrupting, but I'm afraid I've been caught by the dark. I've come from the source; today is

---

The Caprivi at this spot is flat, flat, flat. Not even a bush protrudes above the marsh of low grass and reeds. The water – with flecks of brown foam floating on the surface – looks dirty. It reflects the way I feel. I'm really down.

my 45th day on the river. I didn't know there was a lodge here. If you see torchlight downstream, please don't worry, it'll be me.'

He became almost human. 'Oh – why don't you stop for a moment and buy a drink?'

'I'm afraid the light's going fast and I need to find a spot and get my camp up quickly,' I respond. 'Thanks, anyway'.

'Oh,' he says. I say goodbye and turn downstream to shoot the little rapids. He carries on casting.

Within a few hundred metres of where he is, I see a spot that may do. Beggars can't be choosers, I think. It looks a little like a hippo run and I can hear the hippo already. I get out and check. Off to one side under a thorny shrub and a tall jackalberry tree I decide I will make my bed. I sit for a while thinking about the relativity of hospitality. I am sadly back in the world of wealth again and the quality of care and hospitality reflect it. I think of the poor boat builders and a cup of groundnuts, and then I remind myself of the powerboat, the couple and their interest and concern. But I'm afraid they may be a minority here.

In human age terms, the river here has reached its 30s and 40s. Money has been made, the expensive toys – boats, fly-fishing rods and four-wheel drive vehicles – have been bought, and the human within has begun to withdraw. Everything now is materialism; things have become more important than humanity. Money is more important than principle.

> **In human age terms, the river here has reached its 30s and 40s. Money has been made, the expensive toys – boats, fly-fishing rods and four-wheel drive vehicles – have been bought, and the human within has begun to withdraw.**

I lie under the perfect sky, the sound of a gentle rapid washing by. A hippo starts his bass engine and an elephant's stomach growls. Another answers and then a little trumpet from a calf. A nightjar whizzes by and lands near my kayak. The Southern Cross is just so bright.

I sit on the sand, my back up against the giant jackalberry under which I have made my bed and I drink my tea. I have visitors in the night. The hippos, not three metres from me, below the bank on which I lie, walk upstream snorting and blowing. One stops a few metres from my kayak and looks at it directly, then lets out a loud bellow and a series of grunts and turns sharply away. They take their time ambling up the rapids, and I marvel at their huge forms and the places they can go. The elephants feeding on the other side of the 40-metre-wide channel have me worried for a while, as I think they may cross exactly where I am. I shine my torch into the tree to alert them to my presence and then they slowly move downstream from me as they feed.

In the morning I lie for a while letting the sounds of birds and bush and water wash through me. I also think of the rather unfriendly, inhospitable response from the lodge owner and guests of last night. Perhaps I am being too harsh. After all, I did surprise them and I certainly don't look upper-class at present! I decide to walk upstream and check out my perceptions.

The lodge is spectacular. Set between two baobabs, there is a pool deck overlooking a rapid-filled channel. Another deck pushes out between the trees to the spot I arrived at last night, which is the junction of two channels. It is stunningly beautiful. The wood panelling, the perfect craftsmanship; but something is missing. It lacks heart. It's too perfect. I meet the owner, Simon, who is the fisherman of last night. I greet him with a big smile and say 'I thought I'd pop in and say hello; I'll take you up on that drink you offered last night and have a cup of coffee with you – I've had an amazing journey!'

'Yes, mushie,' he says, which is slang in these parts for 'great'.

I try to help him bridge the divide between what I look like now, and an image he might relate to. 'I'm a retired CEO of a multinational and I thought I'd take a little time out from the office,' I say jokingly. He nods, but does not respond. I quickly say that he has a really beautiful lodge. 'Thanks, do you think so?' he says with interest now. He follows with, 'Did you see … ?' and he rattles off a string of names of places on the river which, I soon find out, are lodge names. 'No, I'm afraid I didn't – I obviously saw them from the river but never went in.' He looks down his nose at me again. 'Oh,' he says.

I am afraid I was right in my first impression last night, and so it's time to leave. He has not offered me coffee or a seat. 'OK then, I must go,' I say and I make my way out. As I walk away I remember something; and, putting my pride in my pocket, I turn and say, 'Oh Simon, I had a bit of bad luck in big water further upstream and lost some of my gear. One of those rather important things is a spoon to eat with. You wouldn't by any chance be able to let me have one would you? I've been carving pieces of wood and bamboo to use until now. I'm happy to pay for it.'

He turns, saying rather unenthusiastically, 'Mmm, lets see.' And we go off to the kitchen. In there he says hello to the white lady chef, ignores the two black men, and says, without any introductions, 'We don't have a low-budget spoon we could give this chap do we?' While asking, he has taken a teaspoon out of a cutlery tray that is sitting on a shelf and he is looking carefully at it, turning it over and over in his two hands. I smile and say hello to the two men and the lady, who looks very embarrassed. The spoon is a flimsy twenty-to-the-dozen item that costs nothing in a bottom-end grocers. 'We don't use these for our guests, do we?' he checks with the chef. 'No,' she answers, a little surprised, and glances at me. 'Here then,' he says, thrusting it in my direction. He makes me feel like a beggar. I take it with thanks, but I just want to leave now. I'm sorry I asked.

I knew there was something missing here and I've just been shown what it is.

I walk down the corridor with him. I just want to get away. Suddenly he talks, his voice full of enthusiasm. 'Oh, I know what you need. Come here,' he orders. He steps into a room and walks purposefully to a cabinet. Yet again, I try to convince myself that I must be mistaken about his manner. He rummages around and emerges with a pretty little piece of paper, neatly tied with bits of raffia. It has a cluster of three combretum seeds tied to one side. It's clearly a standard pillow gift for his guests. It is very delicate. 'Do you have *Nyaminyami* with you?' he asks, as he turns and hands it to me with pride and excitement in his voice. 'You will need this where you are going.'

> I knew there was something missing here and I've just been shown what it is.

'Thank you very much,' I say, tongue in cheek. 'I'll stick it to the nose of my kayak.' He nods with a satisfied smile on his face.

He has given me something on which he places value and I acknowledge this sincerely. But, sadly, it has absolutely no value to me in my little kayak. What would have been very nice was a decent spoon that I could eat with! If not that, then maybe a cup of coffee. I am not ungrateful but I'm saddened.

As I walk through the bush I think about this experience. I'm quite amazed that, running a lodge on the great Zambezi River, he didn't ask me one question about the river. His lodge is actually not here for the river, I realise sadly; it's only here for the money. The river itself means nothing to him. If the river reflects life, if it somehow bears our soul, he seems to have lost touch with it somewhere.

I think of a cupful of groundnuts from a poor man. I think of a bat offered to me in Angola for food. I think of warm smiles and welcomes from Gavin Johnson at Mutemwa, who is in exactly the same situation as this man. And the river just keeps flowing by.

I leave the camp of the low-budget spoon and make my way through the beautiful islands, past hippos, crocodiles and elephants. There are kudus, waterbuck, warthogs and impalas, and through all this the river keeps throwing up little challenges in its rapids. Some are quite big, others a real pleasure. Then I hit a long stretch of dead calm, sticky water. I struggle. My body is tired. It goes on and on. I get excited when a slight breeze picks up for it gives the water a ripple and helps to unglue the boat. It feels as though I am paddling on a heavy waterlogged tree with some of its branches still attached. It is very hot. The sun beats down. The breeze is gone. I keep spraying water over my head and shoulders to try and cool down. The sun dries it off in minutes. I paddle and paddle and paddle. A ridge begins to appear in the distance. This marks the spot where four countries meet at one point: Zambia, Zimbabwe, Botswana and Namibia. Soon I am approaching the confluence of countries. The closest town, Kazangula in Botswana, gives the ferry its name. I watch great trucks with massive loads come and go. This is a crucial lifeline for supplies to countries in the north from the industrial south.

I paddle and paddle. The ridge is now very close and the river begins to break into channels again. Is that what I think it is? Yes – thank goodness – rapids up ahead. I cross at a hippo-populated junction to get the best-looking line. They are little at first, but soon the angle steepens and the water's speed does too.

Some quite big rapids. A very big hole. In I go. My stern sticks for a moment as I paddle hard to get out and then 'pop!', I'm free and whipping down and through the big waves. The side- and under-currents are the problem again, but I hold it together. A long straight section and a sharp turn into a very steep narrow run. Two men are at the top fiddling with fish traps. They gesticulate – no, no – but I am past now and through the churning waves I go. They shout for others to watch but I concentrate only on the water. It is big but great to run.

Evening approaches. There are impala on the bank, then elephant: a herd of about 25 with their calves. The sun sinks lower and with the east–west lie of the river here, it is sinking into the water – a magnificent sight. I pass some hippos and, giving them a wide berth, cross over to the Zimbabwe side to get a better view of the game I see there.

A sunset cruise boat full of tourists passes by going upstream. They look at me curiously. Some of them take photos of me. I wave.

A little further on, and with the sun now sinking fast under a pink and lilac sky, I decide to pull over. But right where I thought I would – another herd of elephants. I am very close. A cow nudges her calf out of the water while watching me. A young bull faces me directly; his ears spread wide, his head high. I carry on for a little, trying to find a safe spot. I stop at a treefall that I think I can crawl under and yes – it's perfect. I carve out a platform for a bed, stack some dry elephant dung, twigs and wood next to my sleeping bag in case I need a fire in a hurry, and I'm ready for the night. A hyena calls. Across the river a radio is turned up and people shout to one another. I hear the lowing of their cattle. The river reflects two of Africa's faces here in this one place. I sit quietly listening to both worlds.

The day unfolds gently on the riverline through Africa. Hippos call and monkeys begin to chatter close by. In the distance, an elephant's rumbling stomach, and birds slowly begin to stir. Across the river, another Africa – a rooster calls the daybreak in and the cattle low. Over there a peaceful, harmonious Zambian people, and over here Zimbabwe – a chaotic, tragic, slowly dying country ruled by a racist despot. Tourists have fled across the river, where lodges are full. Here in Zimbabwe they are failing and closing. No crops have been planted by owners for fear of farms being snatched away from them. Businesses simply stop operating. There are shortages of everything, even basic food items. This, in a country once known as the breadbasket of Africa. The jewel of the region. I sit quietly in the bush next to the river and my heart bleeds.

The river flows through beautiful channels and open stretches. Short rapids, sometimes inhabited by young crocodiles who lie on the rocks, are pleasant running and beautiful to see in the morning light.

Several boats are tied up in a group on the Zimbabwean bank. They are the ones used for the sunset cruises. I approach very quietly. There is a security guard sitting on one, his back to me. His head nods every now and then. I greet him and he gets an enormous fright, then tries to recover and we both laugh. His name is Mike and he is a pleasant fellow. He says he has heard of me. The people have been talking about a lone white man paddling in a kayak. He warns me of the coming rapids and points out where the hippos are. We have a good chat and then I must go. I leave, thinking how friendly the ordinary Zimbabwean people generally are.

Soon more rapids, and all of them take me closer to my family who, by now, will be waiting for me at Victoria Falls. But something else is playing in my mind and I force myself not to lose concentration on my surrounds. It's so easy to do as I am so excited that I will be seeing my loved ones. A long stretch of mirror-like water and around the corner into another long straight section. At the end of this I see buildings and

> The river reflects two of Africa's faces here in this one place. I sit quietly listening to both worlds.

boats. These mark the towns of Livingstone and Victoria Falls, which are on either side of the Falls.

I can hear hippos somewhere ahead to my left so begin crossing to the right. But there are hippos there too. This time I watch them with more purpose. It was somewhere near this spot in 1996 that a river guide by the name of Paul Templar was brutally savaged by a hippo. He lost his left arm in the incident, and one of his colleagues lost his life. I paddle in the middle of the river, lost in thought for quite a while, thinking of this amazing man. Paul's story didn't end with his attack and rescue. In 1998 he led an expedition of five down the Zambezi to raise awareness of the landmine problem in this region and, through sponsorship, to establish facilities for amputees, many of whom are victims of landmines. Their expedition could not get through Angola due to the intensity of the war there at the time, but they paddled the length of the river excluding Angola. Paul did this with one arm and a specially adapted paddle! I am deeply humbled by his courage and his raw humanity. 'I feel I must conquer both my handicap and the river,' he said, as he set off on the 1998 expedition.

A motor boat does a U-turn and follows me for a while – until I realise they want to talk to me. They are absolutely fascinated by my journey, and although I'm trying to be polite, I'm also very anxious to see my family. Once I get going again I can make out figures on the wooden deck of the waterfront. Then I see someone run down some steps to get closer to the jetty and, yes, it looks like Jess! Then I see Annie doing a double-handed wave, hips swaying, arms high up in the air and then come James and Rory. I am wildly excited.

A hippo surfaces behind me and gurgles and snorts, and a big cruise boat pulls out just as I am coming in. I have to sit, frustrated, while it creeps slowly out of the way. But then, only just clear, I paddle as hard as I can for the shore.

We are all delighted, happy, exulted and, I guess, relieved. Full of love, I just wanted to somehow hold them all at the same time. Then I realise there are others as well and, lo and behold, one of those couples is Jeff and June Speichisger – missionaries I had met at Chavuma. What a pleasure to see them here.

We have each other for such a short time. Do we really invest in the now with those that we love? Those that really matter? Somehow, I feel that I am left wanting.

I spend three and a half wonderful days with Annie, Jess, Rory and James at Victoria Falls. They are kind and let me sleep at first while they explore, but soon my energy is back and we run around together. We take a quiet cruise up the river together as a family. I can't stop talking. I show them where I camped the night before meeting them; I point out the hippos, the crocs, the elephants, the bush, the beauty, the rising spray of the Falls. We hold each other a lot. They can't stop talking, either. James catches a huge barbel. We're all proud.

And then it's bungee jumping off the Vic Falls bridge for Jess and James – and who am I to say it might be dangerous! Rory is distraught that he's not allowed to do it as he is still too young, but I see in him a fire and determination, a sensibility and courage that will one day take him on his own adventures. The kids nag Annie but she says, 'I've already done it,' and no-one can argue with that because she has.

Too soon they have to board an aircraft and I have to wave them goodbye. It's school for the children tomorrow and I need to get back to the river.

I sit here now quietly on my own and I miss them so much already. My heart just feels like lead. So much like life in general, I think. We have each other for such a short time. Do we really invest in the now with those that we love? Those that really matter? Somehow, I feel that I am left wanting.

Once their plane leaves, I make my way back into Livingstone. A little at a loss as to what to do, I make my way to the museum. There I find the section dedicated to David Livingstone and see his cape and that most famous of forage caps. His medical box and surgical instruments sit a little forlornly behind the glass. The metal trunk that he had with him when he died shows signs of candle wax in one corner of the lid. I imagine him sitting each night and making his notes, just as I do now.

Opposite: My children, James and Jessica, bungee off Vic Falls bridge. Rory complains bitterly, but he is too young and watches from above. **Above:** Not even trolls are allowed on Vic Falls bridge!

Vic Falls to Kariba

- Scouting the Falls
- Zimbabwe then and now
- The perilous Batoka Gorge

The rapids below Victoria Falls are enormous. They are some of the most severe rapids in the world that are commercially rafted but, of course, they change dramatically with the time of the year and volume of water running though them. At this time of the year, the first nine rapids are unrunnable for both rafts and kayaks. The water is dropping fast and it might be just days before a kayak could run some of them. I have already waited four days while my family was with me, and I choose to continue to wait, though time is becoming a problem. While waiting for Rapids 1 to 9 to settle, I decide I will run some of those further down. I walk and walk, examining the water with great care, choosing lines and deciding what is and is not possible. I'm going to use a boogie board for the lower section and, for safety reasons, will hang around one of the commercial rafting trips, as they do a section from Rapids 10 to 25.

I rise early and make my way to the put-in point. The rafts are inflated and the excited clients arrive, looking at me as though I am quite mad. When they are ready, I push away from the shore

and the mighty grasp of the river takes hold. The water is big and, on a boogie board, difficult to read, as I'm so close to the water. The huge waves completely engulf me, and I look at the holes and whirls I whip by with considerable respect. The rafts are very helpful – shouting or pointing out which side of the river I should make for before each rapid. I decide that most of these are not runnable on my kayak, which is not designed for such extreme water. However, my boogie board trip will do, and my spirits are high.

Boyd – a phenomenal safety kayaker in the gorge.

I would still like to try in a kayak and SAFPAR (Safari Par Excellence) kindly agree to lend me one of their safety kayaks for an attempt. In the meantime, the first nine rapids are still not runnable, but the water is dropping. The professional whitewater kayakers and guides will still not run them at this stage and tell me, quite simply, that if I try I will die.

Over the next two days, I go and take a look at as many of the first 10 rapids as possible from the top of the gorge. Rapid 7 is clearly visible. It has a very long diagonal wave on the right and some extremely unpleasant-looking water on the left, in which there appear to be some serious drops. It looks like a very technical run. The waves in the middle are enormous and I'll need to break through the diagonal wave at a specific spot or I'll end up running into drownable trouble further down. I look at it for a long time. It's difficult to get a clear view of many of the others, but Rapids 4 and 9 are also problems as I am told that they are definitely unrunnable. Rapid 9 is permanently

The professional whitewater kayakers and guides will still not run them at this stage and tell me, quite simply, that if I try I will die.

so. I make my way to the boiling pot right below the falls on the Zambian side and have a look at Rapid 1. It is an interesting one with big waves under enormous pressure that run directly into the wall of the gorge. The water then forms huge pressure boils, hence the name The Boiling Pot, and breaks both left and right at almost equal speed. Right will take you downstream. Left, back into the big eddy. This is the exit point for the entire volume of water coming over the Victoria Falls. The energy and power in it is awesome.

I climb up out of the beautiful rain forests and make my way to the lip of the Falls. I am mesmerised by the beauty and power of the sheets of falling water and enormous cliffs dropping off into tumultuous rapids way below. The spray rises fast in the updrafts and the slight breeze and pressure gusts blow it over me. I take off my shirt and let the droplets form on my bare skin. The mists draw me in and I become a part of it. This is a place that draws one to meditation. To the very essence of life that lies in the place that is also so close to what we call death. Here in this one place, if we allow, all of this fuses.

Perhaps it's this – even more than the incredible experience of beauty – that touched Livingstone so deeply. I imagine him sitting in awe of what lay before him. The Tonga name and, of course, the original name for the Falls is 'Mosi ao Tunya'. It means 'the smoke that thunders'. It describes something of the experience – something of the esoteric that lies so clearly imbedded in the physical. It is a good name.

After discussions and consultation with as many professional kayakers and rafters as possible, it is declared that Rapids 1 to 9 are still way too dangerous. I, therefore, decide to get going again, as I can wait no longer. I borrow a whitewater kayak from SAFPAR Zambia and go back to Rapid 10 where I put in with one of the rafting groups. Boyd, an absolutely superb whitewater kayaker, is the safety kayak for the day and I am very pleased to see him. I have little experience in white water of this calibre but am going to give it a try. I paddle hard, fall out, and swim a lot. I drink a lot of Zambezi water. Then finally humbled by the water and Boyd dragging me out of a whirlpool, I decide the boogie board run will have to suffice and I hitch a ride in a raft. I think this must have terrified the tourists in the raft for they would have thought that I was a safety kayaker for them, and here I was saying, 'Nope, this is too big for me!'

Exiting the gorge on the Zimbabwe side gives me a good opportunity to practise my Ndebele, much to the delight of the local people. The Ndebele language is closely related to the Zulu language of KwaZulu-Natal where I grew up in South Africa.

In Victoria Falls once again, SAFPAR is tremendously helpful. We discuss the Batoka Gorge below Rapid 25 and its considerable dangers. One of the greatest problems is that the gorge narrows periodically, preventing exit. During these stretches one will run several rapids, but the middle or the last one is unrunnable and will definitely kill. Unless one knows where to exit before entering these channels, there is an extremely high chance of death. We discuss whether or not carefully drawn maps or counting of rapids will work, but the risks are just too high. One miscount – easy to do when the rapids follow quickly one after another – and disaster will follow.

Eventually, I'm persuaded to compromise. SAFPAR will take my kayak downstream to below the enormous water and rapids that lie ahead in Batoka Gorge. They will provide me with a raft, a guide, and two other men to assist with the portaging that will be required. I am bowled over by their generosity, but quite clearly they are excited and interested in what I am doing.

> This is a place that draws one to meditation. To the very essence of life that lies in the place that is also so close to what we call death. Here in this one place, if we allow, all of this fuses.

In a final attempt to find a way of doing this section entirely on my own I ask if perhaps a boogie board isn't an option. Brent Williamson is horrified even at the thought. His words are said calmly and seriously, 'If you do that, you will die.' Besides the challenges of the enormous, unrunnable rapids in the steep-sided gorge, the problems are the rocks that I will hit in the enormous water and, in the calm, the very large crocodiles. Brent tells me that a colleague of his, paddling in the flat water at the end of Batoka Gorge near the start of the Kariba Dam, has teeth marks in his kayak where a crocodile got hold of it. Only by beating the crocodile vigorously with his paddle was he able to get it to let go. If he had fallen out he would definitely not have survived.

I decide not to boogie board the lower part of Batoka Gorge!

It's Day 54 on the river and I'm up at 06h00. Eliam, the guide, his brother, David, and David's friend, Taro, will be with me on this section. We climb down into the gorge at yesterdays exit point and soon we are on our way. It is not long before I understand the handling of the raft, but I see that Taro, in particular, remains apprehensive. The water is extremely powerful, full of boils and whirlpools. There are two Class 6 rapids on this section. This means, very simply, that if you run them you are very likely to die. We see a small crocodile, so we tell each other stories of crocodiles.

In the upper part of Batoka Gorge, close to the Falls, there are only very small crocodiles. This is interesting and the reason is quite simple: small crocodiles are able to catch fish. They do this by using their tails to assist in trapping the fish they are chasing. However, as they grow larger they are far less flexible and are unable to eat sufficient fish to survive. They then switch to small mammals and then much larger ones later in their lives. There are, understandably, very few mammals in the gorge; some monkeys and baboons and a few small buck species, such as klipspringer. Thus, one only finds relatively small crocs. As one goes down the gorge and closer to Kariba so the banks become gentler and antelope are everywhere to be seen. Result: big crocodiles!

In chatting about this, Eliam tells me that a few years ago there was one very large crocodile directly below the Falls for quite a while. Where he came from is something of a mystery and the

only feasible explanation is that he was washed over the falls at high water and somehow survived! He was finally shot when he started chasing kayakers.

Eliam Mushambusa is very experienced, having kayaked and rafted this section of the river for 12 years. He has spent time on the rivers in Nepal, and I find his quiet and unassuming nature refreshing. Taro has little experience on this type of water as he works with canoes above the fall.

Rapids are divided into rafting classes according to their severity:

Class 1 – Flat water
Class 2 – Small waves
Class 3 – Large waves, whirlpools and boils
Class 4 – Big stopper waves, whirlpools and boils
Class 5 – Big standing waves, whirlpools and boils
Class 6 – Not navigable

We start at Rapid 23 so I have the pleasure of rerunning 23, 24 and 25, which I boogie-boarded a few days ago. The view from the raft is great. We then run through a rapid called Closed Season (Class 3) and then stop above the next one called Open Season to take a look. It is a Class 4+. Taro takes a good look at the boils and whirlpools and begins walking downstream. He shouts back that he will see us below as he will not run that. It's big, with a very big stopper in the middle. After running it we collect Taro. Further down we stop and recce the next big one called Narrows 1. Taro walks again! We laugh and begin giving him Ndebele praise names – the first being *Mahlale matsheni* (he who sits on rocks). He laughs too. It is, however, a very big Class 4 and the three of us work very hard. The rapids mostly have names here and, we run through Narrows 2, Narrows 3 and then get to one called Chimamba (the snake). Here the force of the entire Zambezi hits a vertical undercut

wall at an angle. We run the top half but are forced to portage the second. The waves and boils built up against the wall run snake-like for a long way. This rapid can definitely bite!

We then run through Upper Mowemba (Class 4) and reach the Class 6 Lower Mowemba. Below the enormous powerful water churning and boiling into massive holes are big eddies that suddenly turn into whirlpools. Four years before, a Kiwi guide by the name of Ray was camping at the rapid with a group of clients. He took a swim in what appears to be a gentle eddy near a beach below the rapid. He was

sucked into the churning water and drowned. His body was kicked out four days later. The river is totally unforgiving.

We portage to a point where we have to lower our raft down a five-metre shelf into the water. We are very close to the hole but the water here is rushing downstream at speed. As soon as we jump in we start moving. Eliam skilfully guides us through the big waves that follow. 'Right, Mike, right – good. Hard left now, very hard.' His calm voice is reassuring and I learn as we go.

Through a Class 2 rapid, and we get to what is simply called Dam Site. This is the spot where, in 1990, Zimbabwe and Zambia began a co-operative venture to dam the gorge for hydro-electricity. Massive pressure from many groups – local and international – eventually stopped the project. But not before drilling survey work was complete and initial diggings were begun. There is still a cage hanging on cables over the water that was used to ferry workers back and forth. The rapids here are enormous: Class 5 and straight into a Class 6 fall. This is one of the spots I had been told about – what looks like a totally unthreatening entrance quickly turns into a terrifying, tumultuous force. The tow back into the falls is terrific and the frothy brown water absolutely awesome.

In 1999 a visiting international kayaker decided it was runnable. His approach was good but when he hit the water below the falls it sucked him straight back into the hole. He was flipped upside-down and tried to roll two or three times. But the water held him fast. Ejecting from his kayak, he was still not kicked free by the water and he drowned, even though he was wearing a life jacket.

Dam Site is a long portage and hard work with only four of us. Just below it we take off again. I look long and hard at the rapid. It's difficult to believe anyone would try it.

We then run Son of Ghost Rider (Class 4) and, shortly thereafter, meet the old man called, predictably, Ghost Rider (Class 4+). Taro's confidence is up now, so he stays aboard for the run. The waves are massive and as we speed down the tongue we all hold on tight. Over the first wave. Through the valley. Over Wave 2 and an ever deeper valley. Just before the crest of the third wave the raft, almost vertical, is given a sharp tap by the great river and we flip over backwards and sideways. I manage to grab onto a line and I am quickly up on the overturned raft. Eliam is already aboard. Taro is swimming as best he can, sometimes above water and sometimes underwater. Eliam just manages to reach him with his hand while I'm trying to find David. He comes up metres away from us, and seeing that he looks OK, if a little wide-eyed, we three quickly right the raft. Only then do we manage to fetch David and pick up the paddles.

Much adrenaline-filled chatter and laughter follows with hilarious descriptions of each of us flying through the air and the looks on our faces. Taro, of course, is unstoppable, having walked two big ones that we successfully ran and then sticking with us on this one that, from the top, didn't look too bad to him. But soon we are at a very narrow, powerful spot that means real trouble. It carries the unfortunate name of Deep Throat, and without doubt it could swallow us in an instant. We portage around the left.

A few small Class 2 rapids, through one called Sleep at the Wheel and onto a beautiful white beach. Here is the magnificent place we will spend the night. Not a metre from where I am the track of a leopard crosses the sand. Monkeys – his prey – were here too. Soon night is upon us.

The big water washes by under the first evening star. Moonrise is spectacular over the gnarled, tree-covered ridge. The fire is high and bright. The sand very white, contrasted by the black of the water-washed basalt. It is as it has always been.

A cold dawn under a disappearing full moon. The sun will not be far behind but we huddle next to our beach fire, which has been quickly rekindled.

Soon our gear is packed and we clamber onto the raft, all paddling hard to break free of the eddy. We go through about four rapids all around Class 2 to 2+ and then run The Wave Train, a series of medium-sized waves that, bracketed by boils and swirls, goes on and on. It's great!

The gorge changes quickly now. The sides, although steep, are less severe. There is more bird life and more crocodiles begin to appear. I see several fish eagle nests, two of which are in mighty baobab trees that cling to the steep slope with talon-like roots.

The day is gentle and calm but hot, and I sweat profusely as I row. We pass our first hippo in this section below the Falls and my three colleagues are anxious and concerned – beating the raft frequently to ward it and any others off. This, by the way, is in the vicinity of Sidinda Lodge, which is also the first lodge after the Falls.

Soon we are at the pick-up point for my three friends and the raft, and the delivery of my kayak. Warm hugs, farewells, and my

friends leave on the pick-up vehicle. This occurs at around 16h00. But my main paddle has not arrived with the kayak! Frantic communications; Annie to the rescue via satellite phone, and at about 21h00 my paddle arrives from Vic Falls on a second vehicle.

In the meantime, however, while it's still light, I have been sitting on the bank and chatting to some local people. Three women are collecting water – one with a baby on her back. Their children with them range in ages from about four to nine years.

Ma Courage Charity Kasomo is an unemployed pre-school teacher. Her friend Lindani Zulu is also well educated, also unemployed. We chat about the situation they find themselves in – desperate and close to starvation – and we talk of how perhaps things in Zimbabwe could improve. They have little hope except for the fact that a white man is putting up a fishing camp close by and they hope it will provide work for some people.

Ma Courage warns sadly, because of how desperate people are now, that I need to be very careful of being robbed. I assure her that I will, but she and her children stay with me until the light is practically gone. Just then a pair of donkeys and some cattle walk by and she proudly points out that the grey one on this side with a bell around its neck is hers. I ask her why she wants donkeys – is it perhaps for helping to carry water and goods? No, she says; she has been saving for a long time to buy a second one so that she can use the two to pull a plough. She would prefer two oxen but they are way out of her financial reach. I ask her how much a donkey costs and am told about Z$5 000 ($20). When she says this, her voice becomes listless and I can see the reality in her eyes and demeanour; she will clearly never have Z$5 000 for another donkey.

I question her still further. What good will two donkeys do her, as clearly she must be able to plant sufficiently using a hoe? She disagrees. It's impossible to prepare and plant sufficient land and crops for a family if one does so by hand. The rains are short and unless one catches them correctly, there simply is not a large enough harvest. Before the rains the ground is too hard. But with a plough, all of this can be overcome.

She then tells me that her husband is a fisherman and normally fishes here at night, so I shouldn't be afraid when they arrive. She tells me his name and the names of other fishermen who may come by in the night. If it is anyone else, I must be very wary. She is loath to leave me alone but soon is forced to by the approaching darkness. I assure her that I'll be fine.

I've found myself a spot under a tree and am busy dragging my kayak closer when one of the little boys who was here earlier comes running back. It is Ma Courage's son of about eight years old. He is very worried that I might experience trouble and insists that he help me to drag my heavily laden kayak even closer. He is only eight! I tell him that he is very strong and he beams and takes a breath with a slight wiggle to his shoulder. But now he too must go, as it is practically dark. I give him a Bic pen in farewell – he is absolutely delighted.

It's the time of full moon but the moon only rises at about 21h30. The night is very dark. Using night-vision binoculars I see two men arrive on the open section some way from me. They gather firewood and begin walking towards me. Then they call out. I greet them from the dark undergrowth in response. It is Ma Courage's husband and the husband of Lindani. I ask where they will be fishing tonight but they tell me they will not be. 'Why?' I ask. 'Because we are worried about you so we have come here to spend the night to make sure you remain safe.'

While we have been talking, one of them has already made a fire – carefully placed I notice – not too close to be intrusive but not too far that they will not be able to watch me and my equipment. I protest, humbled yet again by these poor folks' humanity, but they will have none of it – they are here to stay. They are willing to sacrifice one night's fishing – food that they desperately need – to be able to ensure that I, a complete stranger, am safe.

We chat and I find out that Kayombu, Lindani's husband, is the chairperson of the local community council. He is well read and we converse on a range of topics. He talks of the unfortunate effects of poverty on the environment with the felling of trees for fuel and the over-harvesting of fish. He says they need a 'scientist' to come and show them where the fish lay their eggs so that controls can be put in to stop people fishing there. He is concerned about the future for the children unless the trees, fish and other resources are conserved. We then begin to talk of the situation in Zimbabwe and, perhaps because I am able to speak in Zulu/Sindebele, they slowly open up. In chatting with them, though, I begin to learn some terrible things about this area of Zimbabwe.

The Matabeleland North district voted for the MDC (President Mugabe's opposition) in the controversial 2002 election. The election itself was declared not free and fair by the Commonwealth nations and Mugabe's regime was punished with Zimbabwe's suspension from the Commonwealth for one year. In response, Mugabe made the Grain Makers' Board stop supplying food to all rural areas in which the MDC had a strong showing. In these areas, people are now unable to buy even the most basic foodstuffs. Maize meal, which is a staple food, is not delivered here as it used to be. Instead, it goes to all the larger

I protest, humbled yet again by these poor folks' humanity, but they will have none of it – they are here to stay. They are willing to sacrifice one night's fishing – food that they desperately need – to be able to ensure that I, a complete stranger, am safe.

Birds and animal tracks everywhere.

centres where Grain Board officials (all now Shona) ensure that if it is available at all, it is sold to ruling-party middlemen in the towns who mark it up by massive amounts and then sell it on again.

However, even the on-sell has a glitch, for it is sold only to trusted Mugabe supporters in the deep rural areas. These people are able to buy 20 or 30 of the big 50-kilogram bags at a time and nothing is left for the others. These bulk buyers now hoard the grain; others sell on their excess, once again at a huge mark-up. The poor people simply cannot afford it even if it is available, which mostly it is not.

The two men I talk to are humble but dignified people. But they have families and absolutely no way of ensuring their survival. They catch fish if they are able, but say worms are difficult to obtain for bait. These they have to buy in Hwange some 40 kilometres away. This means a bus fare there and back, plus the cost of the worms – an excessive burden for these poor folk. My heart bleeds for them.

This is the result of them having two major faults in Mugabe's eyes. The first is that they voted for the opposition MDC. The second is that they are Ndebele. Mugabe is of the Shona tribe that accounts for some 75% of Zimbabwe's population. They tell me that in the '80s, Mugabe's infamous North Korean-trained Fifth Brigade annihilated village after village in Matabeleland, which was then an area that supported the Zapu opposition, led by Joshua Nkomo. This I know of from previous research, which shows that in 1982 alone just over 30 000 people were murdered by Mugabe's troops. But now I get a first-hand account. They name the villages in their immediate vicinity: Tilupane, Cholocho, Nkaye.

They tell me of terrible things that happened in these places. People were called together in groups, and parents forced to use the grain pounder to stamp on their children's feet and hands in order to cripple them. Many times this would also occur to their children's heads until they were dead. People's ears and lips or noses were cut off, after which they were released so that they would be visible reminders of what would happen should Mugabe's ZANU-PF be opposed.

I sit quietly and I understand all this so awfully well.

Morning arrives and I greet my two companions. They check that I slept well. It's cold and all they have had to sleep in are two old, torn overalls. I pack as quickly as I can in order not to inconvenience them any longer. They are cheerful and polite, asking questions about my kayak: how the rudder works, how I handle dangerous animals, such as hippos, crocodiles and lions.

They haven't eaten, so I give them food. They are very grateful. As I'm about to leave I give each of them some fishing hooks. Then turning to Sidoya – Ma Courage's husband – I tell him that I can see how much the people are struggling and starving. I explain to both of them that I am unable to help everyone but that I wish to help in some way; I give him $20 to give to his wife. 'This,' I say, 'is so that Ma Courage will be able to buy her second donkey. I hope she ploughs well and grows many vegetables and mielies.' They are both deeply touched and enormously grateful. I don't want that though – I am the one who has been touched. 'God bless you,' I say as I shake their hands to leave. 'May he protect you too,' says Kayombo. 'I will pray for you on your journey.'

A few Class 2 rapids start my day's paddle and a lovely fast-running channel bracketed by dark black volcanic rock. The swirls and boils here are gentle compared to where I have just been but they still knock my kayak sideways. Thinking of Sioma Falls, I don't wave at anyone!

It is not long before I travel past the Deka River and I am soon in the upper reaches of Lake Kariba. It is beautiful almost beyond description. Baobabs grow right to the water's edge. Cliffs drop off into the water. A line of green at water's edge. Harsh dry hills covered in leafless trees make a spectacular contrast under the blue of the sky. Past large bays, I can see that navigation here could be difficult. Just then a boat comes alongside me. It is some fishermen who I had greeted earlier. They say, 'You must be hungry – pull in your boat down there on the right and have some breakfast with us.' Thirty minutes later I get to their houseboat for a wonderful meal and good company.

What is very helpful is that they have charts of the dam. I spend several hours sketching maps and making notes and plotting GPS points. What a great help this has been. They, in turn, tell me of the situation in Zimbabwe as it affects them. I ask what they do and Mike says, with a shrug and a wry smile, 'Nothing at present.' I don't understand at first so he explains. They work in the tourist industry. With the troubles of late there are no tourists, so no work. They have had to lay people off and all they can do is wait and hope things change. I ask about the situation with the farmers. All farmers who have been told their land will be taken are to be off their land by a certain date, approximately three weeks hence. They are not permitted to remove anything from the farms – no implements, equipment or farm goods; only one vehicle and their personal effects. If they do remove anything, they face a jail term of two years. Mugabe continues to wave his oppressive wand. The farmers who have not yet been told to get off their land are not permitted to plant anything or to work the land. The Mugabe system is quite simple. If there is not the time or resource to physically remove all white farmers this season, then simply force them into bankruptcy. The secondary effect is, of course, that the people will starve!

I am told that in Hwange, one has to stand in a queue for a ticket to buy bread and then in another queue to get the bread. This applies only when bread is available, of course. The same applies to maize meal and other items and all of these are almost unaffordable anyway. If this is the case for the more well-to-do middle class, then oh pity, pity for the really poor people.

I paddle into Devil's Gorge – a beautiful narrow stretch of lake that has me in awe of its magnificence. I do not have much choice for a place to camp, as the sides are very steep. At a place where I can get out, I check for tracks as this spot is clearly well used by game as well. Lots of buck here and, yes, it is also used by hippo. I get well away from the water and decide to build a fire. At around 21h00 I hear snorting and grunting. I'm afraid I have put the hippos out for a night but hope they manage to find another spot for a meal.

The night is black, black, black, broken by the flickering fire. I appear to be on an island in space, for only the stars can be seen beyond. I'm disturbed by what I've heard from the locals. Imbalance and hypocrisy are blatantly laid out in this desperate place called Zimbabwe. Such deep poverty and quiet desperation in everyone's eyes, such enormous wealth elsewhere in the world that is held by so few. I don't begrudge the excessively wealthy – I am simply disturbed by the imbalance. Is it racism that keeps the Western world from real action in Africa? Is it a lack of understanding? Is it perhaps that Africa, as a market, is not very attractive and so it is all about money?

The campsite in Devil's Gorge holds me with its beauty and I have difficulty leaving. I repair some gear, try to glue unglueable sunglasses, and only start out around 11h00. The wind is strong and directly into my face but the gorge remains magnificent and helps overcome any weariness. Past the Gwai River and the spot where the gorge splits in two, and suddenly there before me, the start of the big open waters of Kariba.

> Imbalance and hypocrisy are blatantly laid out in this desperate place called Zimbabwe. Such deep poverty and quiet desperation in everyone's eyes, such enormous wealth elsewhere in the world that is held by so few.

Across Lake Kariba

- Days on the lake
- I receive a new name
- African stories
- Elephant encounters

The wind is really pumping now and the waves are very big. I have to cross a four- or five-kilometre stretch from the Zambian side to the Zimbabwean side, so I stop to check my gear.

Once I get going, it is very tough and my forward speed reduces dramatically. It's a little like paddling up a waterfall. Waves break over the bow and spill right over the deck – without a spray deck, the boat would fill with water very quickly. Right out in the middle with no land close by and no people or boats I experience a feeling of elation. It's just me and the elements. It's tough but good. I cover only 25 kilometres but find a spot on the lakeside where two baobabs stand side by side like sentries. Here I make my camp just as the sun is setting over the vast expanse of water. I know today was really just a warm-up, for the lake gets much wider the further east I go and the winds are sure to test my very limits.

I walk the few paces to the baobabs and just stand with them for a while. I place the palms of my hands on the gigantic trunk of one. It is a moment that connects me to this magnificent monolith. Perhaps, in a way, I also connect across the thousand years that this tree must have been standing here alongside its partner.

Baobabs are fascinating ugly-beautiful trees. The San (Bushmen) people say that when God was creating the universe and planting the trees, he made a mistake and stuck the baobab into the ground upside down. It is the roots we can see, and the rest of the tree is all underground. A relatively small baobab, with a diameter of three metres and a girth of 12 metres at breast height, has been dated at just over 1 000 years in the Kamba area. This was done using two methods: identification of annual rings and using the Carbon 14 technique. Tonight I camp alongside two of these giants. Both of them are larger than the one dated above. They were young trees when the first Crusade took place in an attempt to recover Jerusalem for the Christian world. They were alive when Genghis Khan established the Mongol Empire, and William the Conqueror invaded England, some 500 years before America was discovered by Columbus for Europe. I hold the palms of my hands against the ancient trunk and a whirl of animals, people, tribes and time blur in my mind. Alone, we are truly so insignificant: a single atom in a giant organism. But when connected, interdependent, and a part of all that lives, and has ever lived, then we have true meaning.

Alone, we are truly so insignificant: a single atom in a giant organism. But when connected, interdependent, and a part of all that lives, and has ever lived, then we have true meaning.

The baobab fruit is edible and also provides a refreshing drink. Baobabs are also often hollow and the core fills with water during the rainy season. This can be a most welcome source of liquid long after the rains have ceased. Elephants eat the bark – tearing great lengths of it off, using their tusks and trunks to great effect. In fact, this is becoming a very serious problem. For some reason, the elephants have begun singling out baobabs excessively, a behaviour not seen in earlier years. The damage is absolutely tremendous, with some estimates in the Kariba/Mana Pools area indicating that, at the current rate of destruction, baobabs could be extinct in these localities within 30 to 170 years. This is not only happening here but has also been observed in national parks in Tanzania. No plausible explanation for this relatively sudden behaviour shift in the elephant population has yet been found.

But tonight I lie under two of these magnificent ancient totems. They stand here undamaged and I marvel at their lifespan, which makes our human life seem so fleeting.

Out in the water hippo call, and here, on the bank somewhere south of me, the rasping call of a leopard chills the night.

Up before the sun, I try to get in as much distance as I can before the great wind starts to blow. The lake is like glass in this first lagoon but I have noticed how quickly it can change. The first of the daytime fishermen are also out, emptying their nets of last night's catch.

I need to be very careful of my navigation for there is only a narrow channel which connects this part of the lake to the rest. I am successful and into the main body of water I go. The trees here are unusual for a watercourse but what I am seeing is what was, until 40 years ago, the very top of steep hillsides dropping down into the Zambezi River valley. Erosion from wave action has created beautiful rock formations. Periodically, a tumble of boulders marks the place where the undercutting water has caused landslides. Dassies scramble into their rock hideaways as I approach. Fish eagles call and fly ahead of me to perch, as I play catch-up. A green-backed heron allows me to come within just a few metres but flies off as I reach for my camera.

The wind is picking up now and the waves are beginning to get quite big. Tucked under my spray-deck I am safe from flooding but hot. Sweating and pulling hard I struggle into the wind. There is no respite, for if I stop it blows me backwards and there is no shelter. The lake is ever wider and, at times, the water and the sky merge without even the faintest line to indicate where one starts and the other ends. I paddle and paddle.

The spot I find for lunch is a little rock-strewn bay. I paddle my kayak in to the shore and notice that elephants have been here recently. When I look carefully I see that it is an elephant trail. The rock is worn by their enormous feet and piles of dung mark their route. If I am to have a picnic here then this is a little different to having to watch out for doggy do! There is an enormous mound right next to where I have to get out of my kayak. I'm tired, and after my peanut butter and Pro-Vita biscuit lunch, I nap for a few minutes to ready myself for the next leg.

The wind is exhausting, but the beauty of the place and my isolation exhilarates me. I make it to Binga just as the wind begins to quieten down with the sunset. A beach, some tree stumps standing stark in the water, and a camp under a thicket of mopane and thorn. A nightjar serenades the last of the light, and then comes the foreign sound of throbbing engines as capenta rigs begin their nightly work. They are awkward-looking things, and the lake reflects the bright lights of six or seven of them in the vicinity. Capenta are not indigenous to the Zambezi but were introduced after the dam was built. These plankton eaters originate from Lake Tanganyika and are able to thrive in the deep waters of the lake, which no other species will inhabit. The capenta industry is a thriving one, providing jobs and protein to a population desperate for both. The rigs I can see are using lights to attract the capenta. Nets are dropped – then the light is shone on the water. Capenta come to the surface over the net, which is then lifted once a suitable number appear to be in position.

So here I sit on the banks of a lake. Elephants, lions, hippos and crocodiles in the bush and water close by. Out there on the water are commercial fishing boats, which pick their way around the simple nets of the other fishermen in dugout canoes. I hear an aeroplane in the distance at the same time that some baboons begin making a racket in the bush. This must be Africa!

> In the shallow waters I move between long-dead trees, drowned over 40 years before in the rising waters of the newly sealed dam. There are thousands of them and I begin to think of them as frozen forests.

In the morning I paddle through pacific calm. Not a breath of wind. The heat becomes stifling. I keep sponging water over myself but my clothes dry in minutes. On the bank I see elephants, mostly lone bulls, but periodically herds as well. They are all gathered at mud holes, covering themselves with brown, muddy sludge. Just like me, they are trying to cool themselves down. I chuckle at our shared discomfort.

In the shallow waters I move between long-dead trees, drowned over 40 years before in the rising waters of the newly sealed dam. There are thousands of them and I begin to think of them as frozen forests. The sun-bleached limbs are white and motionless in the mirrored water.

Near Chete Gorge I round a corner and surprise a most unusual crocodile. It's very green in colour – so green, in fact, that I'm initially unsure what it is. But its size and speed leave me in no doubt. I wonder whether it is the water nutrients in this part of the lake that have something to do with it.

The night, too, is very hot, and sleep does not come easily. When I awake, my body is stiff and tired, and my shoulders and back ache.

Opposite, top: Just a touch of madness!

Opposite, bottom: Elephant dung, a sign of my lakeside companions.

Top: Capenta fishing boats.

Above: The strength of the wind in my face is formidable.

I catch myself doing all sorts of fiddly things that are not really necessary. I suspect that at a deep psychological level, my subconscious is creating all manner of tricks to avoid paddling. But today is my 60th day on the river. I pull myself together and get going.

Navigation on the lake is not easy. Enormous bays extend off at right angles to the main body of water, and it is easy to find oneself adding hours and hours to a trip that could have been much more direct. I decide to move in closer to the shore to have a better look at a bird. I am very focused on the bird, with my camera, when two hippos surface 15 or 20 metres from me. A little later a group of eight – all sunbathing – rush into the water when they see me.

As evening draws closer, I arrive on an island called Christmas Island. There are lots and lots of elephant and hippo. The wind has now picked up and I have little choice but to stay there. Feeling uneasy in the wind, which makes it impossible for me to hear animals, I build a fire. The fire, in turn, blasts flames and ash this way and that. It is most unpleasant and uncomfortable. In the morning, the wind is even stronger than it was during the night. There is ash on everything. I pour water onto the big log which is still burning and, through the hissing steam and smoke, I see a *mokoro* battling into the wind and heading for me. He barely makes way. The gentleman is a fisherman on his way home. We chat and he says that today is not a good day for me to paddle with the wind so hard. He is trying to get home himself but, luckily for him, he explains, it is not very far now. He asks after my journey and complains about Mugabe. He says there is a partially-built lodge close to his home where everything has just stopped because of the problems in the country. He was hoping that he, or at least one of his family, would have been employed there. He shakes his head and shrugs. Then he looks at me

and with a smile says he must go now, but do I eat fish? I do not wish to deplete his hard-earned catch but he insists, taking what looks like the best bream of his catch and giving it to me. Then with a wave he is gone – back into the waves and winds that await me too.

For a moment I think of the wind: bang on time – it's the first of August and the winds sure know the date.

As I paddle into the wind through the big swells I soon see the lodge of which the fisherman spoke. It's a sad image. Some buildings have their roofs on, others just vertical poles. But clearly no work has been

done here for some months. Who in their right mind would continue if the government could simply take it away from you on a whim, as they have done with the farmers? What tourists will come to such instability anyway?

The going is tough, the wind directly into my face. I decide not to struggle but to enjoy this, so I paddle further from the shore. The swells are bigger here but I don't have to be as concerned about the hippo. I cross a bay and take shelter in the lee of the point at Chipampa Fishing Camp. After my Angolan experience with the crocodiles in the lee of a hill, I paddle right up to the rocky shore and get out. After stretching my legs, I walk around the point to check what lies ahead for me. Another big bay, filled with ominous brown water and big waves. I decide to run the most direct route across. When I walk back to my kayak I see a man on the edge of the water a few hundred metres from me. As I walk towards him two other men arrive carrying fish. The first man's name is Ilija Chambisa. He has travelled here all the way from KweKwe just to buy fish. He holds a bream and a bottlenose and I take a picture. The fishermen tell me to beware of crocodiles, that they are very dangerous here, even taking men out of *mekoro*.

As I paddle around the point, the strength of the wind strikes me hard. It is quite formidable. For a moment I check whether I shouldn't be hugging the shoreline. I decide my original decision is the right one and out into the middle of the bay I go. A group of people on the beach watch in amazement as I go directly into the gale and deep water. This sequence is repeated a few times as I move from point to point.

Below: Ilija Chambisa holding a bream and a bottlenose.

Then, while making my way past some hippos in a frozen forest of dead trees, I see in the distance a Land Rover with several men on the back and two in front bouncing across the veldt towards me. The vehicle stops and I see both men up front looking at me through binoculars. I wave. They wave back and drive closer. I pull into the bank. The driver, carrying a rifle, walks over to me. 'Good afternoon,' I call as I climb out of my kayak in the small waves on the flat shoreline. 'Are you guys an anti-poaching unit?' I ask. 'No,' comes the response, 'We're hunters.' He takes a few more paces to cover the gap between us and extends his hand with a warm, friendly smile. His name is Gavin Rorke and he has an American client by the name of Phil with him. We walk over to the vehicle where I shake everybody's hands. They are amazed. Here they are, in the middle of nowhere, and they come across me.

They tell me they are after hippos and crocodiles. Phil does not want to kill the animals but darts them instead. In this way he has the pleasure of the hunt but the animal stays alive. However, Gavin tells me there is a very large crocodile at Chipampa that they do want to shoot. He's killed nine people already and taken several fishermen out of their *mekoro*. I remember the crocodile warnings I received when I paddled past Chipampa, so I tell them I hope they get him before he attacks any more people. We swap crocodile stories for a while and I take particular note of Gavin's comments. He hunted crocodiles in Mozambique professionally for a while in the late '80s. We discuss where I should stab a croc if I do get attacked by one, but we agree that I would have little chance. However, he mentions their eyes, behind the front legs into the heart and – a new spot I didn't know about – the nostrils and snout.

Gavin explains how the nostrils work and how they connect to the back of the crocodile's throat. This is a sensitive place for the crocodile. 'Basically,' he says, 'just stab the bajeebers out of it, Mike.'

They ply me with food – fruit and carrots and even an avocado. Wow! I'm spoilt. These men are clearly experienced, though, for both Gavin and Phil ask me sensible questions. Do you have enough batteries for your torch? Do you have salt? Do you need a lighter? Would you like antibiotics? 'Here, take this,' says Phil, giving me his complete torch. I refuse it but accept the batteries. 'You should make a call home,' says Gavin, setting up his satellite phone. 'I'm sure they will be pleased to know you are still OK.' I cannot help but compare this reaction to that of Simon of the Low Budget Spoon.

Soon we go our different ways. I watch them bumping across the veldt once more and back into the shoreline. A group of four bull elephants holds my attention for a while. Compare them to elephant cows: the cows are always close to one another, often touching and universally alert. I watch the bulls amble slowly around in one another's general vicinity. They are loners but appear to enjoy at least seeing one another, even if they don't settle down for a good chat.

As I write about them now, where I sit under the mopane canopy, an elephant's rumbling stomach gives him away. I am always amazed at how quiet elephants are as they move through the bush, unless of course they are feeding. Then it sounds like a whole forest is being felled – which it is, I guess.

I paddle through the heavy wind and a frozen forest, mostly mopane and ironwood, and soon arrive at Sengwa. It is an attractive Tonga village. Some of the homesteads have pretty designs painted on their ochre walls. The beach is strewn with boats. Not *mekoro* now, but metal boats. Women are busy collecting water. One stands out for she wears her hair in long braids and is the one who greets and asks me questions. A small crowd gathers. I discuss the route with them but I have a problem. It is only about half an hour till sunset and the bay I will need to cross, the locals tell me, will take four hours in this wind. In my boat, I figure two to three hours, but still that will take me into darkness in a heavy wind right out in the lake.

I have just about decided to stay when a man quietly tells me to be very careful of my stuff, as he is worried about theft. I thank him, but then another person repeats the warning. I look around. I'm on the very northerly point of a peninsula. The wind is blowing from the north, which is the direction I need to travel in. It's too late to try and cross the bay now, but to get to a safe camping spot means backtracking down the peninsula once again. This is all hard distance I will need to make up again in the morning. I decide to stay. I'm trying to find a way to transport all my gear and kayak into the village itself and take my chances there for the night when I receive my third warning. The friendly, pretty young woman – the one with her hair in long braids – says quietly and firmly to me, 'It is better if you do not stay here tonight – there are people here we don't know today. We cannot trust. You are not safe.' She is very nervous. I understand instantly the risk she has taken in even talking to me.

I thank her and my mind is made up. I tell everyone I am backtracking to find a spot nearby in the bush. Once out of sight, I turn for the deep lake and begin paddling hard for the opposite shore, and directly into the wind, some two to three hours' paddling away. I'm feeling strong – and I can see two capenta rigs making their way out. This means that if I'm in trouble out there, I can make for one of them.

As I paddle, I think of the girl in braids and my mind drifts to another woman, also with braids. It is six months earlier and I am doing transformation work, an addition to the work I do as a

I have just about decided to stay when a man quietly tells me to be very careful of my stuff, as he is worried about theft. I thank him, but then another person repeats the warning.

consultant leading a massive culture change project in a large organisation in Southern Africa. I am frequently asked by groups, be they churches, schools or businesses, to assist them with transformation, as everyone struggles to come to terms with the new South Africa. I was very busy but I agreed to do a workshop at a school over a weekend. They were struggling with issues of racism and discrimination, amongst other things, and desperately needed help.

The process I use involves briefly creating a vision and shared values with the group. But before we move on we spend whatever time it takes to release any residual anger, frustration, hurt or pain that still remains with us from the past that may reflect on categories of people in the room now.

In South Africa, there is a lot of baggage from our racially divided past. We are doing well as a nation, but each individual has their story and there is a lot of pain. Many of us labour under stories that have mostly never been told, which keep us locked in our bigotry, anger and discrimination – in those dark places in our hearts. Until we release these, we cannot truly move forward together as a people – as one.

Part of the process I have created is to confront, as directly as possible, issues that are apparently the problem. In this case, as it mostly is in South Africa, it has to do with race. I divide the participants physically into racial groups. Each group has a turn to tell the other group what they think of them. It is a carefully facilitated process, which needs to be handled very sensitively. Initially, people laugh and let fly with classic stereotypes, but soon these pass and the stories get very deep; awful in their tragedy. Painful – so painful it strikes to the very core of our humanity.

Many of us labour under stories that have mostly never been told, which keep us locked in our bigotry, anger and discrimination...

On the banks of Lake Kariba I am warned by a young woman wearing her hair in braids. In a different place, a different group of people, an attractive woman – her hair in braids – is about to speak. I have watched her as others have been talking. She is twirling a braid of hair in her fingers. I have seen the deep inner struggle occurring. But the moment has arrived and now it must come out.

'When I was a little girl,' she starts, 'I used to live in a rural area on the farms. I carried firewood on my head and went to a small farm school. It was my job to collect the milk each day. My sister and I, and sometimes my cousin, used to go and collect it after school. There were two farms between where we lived and the dairy farm. Sometimes, when we were walking along the gravel road we would see the farmer's wife in the garden. She used to wave but we never saw her from close. We were quite scared of the farmer from this farm. He would drive by near our house in his bakkie.

'On this particular day we got home late from school and so were late to collect milk. On the way back, we passed the farmer's house as we always did. This time, his wife was not there but he was. He saw us and shouted. We were very scared and I think we made a terrible mistake. We started to run. He ran out after us and then there were shots. My cousin was hit and fell. I dropped the milk.

It spilt all over the road. My sister also fell now. I was very scared. The farmer came running up to where my cousin and sister lay. I was terrified. He pushed me, hard, with his boot, where I sat on the ground. Then he said I was lucky – "fucking lucky" – that I was a coloured, or the same would have happened to me. My hair was in braids and my skin was much lighter than that of my sister and cousin. I was ten years old.'

Almost everybody in the room is crying. There is a long heart-wrenching time when no-one talks. 'That's why I always wear my hair this way,' the woman continues. 'I have ever since then.'

It is very dark now and the swells are big. I paddle past a capenta rig wallowing in the waves. I can see the crew in the bright light which they shine on the water 300 metres away, but they do not see me in the black night. Under the stars and into the heavy wind I keep paddling. It is tough.

Another woman – this one is white – begins to talk. 'I grew up on a farm. My parents carried on living there until two years ago. It was a Sunday and they had been to church. They went into the house through the back door as we always did. There were four men inside. They beat my father and then also my mother. Then they tied up my father and he was forced to watch while they all raped my mother. She was 78 years old. Then they throttled her and stabbed her until she was dead. They stabbed my father too. The chair he was tied to fell on its side and they kicked his head and face and stabbed him again and again and again. He was 82 years old. Then they left. But my father was not dead. Neighbours came by, and my father lived long enough to explain what happened. I saw him in hospital before he died. The men that did this were black.'

There is a long pause, I think for a moment it's over but then she continues. 'Six months ago my son was driving on the M2. At the traffic light after an off-ramp, two men approached his car. One shot him in the face through the window and then they dragged his body out, leaving it in the road. Then they took the car. The men that did this were black.' She pauses again and the listeners barely breathe, then she continues. 'But I don't think that matters now. They are sad, sad people, just people. I'm sorry for them, sorry for what drove them to this.'

Their voices and more voices go on and on in my head, but then they begin to fade. I let it go.

The wind has practically gone and it is very quiet. I listen carefully for the sounds of hippos and approach the land quite fast to avoid crocodiles. It was a very, very tough stretch but I am glad I did it and it turns out to be a good place I have got to. There is a peace about this place in which I now am.

Opposite: The pretty young woman with her hair in braids says, 'There are people here we cannot trust. You are not safe.' She is very nervous. I understand instantly the risk she is taking even talking to me.

Their voices and more voices go on and on in my head, but then they begin to fade. I let it go.

The morning greets me with a howling wind. I walk to a higher point from which I can plan my route and make some decisions. I decide to go straight across the bay again. It will be directly into the wind but I'm well rested now. For three and a half hours I paddle. If I stop paddling for just a moment I'm blown backwards. The waves are sometimes very big indeed. But it's good to be here. I revel in it, in the water breaking over the length of my little craft, in the wind in my face, in the isolation of being here far, far from the shore. It's just me now but I feel good in it. It washes over and through me.

I have needed this so badly. I sing loudly. All on my own far out on Lake Kariba in a strong, strong wind I sing. I laugh at myself and I sing. It is good.

Once again quiet on a boulder-strewn beach. Evening is here and now the water is calm. Over towards Bumi Hills a lion calls. I lie still and quiet under the stars. No mosquitoes to worry me tonight. It is blessedly calm. The lion calls again. Oh, how I love the sound. I see two shooting stars in close succession and I make my wishes. They are my secret.

It's Day 63 and I'm weaving in and out of the islands. They are dry, rocky and inhospitable. But I like the names – Namambere Island, Elephant Point, Bumi Hills and Matusadona. On the mainland I see animals, so I paddle in closer. A herd of buffalo, not too concerned by my presence, but simply curious, like cattle. A group of waterbuck flee, but one loner across a channel stays where he is.

Impalas take flight as well, but the elephants stand where they are. There is the tiniest calf. I paddle in closer but am wary. The water is shallow and its mother is watching me very closely. A pod of hippos on the bank decide to take to the water, creating a wave effect as they do. I take some pictures but mostly just enjoy the moment. A hippo grunts and burbles directly behind me. With elephants in front, hippos all around me and not much room to manoeuvre, I decide to leave. It is exhilarating but I am also very wary of crocodiles now; with this much game, there are sure to be big ones all around me.

Once back in the deep water I stop and look back. I imprint the picture that lies before me on my mind. The blue water, the hippos. The open, sandy, treeless strip on which stands a herd of elephants, with buffalos off to the right and the lone waterbuck on the left. Behind that, a gentle ridge covered in mopane, and a magnificent African sky.

I keep a sharp lookout for a cruise-boat, as I know my friend John is on Kariba at this time. I know he is looking out for me, too, and that Annie has relayed my co-ordinates. Hours go by and I start to think that meeting with him is not very likely. Then, in the distance, I see a boat that is not a capenta rig. It draws closer then, seeing me, changes course towards me. I am excited and, yes, it is his boat. They hail me and welcome me aboard. We take note of the position, as I need to start from this point again when they put me back in the water.

Then – a wonderful meal, great company, a comfortable chair (with a cushion!) and time spent catching up on news. All this luxury after my most basic life is difficult to deal with. John and his wife Gaye have six friends with them. All are white Zimbabweans. This shouldn't matter in the greater scheme of things but in Zimbabwe at this time it does. They are locals of a different ilk to those I have met elsewhere on the river. They are all fairly wealthy and are all well-read and educated. But they are a group torn apart by so many influences. They love their country. They love Africa. But their children have mostly fled to distant lands already: the UK, New Zealand, Australia and Canada. One of the couples has decided to follow their children to New Zealand. But they are hurting and angry. They are powerless against the tyranny that prevails; they don't want to leave, but feel that they no longer have a future in Zimbabwe. It's just too risky to stay. But they don't want to go. The others are staying, but they know it is going to remain tough for a while.

They are all so warm and friendly and concerned for me. I get quite emotional. It's wonderful to see John and Gaye. They have a beautiful houseboat and I marvel at it. My little kayak sits perched temporarily on the stern plate. I chuckle at the journey my kayak has had: the roof rack of a Land Rover, rapids, waterfalls, a plane trip in a military aircraft in Angola, the back of a Russian GAZ truck, and now a gentle ride on a beautiful houseboat. I hope it's enjoying this little breather as much as I am.

I have a wonderful hot shower. But within an hour or two I must get going again. It puts my little craft into perspective when I once again sit in my kayak so close to this great vessel. I wave and call my goodbyes to these wonderful people and begin to paddle.

Frozen forests and elephants. Lone bulls and breeding herds. Hippos and waterbuck. Impalas and buffalos. All pass by as I paddle. Towards evening I cross a very wide bay and approach a large island out of the west, the sun directly behind me. And very soon I'm looking for a place to overnight. As I draw closer to the point I've selected for a camp, I realise there is a small motorboat moored at exactly that spot. I can't understand where the boat has come from, or where it will be going at this late hour, but I shrug inwardly and approach it quietly. I make out two figures. One has his back to me, the other, facing him, is looking my way. I approach slowly and then realise that they have seen me too. The person with their back to me is cautiously turning around. I call out a greeting which is immediately followed by a man saying, 'He is cooked – good grief!' And they both quickly stand up to face me. They are both clearly startled, so I hastily strip off my Arab-like headdress and sunglasses to show them my face. They have a good look at me and then the man says, 'Good gracious, you gave us a fright. Where in the world have you come from?' The woman begins to laugh nervously and pretty soon we're all laughing at the strangeness of the situation and each other's reactions.

The people are Sue and Lawrence de Grandhommes, and they are here on holiday from Harare. They simply cannot believe what they are seeing and keep asking me to repeat where I have come

> I chuckle at the journey my kayak has had: the roof rack of a Land Rover, rapids, waterfalls, a plane trip in a military aircraft in Angola, the back of a Russian GAZ truck, and now a gentle ride on a beautiful houseboat. I hope it's enjoying this little breather as much as I am.

from, and to confirm that I am completely alone. After a brief but enjoyable chat, I ask if they would mind taking a picture of me with my camera. Then they tell me they have to go and that there is a lodge called Fothergills not far from this spot. This is where they are staying. They ask me where I will be staying and I point at the bank and say, 'Over there.' There happens to be a lone bull elephant there at the time, and they protest, concerned for my safety. I try to reassure them by saying I have been doing this now for over two months and I am just fine.

They begin to pull away in their boat as I land. I walk around a little and find a reasonable spot. Then, doing what I always do, I walk over towards the elephant and quietly chat to him – to let him hear my voice and to be sure that he has seen me and is not startled by my presence.

I set up my mosquito net as I can already feel the first of them, and lay out my sleeping bag. I have just finished washing and have some water on the stove when I see the headlights of a vehicle bumping its way towards my camp. It turns out to be Rod Stedman, the manager of Fothergills Lodge, who politely insists that I come over to his lodge for supper and to spend the night. I cannot really say no, and so I leave my gear just where it is (no-one here to steal it and only dry food inside the sealed kayak) and off we go.

At the lodge I find the de Grandhommes, who had alerted Rod to my presence. They proceed to tell the story of our earlier meeting, to much hilarity from the others. 'I tell you, we were convinced we were dealing with a maniac,' he says. 'I thought this guy really had to be cooked. He came straight out of the middle of nowhere.' We all laugh, and he continues, 'And then we watch him and he lands next to this bloody great elephant and walks over to it, and I swear it looked like he was having a chat with it.' To everyone's utter astonishment, I explain that I actually was talking to him, and I explain why. 'You see,' says Lawrence, 'he is cooked.' And everyone roars with laughter again.

I spend the morning catching up on my logbook, and talking to local people about the animals, the lake and the situation in Zimbabwe. I also have time to read a little – digging into Fothergills' great collection of books on the river and the area. I talk with some of the game scouts about various animal behaviours. They're absolutely amazed by my story of the crocodile coming out of the water and killing a man at Mutemwa in Zambia. They sit quietly for a while, then one says, seriously, 'That was not a crocodile. It was a man who, having been cursed, was turned into a crocodile. Crocodiles do not act in that way.'

We swap stories and talk about the rogue lion that was shot the day before I arrived. It had begun attacking villagers and, two days before, had nearly killed a headman in the area. Mary Masendeke, who had listened to my stories the night before, looks at me deeply and says, 'You are Chekanyika – that is your name.' When I ask her what it means, she says she will tell me the story. Chekanyika, her tale goes, was the son of a powerful king who ruled a great empire. The king was known as the most courageous and capable warrior, but was also respected for his humility, fairness and kindness. His totem, the crocodile, was tattooed on his chest and, when Chekanyika was still a baby, his father had it tattooed on his little chest, too.

Then there came a time when all the tribes were torn apart by great wars. The king and his wife, Chekanyika's mother, were separated in the terrible confusion. So awful were these times and so dangerous, that the scattered people were forced to sleep in trees. Lions, hyenas, crocodiles and all the predatory animals lost their fear of people and a time of terror ensued. Bandits, too, plagued the land – killing at will – and taking whatever they wanted.

Chekanyika had been protected during this time by his mother, who eventually joined with others. Together they struggled to survive, never knowing which of their family or even if Chekanyika's father had survived or where they were. Always, though, Chekanyika hoped that one day his father would be reunited with them. Many years passed. Old enough now to decide his own destiny, Chekanyika decided that this was no way to live. So he told his people that he would go on a journey in search of a better life. As a young boy, his father had taught him some combat tactics and techniques, and these he worked on and perfected until he felt he was ready. Then he bade his mother and friends farewell and set off on his journey.

Each time he came across another tribe, there would be hostility. 'Where do you think you are going?' they would ask, but he would simply say, 'I am walking.' Always he would be forced to do battle with their champion. In every case, he overcame the most skilled warriors. But then he would do an interesting thing. He would help the people whose champion he had defeated to rise above their suspicion and misery. Then he would be gone, to repeat this over and over again. 'I am walking,' he would say, and defeat and assist, defeat and assist. Many offered him cattle to entice him to stay, and the most beautiful women wanted to marry him, but always he would say, 'No, my mission is not complete.'

Then one day he arrived at a massive settlement. He was warned not to approach for the chief of this place was the best warrior in the

They sit quietly for a while, then one says, seriously, 'That was not a crocodile. It was a man who, having been cursed, was turned into a crocodile. Crocodiles do not act in that way.'

Opposite: Spending a few wonderful hours with my friends John and Gaye.

land and would do anything to protect his people. Chekanyika chose to take the road through this place, but came upon a junction at the same time as another warrior leading a group of men.

'Where are you going?' the man asked him, and he answered, 'To see the chief of this great settlement.'

'The chief will not see you,' he was told.

'Then I will see him,' he replied.

The warrior stood squarely in his path. Both were armed with clubs and swords. And soon they were upon each other.

They were well matched, similar in stature and skill. Chekanyika, more youthful and perhaps a little stronger, inflicted the first wounds. But his opponent used his age and experience to his advantage. Both were soon wounded and bleeding, and the fight had been intense indeed.

Eventually, at a critical moment, the older man plunged his sword into Chekanyika's side and Chekanyika began to fall. Withdrawing the sword, the older man lunged onto Chekanyika to deliver the killing blow, but as he did so Chekanyika caught a glimpse of a crocodile tattooed on his opponent's chest.

'Father!' he cried, and the older man hesitated and stood back. Cautiously, he kicked away Chekanyika's weapons and ripped open the garment covering the younger man's chest; and there, too, was a crocodile.

'What does this all mean?' I ask Mary. *Cheka*, she tells me, means 'to cut'. *Nyika* means 'the world'. So Chekanyika 'cut the world'. He moved through the world, going to different places on a difficult journey, seeking not only his father but himself, and he was courageous enough to do it. Most people will just stay in the trees. 'This,' says Mary, 'is just like you.' I'm deeply humbled and appreciative of these beautiful gifts she gives me: recognition, acknowledgement, a context, and a name.

After lunch, Rod drives me back to my kayak and waves me goodbye. My bull elephant from yesterday has a friend with him today. He eyes me but keeps his distance. Once packed up, I walk over towards them to investigate some bones I see strewn around. It is the remains of a hippo. Long dead, the bones lie pure white under the African sun. Then I break the rules of yesterday's co-existence agreement and walk a little closer to the elephant for a photograph. He definitely doesn't like this. One bull, his one ear torn, the other with a neat bullet-like hole in the middle, shakes his head at me. When I don't leave he chooses to see me off. Head held high, ears extended he starts walking purposefully at me and then breaks into his charge. I take my picture, wait and, when he keeps coming, I decide to stop him. Bellowing at the top of my voice, waving my shirt – which I have carried in my hand specifically in case this happened – I run straight at him. He stops short, total surprise on his face. Then, huge as he is, he slaps his ears flat against his body, turns sideways and flees. The great white eye on the side closest to me watches me in consternation as he goes.

My heart beats a little faster. Even a mock charge from an elephant is an awesome experience, especially when you're all on your own on a totally bare peninsula. I walk over to check out his friend and, lo and behold, there is a hippo walking stiff-legged close behind him. What a lovely sight. I take another look at the hippo bones and can see where lions have gnawed at some. Lion kills of hippo are not unusual in the Matusadona area. Before Kariba was built in 1963, the low-lying areas used to support great herds of buffalo. As the water rose and covered the grasses, so the buffalo were forced to seek other grazing areas and moved away. In this way, the lions lost one of their traditional food sources. Hence, the frequency of hippo appearing on their menus!

I paddle the eight kilometres out to Long Island and arrive as the sun is setting. It is just a small bump on the surface of the great lake. No more than one kilometre long and perhaps 50 to 80 metres wide. I check carefully for tracks as I want to know what company I have. I'm amazed to find hippo and elephant tracks, both fairly recent. I look around for them but they're not on the island now. Both of these creatures have had to swim eight kilometres to get here, after first swimming the distance to Fothergill Island; the same route that I paddled earlier. It took me just over an hour in a kayak. Incredible that an elephant would undertake such a trip. This reflects the state of drought on the mainland and the great challenge the elephants face in trying to find the 100-odd kilograms of food they need each day. However, there is also another explanation. Even though it is 40 years since the construction of the dam, elephants are still periodically found swimming across from one side to the other. This is thought to relate to traditional migratory routes that the elephants are instinctively drawn to. Also, of course, an elephant who was 20, 30, or even 40 years old when the dam was constructed would have walked the ancient routes itself. So now, between 60 and 80 years old, they continue their ancient behaviour.

I find the bones of another long dead hippo, led to it by the tracks of an elephant. He had stood here for some time, the elephant – just stood. I have seen elephant do that before at the bones of one of their own kind, but here he did it with the bones of a hippo; a kind of acknowledgement of another's death.

I choose a campsite not far away from this spot. Across the way, I can see the lights of Kariba town. I feel like another chapter in this wonderful journey is coming to an end. I am sad, but excited by what lies ahead.

Top: Elephant in flight after charging me.

Above: A very exposed and windy camp.

Below: Just off Fothergills Island.

Kariba to the Mozambican border

- Kariba Gorge
- Fishy stories
- Mupata Gorge
- Refugees of racism
- In and out of Eden

I spend the morning exploring the island and gathering gifts for Annie. Mostly these consist of feathers from Egyptian and spur-winged geese, white crowned plovers, grey herons, darters and little egrets. I use cotton and a leather thong and fashion these into little decorations which Annie will be able to wear in her hair or hang in her 'special' room.

The crossing from Long Island to Kariba town takes three hours but feels very long. My body is weary and, even though I am excited to be seeing Annie soon, I struggle. I make my way to the point closest to the dam wall. A police launch comes out to check on me but the policemen are not unfriendly. I have got as close to the wall as I possibly can. Turning east I paddle to where I know Annie will be.

Annie has flown from Johannesburg to Lusaka, Zambia, where she was collected by Chris Botes. Chris befriended us at Victoria Falls, where he was working on the Zambian side. He has kindly collected her in Lusaka and driven here to Kariba to meet me and, even though it is only for one day, it is wonderful for us to see each other.

I spend a large part of the morning arranging permissions to portage the dam wall, notify Parks and Wildlife of my presence on the river and, from the Zambezi River Authority, find out a lot more about Kariba Dam itself, the entire catchment of the dam and other sources of information.

The wall was built between 1956 and 1959, and is 128 metres high and 24 metres wide at the base. The plunge pool below the dam is 84 metres deep, having carved its way vertically into solid rock: a testament to the awesome power of water. Even more interesting to me, however, are the natural phenomena that occur and the adjustments of life when such a huge barrier is constructed. One of these is the presence in Kariba Dam of the African mottled eel. These eels, and indeed all eels found in Southern African rivers, need seawater in which to breed, and they do so only in a well-researched and confined area off the northern and eastern coast of Madagascar. The male eel spends between 10 and 19 years in fresh water and the females six to eight years before returning to the sea. After breeding, the adults die. Their larvae, with no propulsion capabilities, drift for months or even years before the ocean currents transport them finally to the African coast. There they gradually change size and shape. By the time the larvae are 18 months old, they are about as thick as a matchstick and five to seven centimetres long. At this stage, they become known as elver, and it is the elver that locate a river mouth and begin to make their way upstream. They are driven by instinct to continue travelling upstream until further progress is impossible, and are able to cross and climb rapids and waterfalls of considerable size. But the further from the sea and, therefore, the larger the eel, the more difficult the exercise becomes. So, large waterfalls close to the sea will be no problem for elver to overcome as they are still small and very flexible.

Kariba Dam, over 1 000 kilometres from the sea and sealed off in 1958, represents a formidable barrier and, one would think, an impossible obstacle. Obviously, any eel born after that date would have had to find its way past the wall. In 1986 a 15-kilogram eel was caught near the Deka River mouth. Bearing in mind that the adults die after breeding, this one must have been relatively young and had to have entered Kariba dam after the wall was closed 28 years before.

Dr E.K. Balon has conducted extensive research on eels in the area of Kariba, and he believes that they would be between six and 10 centimetres long by the time they reached the wall from the sea in the second year of their lives. His research demonstrated that there would need to be 300 juveniles per square kilometre in the dam to sustain the population. Simply put, this means that over 400 000 young eels would need to get over or through the dam wall each year!

A man by the name of Frank Junor and other fisheries' staff watched eels as they climbed nearly halfway up the height of the dam wall. John Minshull, the keeper of ichthyology at the Bulawayo Museum in Zimbabwe at the time of further research, watched eels make their way up step-like ledges on the south side of Kariba. They were following a tiny trickle of water that was also serving to keep their skins moist. Beyond 110 metres, though, it was quite impossible for them to continue. An interesting aside is that eels are able to absorb oxygen through their skins. In water, only 10% of their requirement is met in this way, but out of the water, some 60% is absorbed through their skin. The balance, of course, is through the gills.

No eels have ever been seen crossing the road at the top of the dam wall. If Balon's figures are followed, then 1 000 a day would need to do so. Clearly then, there is only one other explanation: they somehow go through the wall! In 1965, for the first time, 55 dead eels were found on the upstream side of an idle hydro-electric turbine inside the wall. They had been killed by a sudden change in water pressure, which had sucked them up against a metal strainer. Amazing as it may seem, the little eels manage to get themselves through the massive turbines at Kariba and swim up the vertical water intakes against the enormous pressure in those narrow confines. Not only do they achieve this here but, incredibly, further downstream at Cahora Bassa dam in Mozambique as well. How the large adult eels make their way back over or through these huge obstacles on their way back to the breeding grounds in the sea can only be imagined.

His research demonstrated that there would need to be 300 juveniles per square kilometre in the dam to sustain the population. Simply put, this means that over 400 000 young eels would need to get over or through the dam wall each year!

Annie and I lie in each others' arms and talk. Much has to do with simply holding one another and being close. The intensity of early anxiety is past now, but we both know that there are still considerable dangers and challenges that lie ahead. I won't see her again until I have reached the mouth, but we recommit now to meeting there somehow. She has shown such capability through this journey and her own inner journey has strengthened, developed and deepened her just as much as mine has me.

I put in below Kariba with the help of Annie and Chris. It is early morning and they leave almost immediately for Lusaka, where Annie will board a plane for South Africa.

Kariba Gorge is very beautiful; similar to Batoka Gorge below Victoria Falls but more gentle somehow. In the gorge I begin to see many more crocodiles and hippos than I have previously seen on the river. It's not only the numbers but also that they are more willing to be seen than those further up. The exit from the gorge is quite abrupt, and suddenly I'm onto a flat flood plain. It is exceptionally beautiful with sand bars and islands popping up here and there, interspersed with the odd steep bank upon which baobab and wild mango are displayed.

From the exit of the gorge I begin to count hippo and over the next 20 kilometres have tallied up 280 of them in the channels in which I travel. There are obviously still many more that I don't see in other channels of the river. The water is so clear I can see the fish swimming beneath my kayak. The red-green weed all bends downstream in the current and little fish use it as cover as big tiger fish whip by.

A group of Zambian fishermen use a very long net. They paddle it around in a great semi-circle in dugout canoes, then drag it onto a sandbar. It's hard work for them and they don't catch very much.

Later on I see two more people fishing. They, however, are seated in a small motorboat and hail me as I draw closer. It's a couple by the name of Gavin and Sarah St Leger, and they tell me that they have a fishing camp not too far downstream. Gavin says, 'It's getting late anyway, so pull in and spend the night with us. We want to hear your stories.' It's very kind of them and I take them up on their offer.

Their camp is called simply C Camp and they hold the fishing concession for this 60-kilometre stretch of the river. What is really unusual is that they encourage their guests to bring their children. They have three children of their own: Samantha who is seven, Lance, five, and Christy, three. They are a really lovely, special family. Gavin laughs when talking of his camp. It's simple but very comfortable and, when comparing it to the luxury lodges that abound, he calls it 'Peasantville'. The lawns under the lovely shade trees are very green against the dry surrounds. It is relaxed, friendly and perfect for families who love the bush and who want to share it with their children.

Gavin and Sarah St Leger with their children and me at C Camp.

I have a long deep sleep and don't even hear the lion that I am told was making a real racket close by. I needed this rest, and here I could properly relax.

Before leaving in the morning, I spend some time chatting with Gavin and Sarah. They have already experienced the loss of a farm to the 'war veterans', and then they lost Gavin's milling business. He is angry and bitter but refuses to leave. 'I was born here and this is our country, too,' he says. One of the reasons that they are now at this lodge is because Sarah and the children were threatened directly. As a couple, they decided to find a place as far away from any trouble as possible, and here they are, in this remote and idyllic place. The children are all schooled by Sarah using a home correspondence system. They are refugees in their own country.

Today, 9 August, is a critical and sad day for white Zimbabwean farmers. Some 80% of them have been notified that they have to be off their farms by this date. They can only take their personal clothing with them. It is illegal to remove any farming equipment or to damage it in any way. Doing so will land the farmer in jail. There will be no compensation paid, or at least that's what the farmers believe.

The wind blows very hard from the east, directly into my face. The chop on the water makes locating hippo pods a little more difficult and I soon find out that it makes it more difficult for them to see intruders as well. I have some close calls.

There are lots of crocodiles here but they are very alert and, unlike those further upstream, run into the water long before I am any threat to them. I watch the water carefully, much more concerned about the threat they are to me.

The sun begins to set as I approach the first hills next to the river for over 100 kilometres. They are two nicely formed bumps that lie side by side. I call my camp 'Jungfrau Camp' and think of my friends Karl and Dieter in Switzerland.

It's Day 70. I'm awake before the dawn, watching the stars slowly fade. Then the francolin start, followed by the good-morning calls of the wonderful range of feathered creatures in the area. My home under the heavy thorn bush has been comfortable and secure and I have slept well. Four guinea fowl walk by, just a few metres away, calling as they go. They don't see me, although they look a little suspiciously my way. Hippos herald in the day as the sun peers over the horizon.

The river downstream around Chirundu is busy with lots of motor boats and fishermen. It's a long weekend in Zimbabwe and the one on which farmers have been told to get off their land. Many of them, and of course people from towns and cities, have come to the river to try and get away from those pressures for a while and to seek some degree of safety for their families.

They talk of the truck loads of so-called war veterans being dropped off at farm turn-offs all the way along the various roads en route here, and directly at their farms. They are bitter, angry and upset. They berate the world community for doing nothing. The hypocrisy and double standards are so obvious.

A fisherman calls to me from the bank where he fishes next to the cottage he is staying in with friends. He is an Indian from Harare and his name is Noddy. He insists that I go ashore and he calls to all his friends to come over. 'Hey man, come and look here. This is not a TV show, man. This is National Geographic for real, man!' He bubbles with excitement and enthusiasm for my adventure. He wants photographs taken standing next to me and the kayak. He wants to feed me. He wants to give me things. 'National Geographic for real, man – not a TV show, man!' he keeps saying. He and his friends are kind, welcoming and friendly. They, too, are escaping the weekend difficulties of the country. As I probe further, I find that these people's fears are that once the whites are off the land, their businesses crushed, and they are gone, the focus will turn on the Indian community. It seems that it has started to a degree already, with Noddy telling me that some of his Indian business friends have already had their homes and businesses raided by Mugabe's rather shadowy Central Intelligence Organisation. He says that this is so difficult to understand as the Indians have consistently contributed to the economy and have even contributed millions of US dollars in previous years to keep Mugabe in office. 'We are Zimbabweans, man,' he says. 'It's bad, man. We'll just have to wait and see what happens.'

Further downstream a motor boat drifts. One man fiddles with the engine while the others chat and watch me approach. One of them is a farmer, the other three are from Harare. The farmer – his name is Murray – is going to Malawi, he tells me. 'This place is stuffed!' I ask what his experience of the forced removal has been. He tells me that they received notice that their farm was on the list. Then they were told they could remove nothing but their personal effects. However, when they tried to do that, the war vets demanded money. No money, no personal effects. They stayed on their farm as long as they could. As it became ever more threatening, he sent this wife away but he stayed, hoping that perhaps the storm would blow over. But it didn't. Some other men arrived and told him to get off or he would be arrested. 'This farm belongs to … ' and they mentioned the name of a high-ranking government official. 'So much for distributing the land to the peasants,' he spits out, his face twisted with disgust.

A very big pod of hippos lies across the channel I have taken. There are also about 25 up on the bank sunning themselves. I drift closer while taking pictures. There is no way around them, so I have to disturb their slumber. I clap my hands quietly and call out to them. Those on the bank flee for the water, their skins glistening as the spray from those ahead of them hits their bodies. Dust rises from the bank and, halo-like, drifts over the boiling mass of water and great bodies. It clears the bank and now they are practically all submerged. I paddle very close to the bank where they were. It is quite safe as, feeling threatened, they will stay in the deeper part of the channel. Even so, there is a risk, and I move through quickly. As I pass they begin popping up their enormous heads, snorting and blowing as hippos do.

Waterbuck, impalas, pukus, elephants, hippos – as far as the eye can see. African lily trotters and Egyptian geese, giant herons and lilac-breasted rollers in their riverbank colonies.

A very strong wind blows into my face. The current helps me but it is still heavy going. I see a lodge on my left and look at it through my binoculars. Someone is looking directly back at me. I wave. She waves back and then waves her arm to call me over. I simply wave, not wanting to be held up, but she persists – jumping into a motor boat to come out and talk to me. She introduces herself as Elizabeth Baillie, explaining that they had heard I was on my way and insisting I come over and join them. Her kindness and interest is irresistible and I am soon paddling back upstream to their lodge. She and Dave Winhall run a lovely camp called Kayila, situated under a grove of great baobabs in an area that has an interesting story.

During the 1980s a fast-talking gentleman managed to convince the then-President Kaunda's government in Zambia that he had a process, well under development, that could turn grass into diesel. He ran a near-perfect con, and managed to convince the government to let him have 10 000 hectares of land for this purpose across the river from the Zimbabwean Mana Pools. He was granted this for almost nothing on a 99-year lease.

During the late 80s and early 90s I remember seeing great windmill-type structures along the river on the Zambian side, and wondered back then what they were. This, I now discover, was part of the con; something tangible to show any government inspectors or visitors a semblance of a process. In fact, nothing of the sort was occurring and he used it simply as his private estate on the Zambezi. Situated directly across from the Zimbabwean Mana Pools heritage site, not far from the Zambian Lower Zambezi National Park, this was a prime piece of African real estate. He had partners in the company that owned the land who knew nothing of how he had come to acquire it in the first place. A change in government in Zambia and a real look-in by the authorities revealed the truth, and the conman was forced to flee. The land, however, was now legally leased to a company. His share in this company, in turn, was acquired by a syndicate and is now one of the few pieces of privately owned land of such size on the entire Zambezi River.

> Although it is difficult to acknowledge, I realise that in life some of the things our enemies say of us really are true. If we listen to those things and we deal with them, we truly grow in our humanity and integrity.

I stand on the bank with Dave and we watch a boat go by. We wave and Dave says to me, 'That was … , the most highly decorated soldier in the Rhodesian Army.'

'The Phantom Major?' I ask.

'The very one.'

I think of the irony of the situation. I know that he served in the Rhodesian SAS, so Zambia for him back then would have been hostile territory. Now here he is in Zambia, apparently staying just one camp downstream from where I am; relaxing, looking across at the now-hostile Zimbabwe. His erstwhile white countrymen, 22 years after the end of that war, being stripped of their land and everything they own. Is it this tyranny – blatant Stalinism – that he fought with such courage to prevent? Or was there another reason?

I reflect on all the men I knew, and now know, who fought throughout Southern Africa. Whatever the structure they were in – MK, the SADF, Azapo, Swapo, the Rhodesian army, Zanla, Zipra, Inkatha – they all had a clear cause. In each of these structures there were idealists. There were also blatant racists, tribalists, and opportunists. There were people who went into military structures because they were forced to go and others who went gladly. There were heroes and cowards on all sides. There were those who volunteered for everything, and those who tried to do as little as possible. Of all sides this is true. It is difficult to acknowledge this. We all want 'our side' to be right in every way; but it never was or is. Although it is difficult to acknowledge, I realise that in life some of the things our enemies say of us really are true. If we listen to those things and we deal with them, we truly grow in our humanity and integrity.

I watch the Phantom Major go by in a boat and I honour him. I don't know why he fought – I have never had the chance to talk to him and ask him, so I will make no assumptions. But I honour his dignity and courage. Even if I were to disagree with why he fought – I honour these things in him.

I know why I fought and have, over the years, also discovered the lies I was fed. But the things I fought against were communism and fascism. I still do. The Iron Curtain was still up back then. It was not a myth, although the propaganda machines made a real meal of this one. Mugabe is a Stalinist. He is ensuring that the riches will be held by the ruling elite and the people will be reduced to peasants. This is not a myth. It is happening now. It will happen over and over again, long after Mugabe has gone; not only here but around the world, until we recreate our human interdependence and the disciplines of the rule of law and of human rights. Surely this is what the United Nations should be, and it needs to have teeth! I think that it's time for statesmanship not politics. It's time for courage and truth. If we did wrong, let us acknowledge it. If we did right, let it be seen. Not everything in a person is good or bad. We can accept some things in a person's views and disagree with others. Yet we are taught to be bigots in the name of politics. An instant positioning of the person in our minds, and the truth of the person's wholeness stays hidden from us. I fight against this now. It is a deep mission for me. I fight for meaning and truth, for a shared future and a dignified place for everyone. An ancient wisdom of Africa gives us these words – *umuntu ngumuntu ngabantu*, a person is a person because of other people. We are all interdependent; not this group or that group but all humanity.

I paddle into the lovely evening. I creep silently up on a smallish crocodile who sees me only at the last minute and splashes into the water just metres from my boat. I paddle past a pod of hippos, one of whom I discover is directly under me. As the great bubbles boil from his massive body and released air breaks around my craft, my chest compacts in a tight squeeze for a moment. I paddle hard as he comes up right behind me. That was close!

I come across an elephant of the almost extinct genetic line with massive tusks. He is old and ignores me even though I am very close to him. Across the river and back on the Zambian side I seek a place to camp. Now, under a cover of thorn, I listen as hippos emerge for their nightly feed and elephants strip the trees and bush close by. It is new moon. The stars are bright and I would not want to be anywhere else in the world.

Up and away early, I come across the spot where the headquarters of an NGO called Conservation Lower Zambezi is situated. I pull in

> I think that it's time for statesmanship not politics. It's time for courage and truth. If we did wrong, let us acknowledge it. If we did right, let it be seen.

Chirindu.

and have an early cup of tea with Ian Stevenson. Conservation Lower Zambezi was established to assist the Zambian government in its conservation drive. It is active both in education and anti-poaching activities and the work they do is quite remarkable. From them, I am able to understand some of the challenges confronting the valley. Ian describes it as a mini war out there – but it's not the people who are pulling the triggers, it's their masters.

Also working out of their camp is a researcher by the name of Lea. She is tracking the wild dog population in the area. There are two packs; a female in one has just produced nine pups. Everyone is very excited as the wild dog is, of course, under serious threat of extinction.

Leaving them, I choose to paddle along the smaller, less obvious channels. The day is calm and the water pushes quite strongly. I paddle, then stop and drift, quietly coming up on a range of animals and birds that make the day spectacular indeed. Saddle-billed storks, giant herons, buffalos, kudus, waterbuck, hippos, of course, and crocodiles. Big crocodiles, which are so difficult to surprise. Quiet as I am, they sense my approach and slither into the water before I am close enough for a good picture. But every now and then I get it right.

As evening approaches I am still in the channels, but then as the sun begins to set I find myself in an open area with hippos everywhere. They yawn and stretch their jaws. They gambol and run in the shallows, creating bow waves that break the mirror of the sun. I paddle up close, through and around them. Then I turn and, paddling upstream periodically to stay close to them, I watch the magnificent scene unfold. No moment is like the next. No one set of colours like those that follow. 'Age cannot wither her, nor custom stale her infinite variety', said Shakespeare in *Anthony & Cleopatra*. I apply it here – for in this place there is truly infinite beauty and variety. It was here before man existed and will be long after we are gone from the face of the earth.

I linger midstream as along as I can. Then I make for a tree-laden point next to the river with grass so short and green it could be lawn. Behind this lies a reed-filled floodplain. Elephants, it seems, come here frequently to feast on the acacia pods and leaves. So do hippos, which is why the grass is so neatly trimmed.

I drag my kayak out of the water, leaving only the rudder in the water. Busy in my hull, removing my writing equipment, I'm startled by a hippo that emerges in the water not two metres from where I am on the bank. He is equally startled by my presence and lunges back towards deep water. Both our hearts, I'm sure, beat faster for a while.

The Southern Cross lies at its jaunty angle directly in my line of sight. I reach out and touch my family in my mind's eye, and I think of the musicians Crosby, Stills and Nash and their songs. All the friends who, over the years, have enjoyed their music with me come to mind, and I think of them warmly.

The early evening is replaced by a deep darkness and the night sounds are loud. Gradually they quieten down. The frogs and toads pick up the chorus line and hippos blow periodically. Darkness is now merged with the new moon and it is beautiful all over again.

The night is busy around my camp. A herd of buffalo keeps close company, hippos tear the grass, splashing and lowing in the water. A cacophony that keeps me from deep sleep. Afrikaners call hippos *seekoeie* (sea cows) – a good name for them, especially when you hear them in pods, lowing like cattle. When they work in unison the noise is phenomenal.

In the magnificent dawn, I take a walk through God's garden, this little part of it that was left in our care. The sun has not yet risen, but it is light and the mood gentle. This is the time of momentary silence. The time of the changing of the guard. The night-time frogs are silent now, and the last of the hippos are sliding their

> In the magnificent dawn, I take a walk through God's garden, this little part of it that was left in our care. The sun has not yet risen, but it is light and the mood gentle. This is the time of momentary silence.

Opposite: Unpacking for the night.
Below: A typical camp - this one in Mana Pools Zimbabwe/Zambia.

cumbersome forms back into the river after their night's feeding. The splashes and snorts are loud amidst the quiet. Then a gap of complete silence, and suddenly the birds begin where the frogs left off. Doves and pigeons, francolins and guinea fowls, the constant calls are overlaid by others as they join the day.

I walk towards the deep, windy, bass sound of a ground hornbill call and soon see them: enormous, heavy birds with long scimitar beaks. They are shy and fly ahead of me. The sun peeps over the tree line giving life to the dust kicked up by impala and waterbuck. I come upon a lone bull hippo which stands in reeds near a long narrow pool of water. He sees me but does not move. I stand with him for a while, he on his side of the trough, me on mine.

There is little wilderness left in the world; so few places where the real adventure of living in concert with nature can be expressed. Peel away our material 'things' and what is left? I am deeply concerned for mankind. He of the 'low budget spoon' comes to mind. And I dwell on the contrast between rank materialism and the poignant statement of the Cree Indians of North America:

Only after the last tree has been cut down
Only after the last river has been poisoned
Only after the last fish has been caught
Only then will you find
That money cannot be eaten.

I believe World Heritage sites and places critical to the survival of life on earth should not belong to the country in which they exist. They belong to the world community and should be protected by the world community. So if they are destroyed by local people or renegade leaders, the world needs to take action. This is not the way it is at present!

I paddle along in the fast-flowing current, enjoying the sights and sounds. At the spot I choose for lunch, a crocodile takes to the water. But this one doesn't disappear. It keeps its eyes on me and advances fast toward my kayak. I paddle hard for the land only metres away and climb quickly out of the boat. The crocodile disappears underwater now, while still coming at speed in my direction. I drag the kayak well clear, watch the water carefully for a while, then dig for my lunch: granola bars, Pro-Vita biscuits and peanut butter, washed down with cold tea. I explore the area and find that the crocodile has been all over on the land. I follow her tracks and find two spots that could be nests. Perhaps that is why her behaviour was somewhat aggressive. Or was it just inquisitive? Either way, I remain cautious. Once I am ready to leave, my most vulnerable moment is when I have to get into my tight cockpit and push away from the bank. I do so as fast as I can and paddle hard to get some distance between me and the crocodile's territory as quickly as possible.

As I reach the area which leads into Mupata Gorge, hills begin to reach into the river. Slowly the river narrows and there are fewer hippos. But the number of crocodiles increases dramatically.

It's probably just that they are easier to spot here, but on every sandbank or sunny spot they lie, sometimes in twos and threes. Most of them are under three metres long but every now and again there is a really big one. Their colouring is really quite pretty – yellowish with dark splotch stripes all down the underside of the tail.

The river narrows even more. A bachelor herd of elephants draws my attention and I visit them for a while. The bank is steep here and I watch a young bull with interest as he balances his huge frame on a 45° slope to get the choicest branches. He tolerates me below him for quite a while and then suggests I leave! He suddenly turns at me, ears held wide, and shakes his head sharply, dust billowing up all around him. I accede and drift off downstream.

The area becomes wilder still. Just as I am celebrating the lack of development and the sounds of nature, a motor boat going very fast zooms up from behind and disappears into the gorge. I'm sad. There are so few places like this, where we can be free of noisy man-made clutter. Yet it is brought here too.

As I move deeper into this wild and wonderful place I begin to feel just a little twinge of sadness. This chapter of my journey is drawing to an end. Soon I will enter Mozambique and cross another great lake. But here I have seen so much. Our world and the way we treat her lies bare before us in this place. Our care and integrity lie exposed, either in its lack or in its fullness. So many times we simply turn a blind eye to terrible things around us. Look at the wars we have fought (which I have fought!), so many pointless wars of politicians. I think of the courage I have seen, the dignity and humility, the poverty, generosity, meanness and stupidity. The corruption and selflessness. The pristine beauty and its destruction. All this lies here on this journey.

I choose a spot for my camp. There are limited places as the sides are now quite steep. As luck would have it, a pod of hippos are tucked into a little eddy, clearly waiting for nightfall to exit at the exact spot I have chosen. I look around. It is a perfect place for me. But I can see that it is also one of

the few places these hippos can exit the valley for food. I take pity on them, bid them a good night's feeding, and begin paddling hard downstream. It's getting pretty dark now, and I'm a little stressed, but with some relief I soon see an island and I make for it, hoping it will do. It turns out to be a good spot. It is the first island I have slept on in the river itself, and it is ironic that I do so just as I begin to leave the big game areas. It occurs to me that, with all the challenges and problems that surround us in the world, this is exactly what we can so easily and frequently do in our lives – withdraw to our islands: our home, our circle of friends, our religions, our work. Our island is where we feel safe. We can even control our island: what it looks like and who does what on it. But the reality is that in the next rainy season this island will be inundated by floods. The brush several metres above my head and high in the tree bears this truth. Just like the ozone layer and the great forests, we can ignore the greater reality that surrounds us if we wish. We can look after ourselves here and now – carving lovely homes and lives for ourselves. But our world is telling us quite another story and we ignore the greater truth at our peril. Best leave the island and get involved in overcoming the challenges and major areas of destruction in our world, or we won't have a world, let alone an island.

During the early part of the night a lone hippo approaches the island and begins snorting and demonstrating in the water. He is not more than a few metres from where I lie. I talk to him, 'OK, OK, I know it's terrible. I'm sorry to put you out like this, but I have nowhere else to go and I'll only be here one night.' He is not impressed. Clearly I have chosen his favourite spot. Several times he emerges from the water, moving fast towards me in the shallows – a kind of mock charge. Eventually our stand-off must end or I'll get no sleep, and it could get much more dangerous. I wait until he rushes again, then I jump up and switch on my torch, shouting loudly, and throw a branch at him. He gets a real fright and flees, appearing again about 50 metres downstream and still staring at me on my, or should I say his, little island. He stays there for a long time, and I eventually finish writing up my log and go to sleep.

I watch the dawn unfold from my island home. Beautiful and comfortable as it is, I know I must leave and 'get involved'. The noisy hippo who kept me company through the night is only ten metres from my camp. He rests in the lee of the island with just his eyes, ears and nostrils protruding. He watches me with interest.

The river flows fast here and whirls and undercurrents begin to occur. They are not serious but I keep an eye on them. Mupata Gorge is truly magnificent. Here there are lots of bushbuck, warthogs, waterbuck and, periodically, impalas. As is often the case, baboons are close to the impalas, and vervet monkeys peer at me from sausage trees (*Kigelia africana*). A giant kingfisher hits the water not three metres from me and emerges with a fish. I sit quite still and the current carries me to where he is now, perched on a dead branch overhanging the water. I think telepathically, 'I wouldn't do that if I were you – if you drop it, it'll land in the water.' The fish is a small tiger, which is at least as long as he is. He shakes his head and hits the fish hard against the branch to stun or kill it. He does this many times and between blows he keeps an eye on me. I can't move as he will fly away and the current is carrying me past him now. I simply watch in awe and wonder how in the world he is going to fit that fish into his body. I drift around the bend and out of sight.

I try to sneak up on several crocodiles by just drifting towards them, but they are very alert – slowly disappearing into the water without a ripple.

I pass by the survey site of what was, for a while, a possible dam. The geological and ecological impact both mitigated against its construction. I am pleased, for its construction would have covered Mana Pools, a World Heritage Site, and all its natural magnificence.

Through the 'Gates', aptly named as the river squeezes through a narrow break in the steep ridges and hills and then near a place called The Red Cliffs, I am hailed by a couple who are fishing from a motor boat. They are elderly and, while he fishes, she sits comfortably near him on the boat and does embroidery. They are totally happy in one another's company and I enjoy my short inclusion in their warmth for each other. I feel as if I am a little boy, cuddled up on granny's lap.

The border to exit Zambia and enter Mozambique arrives with late afternoon. First I pull over next to a dugout and a motor boat, and climb up a winding path to the Zambian Passport control. Then, formalities complete and after a 30-minute paddle, I approach Zumbu on the Mozambique side.

Border crossing from Zambia to Mozambique.

Across Cahora Bassa

- Mozambique or Mexico?
- Into the lake
- Reed beds and fires
- On the fringes of despair

The Mozambique frontier village of Zumbu looks just like a scene from an old Western movie set somewhere on the Mexican border. The tune of 'The Good, The Bad and The Ugly' plays for a while in my head and I smile to myself. The Portuguese influence remains strong, and can be seen in the style of the buildings and the way the town itself is laid out – neat and utilitarian. But although the village is very tiny and remote, the post office has recently received a new coat of paint, and whitewashed stones mark the edges of the roadways. Indeed, without them it would just be a barren piece of earth with buildings dotted here and there.

Friendly villagers come over to watch me pull in and point out where I must go. Two little boys proudly lead the way. As I am about to take a picture of them in front of a building, a gentleman walking ahead of us turns and says, 'No picture!' It turns out that he is the Immigration official

and this is a government building. Never, never in Africa point a camera at a government building! I apologise. There is no further problem, but with that warning I know for sure that I am now officially in Mozambique.

The grey-uniformed customs official leads me up the stairs of the building and past a long row of empty rooms. He shows me into an office where I am told to sit down, then he leaves the room. It is deathly quiet. Not another soul appears to be in the vicinity. A cat meows, and what sounds like a rat scurries across the ceiling above me. Then I hear the sound of hard boots on the cement veranda and my guide, with another man, enters the room. I stand up politely and shake hands and, although I get a reasonably friendly response, this is clearly serious business. We all peer at my passport and visa. The official pages back and forth and back and forth. Then, with great style, he stamps my passport for 10 days and tells me that I must report to Sengu, the town closest to Cahora Bassa Dam, to renew my visa. I am taken aback and complain, explaining my journey. I'm not even sure I will be able to get to Sengu in 10 days and, even if I do, how will I be able to leave my kayak safely and travel into town to do this administration? He says he is very sorry, but that's it. I have been issued with the wrong visa – a multiple re-entry visa – which only allows for 10-day stays. Then I have to leave the country and can return again for another 10 days and so on. This is a real problem for me as logistics on the river will simply make this impossible.

I politely request that my visa be changed, but to no avail. I must report to Sengu within 10 days. I ask if I can perhaps talk to the person in charge. He *is* the person in charge. I can see I am going nowhere with this, so I gather up my papers, bid them a good evening, and walk back down to the 'port' where my kayak is surrounded by a throng of curious onlookers. Although irritated, I calm myself and accept what cannot be changed. I will try again in Sengu.

> **Never, never in Africa point a camera at a government building!**

At my kayak, I watch a woman separating the chaff from the grain in the age-old way of tossing it in the air. The chaff blows away in the breeze and the grain remains. Her face is white with grain powder, and she gives me a huge, friendly smile and a coy look. I paddle out into the middle of the channel and turn and look back upstream. There I can see the magnificent hills that hide Mupata Gorge. On the south bank, Zimbabwe with all its problems; on the north, Zambia with some of the most peaceable and friendly people in the world. Between these two countries lies a magnificent piece of wild, natural Africa. But it is under severe pressure.

I look back upstream and as the sun begins to set I feel a sense of sadness – of loss even. This is a chapter that is behind me now – beautiful as it was. If the river represents life, then my youth lies behind me.

I enter the floodplains and its many channels at the start of this new chapter just a little depressed. There are people everywhere. The reed banks are all burning or have recently been burnt. My enquiries tell me that it is to chase off the hippos and clear the islands for crops. Isn't there a different way? The reeds play a crucial role in the ecology of the floodplains, filtering the water and giving habitat to so many fish and bird species. As they are removed, so the fish populations will be affected. The people here need the fish, it is a primary source of protein for them; but they burn the reeds that feed the fish! There must be ways, indeed there are many ways, in which the people can feed themselves, and the river and its creatures can be protected at the same time.

I exit on a hippo run – one of the few places that I can get out of the water. I watch the fires burning late into the night, and as the hippos call to one another it is not difficult to imagine their consternation. Where can they go? This part of God's garden is on fire. All night long the local people beat drums and hit tins together, making an awful din to frighten off elephants and hippos. I don't get much sleep.

As I am about to leave I see that the people across the channel have now noticed me and are all watching me with interest. I paddle upstream and over to them and give them some fish hooks and a canister of spices I don't need.

The floodplain is reminiscent of Barotseland in miniature. There are still hippos and quite a lot of crocodiles. Elephants also come in from the southern side. I see a large crocodile lying casually beneath a bank. Well past him, I pull in to the shore and then make my way back upstream on foot and well out of his line of sight to try and get a picture of him. Despite the fact that I am so quiet and careful with my footfalls, when I look carefully over the top of the bank – my camera poised – he is gone. No wonder crocodiles have survived since the time of the dinosaurs!

I pass what looks like a Westerners' fishing camp and shortly thereafter get to Kafagudzi. This is a fishing camp used mainly by Zambian fisher-folk. I pull over and have a chat. They're all Zambian and

come here specifically to catch fish for market. One gentleman comes from Lukulu and is excited when I'm able to relate to places he knows well. I spend some time with them and see the fish-smoking process underway. We sit and chat while fish are split down the middle and put directly on a low rack over a smoky fire. No salt is used.

I discover that the camp I passed not to far away is owned by a man named Peter, who is a 'Boer' and who is 'not a nice man'. He shot somebody in the bush and killed him, I am told. Now he is apparently hiding in Zimbabwe. 'He told us if we come close by he will shoot us too.' We talk of cultures and attitudes to one another. Charles Mwanza says he thinks it must be education that keeps white and black apart. I say that even uneducated people can still be intelligent, honest, loving, caring and kind. They agree so we explore what it is that keeps us apart. There seems to be consensus that it may be money – the 'haves' and 'have-nots' syndrome. It is a difficult issue because I then raise the point that there are wealthy black people and poor whites. We all shake our heads.

I laugh eventually and say, 'But none of this matters; on the inside our blood is all the same colour anyway.' They laugh too but say, 'The others are not like you – they would not sit here on the mat with us and talk in this way.' I'm afraid that inwardly I have to agree, but what I say is that we need to keep trying. Everyone nods sagely.

We discuss elephants and they say that they were awake all night beating tins because elephants were close. I explain that this is not

Charles Mwanza says he thinks it must be education that keeps white and black apart. I say that even uneducated people can still be intelligent, honest, loving, caring and kind.

necessary in a fishing camp where crops are not grown and that they will not harm people if left alone. They are incredulous. I take it further and talk about the animals' need for food and water too. It is a fascinating discussion – I hope it helps both the elephants and these people.

The wind is blowing very hard now and the going is extremely tough. A little finger of land protrudes into the lake. I take shelter in the lee and then decide to give myself a break and have something to eat. I discover that there is an old cement beacon on the point – probably a high water marker. It has been knocked over by the water and wind. I'm not surprised – they are both formidable here.

As I paddle I think of my friends and how important they are to me. I let the concept of time once again drift through my mind and I draw analogies to the river.

If time is a progression then the river can be likened to our lives.

The birth of the river, just like a human birth, is a deeply meaningful spiritual moment. We stand in awe at the profundity of life and in wonder at the life that will be lived. I think of that special place on the river and relive its glory. The tiny stream that holds so much promise as it burbles and bubbles its way in the first hours.

Childhood: in which we explore, testing the parameters of acceptability and gaining our first experiences of action and consequence. A time of reckless joy and sometimes terror, of great change and growth. From the Angolan border in the north to Cazombo, the river, too, lures us with beauty and calm, periodically broken and changed by little rapids and true falls. Once or twice – a real threat. But mostly it is fun, weaving this way and that – a constant routine, spectacular in its sparkling water and magnificent surrounds.

Adolescence: the search for meaning. The time when we begin to assert independence and break away. Just like the river from north of Cazombo, Angola, to Sioma. The calm stretches of beautiful water, the tumultuous rapids, falls and dangerous whirlpools. The finding of a new confidence, a new space – only to be struck, out of the blue, by military intervention and arrest, a surprise apparently unrelated to the river's journey, but very much a part of life. With this broadened experience, a new self emerges, based on personal experience. The emotional swings from delight to depression are clear. Our confidence grows and we begin to know who we are, to trust our own capabilities when forced by physical and psychological trials.

Early adulthood: the founding of long-term relationships, families and careers. All this is well symbolised by the sudden change in the river below Sioma Falls. We have to leave the comfort of our routine and, on our own, portage into challenging, difficult, but spectacularly beautiful moments.

Middle age: that time when we begin reaping the rewards of our efforts, when we have learnt about the routine nature of change in our lives. When we realise that meaning does not come from isolation but from greater involvement in community and society, in life itself. Just like the new river below Kariba. Suddenly our family is no longer there in our home. Just like this, the lake is behind us. The river narrows and we begin to experience a good current that pushes us along, and work in the kayak is no longer so stressful. There is a deep inner enjoyment of the phenomenal beauty around us.

Old age. The dilemmas of retirement. The challenge of how to stay productive. The integration of what we have learnt in life and its conversion to wisdom, or the descent into despair and meaninglessness. I experience the start of this now as I move through Mupata Gorge. Slowly leaving the variety and magnificence of the true wilderness behind and being confronted by more and more people. The border – 'forced retirement' – and a need to re-evaluate and reposition the reason we are on the river at all. It is quite different to that earlier stretch yesterday, just upstream, and I sit in the middle of the river, looking back upstream and, for a while, long for what was. The fires and barrenness of the current situation. The river leads us into new floodplains, but they are not fresh and alive with natural life like the Barotseland of our youth. They are burnt and black and struggling to survive. It is depressing and we search for meaning. Changing channels and talking about life and existence with those lonely people we meet in this place, who also somehow reflect this darkness.

I think about the progress of life and the river in this way and realise that, just like life, I cannot yet truly talk of old age – the last part of the river – for I have not yet fully experienced it. I am still dealing with retirement. The balance of this analogy is going to have to wait.

Zumbu border post harbour.

I pull over in the heavy wind and seek shelter in a little cove. Here I make my camp amidst a tumble of boulders and newly washed sand.

Morning brings with it some visitors who, arriving on the shore, wait respectfully while I finish my breakfast. When they do approach they bring with them a fish as a gift. How can I not love and admire these people? These are only youngsters. There are four of them. The oldest is about 15 and the youngest probably 10 or 11. Here they are, days' paddling from their home in Zumbu, fishing for a living. They are only children!

I give them gifts too: biscuits, sweets and fish hooks. But the gift that they really love is paper and pencil. They are delighted – carefully measuring out the pad so that they all get the same number of pages. The little one, in particular, cannot stop smiling. He is so excited. This is what he should be doing at this time of his life. Learning to write and draw and add. But he is a fisherman, already working to survive. Which skill, I wonder, is, in fact, more important to him?

Lake Cahora Bassa.

I paddle out into the massive Cahora Bassa lake. The wind is very strong. Across long stretches, far from the land, I sing. Pummelled by the wind and waves and on the fringe of madness, I laugh and shout in the wind. Waves, driven by the pumping wind, break over my bow and hit me in the chest. I keep ducking my head – using the peak of my cap to keep the water from my eyes and face. I sing loudly and make up poems, which I recite at the top of my voice. I play with different accents and I talk to the

wild. Frothy wave crests like white horses run in the opposite direction to me. I have escaped that 'quiet desperation' I feel in the city. I am free of it. I live. The moment is now. God is great!

This place is harsh and forbidding. It reminds me of earlier expeditions on Lake Turkana, the Jade Sea in northern Kenya. The water – churned up by the waves – is green. The countryside is tinder dry; the bush barren. Wind and waves ensure there is no comfort, no respite. Yet comfort I feel. It is beyond the physical. I live. I truly live!

My body is fit and hard now. Two and a half months of physical effort have carved it well. I am completely in tune with it, feeling every fibre as it works. Every twinge or pull is understood. I am strong and healthy. The wind – hard as it is – is a feature of this place. It is not an obstacle. I know that anything can be accomplished if I just decide to do it. To just exist is, in a way, to be in a state of death. Death itself is a part of life. But a state of death while still living is hell.

The wind grows ever stronger. After two hours of paddling straight into it across a bay, I pull in to the lee of an island. I write. The lake lies under a pall of smoky haze. The hills to the north are exquisite; layered and broken, different blues and grey emphasise each layer. Waves rock my kayak, which rolls against my foot as I sit on the beach. New soil – reduced from rock by 30 years of wave action – is forming here, and I marvel at the resilience and capability of nature to transform. What will the shoreline show in 1 000 years' time? Riverine trees and bush, perhaps, with all the birds and animals that accompany it. I hope so.

> To just exist is, in a way, to be in a state of death. Death itself is a part of life. But a state of death while still living is hell.

The wind grows even stronger. I paddle hard. Another four hours go by and I stop again at a point. Here I discover a dead crocodile. Just over three metres long, it lies next to my kayak. This crocodile got tangled in the fishing nets in the bay close by. Erastaw Malungu, whom I meet later, tells me that they killed it with great difficulty and then dragged its body here. I remove the head and clean the flesh from the skull. I tie this rather macabre trophy to the stern of my kayak and paddle into the evening. Because of the smoke the sunset is spectacular. But I must make up distance and I paddle into the darkness. Two hours after sunset, with the wind still pushing as hard as ever, I make for the shore. A comfortable beach awaits me and I seek shelter under a lonely bush that clings to the ground on this windswept dune.

It is dark and while I write under torchlight, the enormous 'crump' of a heavy explosion rends the air. It comes from the north and, with the start I get, my pencil slips across the page. Torchlight off, I listen. It sounded like an 81-mm mortar or a TM46 anti-tank landmine going off. I sit quietly alert for a while. I hope that it is not a long-ago-laid landmine that has just found a victim.

The wind blows hard all night and is still blowing as the sun rises. I see a person along the shore and, wading through the water between us, make my way over to him. He warns me of a 'big crocodile' that frequents the area where I spent the night. I wonder what that big crocodile thought of the crocodile skull tied to my kayak. I leave the sheltered bay I am in and the force of the wind hits me with a hard blow. The waves are rolling in-shore and they are big! I struggle to make enough distance through them to avoid the frothy crests that roll over me. The swells remain large even though I have managed to get free of the shore. It is impossible to stop paddling even for a moment as the wind almost immediately swings the boat sideways and pushes me backwards. According to my GPS I am only moving forwards at between two and three kilometres per hour.

The crossing I need to do is a big one and I am facing directly into the wind. I work hard and then begin to sing. I like some of the melodies I make up and I sing them over. They are cheerful and folksy. What I really need is a fiddler to accompany me!

The seven-odd-kilometre crossing takes me over three agonising hours. But now – in the lee of an island – it goes a little easier, though even here the wind still finds the water. I get to the co-ords that Andy has given me for the fishing camp he is beginning to develop with a friend. No camp! I paddle a little further and then decide to recce on foot. I walk in a big semicircle and see absolutely no sign of it. About to give up, I spot what I think is a vehicle track. Closer inspection confirms this but now, which way to go? I choose left. The track takes me right across the island to the opposite shore but there it just stops.

Some fishermen there tell me that there is something in the direction from which I have just come. I retrace my steps – back the two or so kilometres – and then walk the other way. After a few more

kilometres, I come across a dwelling erected as a shelter by some locals. I ask them if they know of the camp. I am directed back again – but the gentleman is pointing in another direction – up and across the island again. I choose to follow where he points. Climbing up a fairly steep hill past baobabs and mopanes, I once again marvel at how quickly the bush changes. Just yesterday there was barren wasteland. Here, now, real beauty. I find another track, and am quite determined to follow this one. It leads me to Andy's new spot and I feel quite satisfied with myself for having found it. I had a good walk, too.

I don't want my kayak left on its own, so we go and collect it. It's heavy!

There is very little at the new camp as yet: two little tents, a toilet, six labourers and a shower! I introduce myself to Edward, the leader of the team. As it is late now, I ask if I can camp with them. I don't want my kayak left on its own, so we go and collect it. It's heavy! Soon I am in that shower, and what a pleasure it is. It is a typical bush shower: grass tied to wire latitudinals makes for the sidewalls and the sky itself is the roof. The water is cold and refreshing and I scrub and polish myself back to shiny new.

But, I have not been feeling well. My neck is stiff and sore and I have a headache along with a slightly nauseous feeling. I decide I had better watch this carefully in case it's malaria. I dig around for my malaria test equipment, only to find that the liquid in a crucial container has somehow leaked out. So I decide to wait until nightfall to see how I feel.

The business of setting up a camp or lodge in a truly remote area is no simple task. Here, vehicle tracks have been carved and trees removed to facilitate the development. Every item here has been brought in by boat or Unimog through trackless bush. In its existing state, there are two tents, a tarpaulin stretched between trees to make a kitchen area, a small gas fridge and freezer. A second tarpaulin makes another roof to cover tools: a welding machine, picks, spades and axes, a saw unit that can be driven by a tractor, and an old tractor. There are also two boats. A water tank up above the camp supplies running water to the kitchen, shower and toilet. The pump to get the water up there is also driven by the tractor.

Every single item is crucial to the camp and was delivered here with extreme difficulty. It is impressive and bold, for Cahora Bassa is completely undeveloped and very remote. Edward tells me that they are busy making an airstrip. Very hard work indeed and it is all done by hand.

I am not well, though, and feel absolutely awful throughout the evening. Really concerned about malaria, I lay out all my medication in order, so that if I end up slightly delirious I have little to do other than swallow tablets and drink the water I have stashed next to my sleeping bag.

I feel better in the morning and, after a few hours while I watch for further health problems, I decide that it was probably mild sunstroke, which won't kill me now that I am rehydrated. I wave Edward and his team goodbye, but everything in me is crying out to stay and rest. I push off into the howling wind and go.

Down, down close to that black awful hole I go; depressed and struggling into the wind I fight. The battle lies within, not only with the wind. I struggle – digging myself away from the edge, clawing my way forward. I consciously make myself sing. It is difficult and the wind so hard. Across the green, relentless waves, slowly, slowly I drag myself free. I go deep inside. I paddle through the pain. I paddle and it just becomes the way it is. My mind – now recovering itself slowly – begins to make fun of my situation. It jokes with itself, it acknowledges the hole. Three hours of relentless struggle go by and then I break free. I feel it go. I know I am back.

I begin to sing again – a little forced in the beginning, and then with ease. I make up new words to old songs. I begin to play. I do Monty Python skits in my mind, I goof around with strange questions – like how do crocodiles mate? I've never given this a thought. Do they face each other? Nah! Do they do it in the water? And what a tangle of tails it must be, what a twisting writhing mass of claws and awful smiles! I chuckle at my own warped sense of humour – but I am back!

The first point I reach allows me a break and I pull into the sheltering lee. Soon I am wandering around amidst the jumbled sandstone, marvelling at the shapes and textures. I watch little lizards with bright, almost luminous, blue tails. They run at incredible angles – defying gravity. They are ever alert, agile, dextrous little creatures that are quick to spot a meal and an intruder like me. Not four or five metres from where they skitter, their much bigger cousins display the same characteristics. I know they see me way before I see them. They, too, are lightning fast, agile and focused. As I think these things I come across the upper part of a crocodile skull. I look at the water and smile. 'I know you're there,' I say out loud and keep my distance from the water.

After a snack it's time to go. I strap the newfound skull to the front of my boat. The existing one faces to the rear. My kayak looks like a yellow crocodile with a head at both ends. I know this is

a little dangerous, because crocodiles are territorial and I could be taken as a real competitor by resident crocodiles. But it is not quite breeding season and I would like the skulls.

Some of the 'frozen forests' of Cahora Bassa.

The area begins to get more picturesque. Mountains begin to emerge on the north bank. One looks like a pyramid, another like a pudding. Still another a bit like Table Mountain. The bush is mopane scrub now and it rests on sandstone. Along the edges of the lake this has broken into huge blocks and slabs making the coastline most interesting and fascinating. Tree roots are exposed – like giant octopi making their way out of the deep.

As evening approaches I finally complete another long open water stretch and, when I check the time, I see I have paddled for eight hours. I had only one brief break today – that was my lunch stop – so no wonder I'm feeling tired! My landing is in a sheltered bay overlooked by a baobab and a sprinkle of boulders. I check for tracks as I always do on arrival. Here we have hippos, kudus, baboons and something smaller, like impalas. A fish eagle watches me arrive, and a green-backed heron – my companion for almost the entire length of the river – flies off squawking across the bay.

Out – well away from the shore – what looks like a pied kingfisher hovers and dives, hovers and dives. I can only imagine that there are capentas out there as they normally fish along the shore.

The sun is magnificent in its deep amber and pink-purple hue and I watch it sink slowly over a frozen forest. A francolin flies up, calling as she goes. And then the cry of a fish eagle.

I'm back in God's garden.

The sun is magnificent in its deep amber and pink-purple hue and I watch it sink slowly over a frozen forest. A francolin flies up, calling as she goes. And then the cry of a fish eagle.

Day 79. I emerge from the lovely spot in which I spent the night, into the harsh, relentless wind. The swells are so large that when I'm in a valley between two waves I can't see the horizon. It is tough, tough, tough. My body aches. My right shoulder – a deep pain – right in the joint. I stop for a moment to rest and massage it a little and I am swept backwards fast. I immediately start to paddle again.

I reach the relative quiet of a bay and pull in for a rest. Tucked away in the shelter of some trees is a fisherman's shelter. I walk the few hundred metres over to it to say hello. It looks rather deserted but, as I approach, I see a man lying on his side propped up on an elbow. He is talking to someone who sits in the shade where I cannot see him. I call out in order not to startle him but he does not hear me in the wind. I walk closer. He sees me and, lightning fast, in real fear, he is on his feet and begins to flee. I stand still, a big smile on my face, hands held up and open in greeting, trying to calm him. The other man peers at me from the shadows. A quick assessment and he emerges, coming cautiously towards me. The concern on his face disappears when he sees my placating body language and we smile and greet. His name is Alberto Esquinar Chumbo and he has been using this fishing spot for 10 years. I break the ice by joking about his friend's reaction to seeing a white man. We laugh but the other still keeps his distance for a while.

This reaction is because of the war, he tells me. We speak a mixture of Portuguese, English and Chilapalapa. There was much fighting in this area – '*mucho hondo*,' he says, 'much war'. I am curious, however, at his reaction to me as a white man, so I ask about this. He tells me that white soldiers '*phuma lapa ndeki*' (came out of the back of an aeroplane). At first, I think he is referring to what would have been SAS operations during the Rhodesian bush war which ended in 1980. But he says he saw them twice: in 1984 and 1987. I realise that it can only have been South Africans. Special Forces units were active in their support of Renamo back then. I ask him exactly where he saw them and he points. He tells me that they 'flew their parachutes like birds,' all landing in the same place. There were five or six of them on both occasions. I look at the mountains to my north a little harder and more thoughtfully now. I ask about the south side of Cahora Bassa. 'Was there fighting here too?'

'*Hondo* beeg,' he says, shaking his head sadly. He tells me that all the people from the area ran away to other areas to escape the fighting.

'What about landmines?' I ask, thinking of the blast I heard two nights ago.

'No, not here.' He point across to the north side of the dam and demonstrates. I understand – there are mines there. Then he adds: 'Zimbabwe *frontiera*, many, many!' He makes a cutting motion on the upper part of his leg, shaking his head and making a hissing sound to express his fear.

I check carefully: 'Not here. Are you sure?'

He is quite clear on this – 'No mines here!'

We discuss the wind. He thinks it is better to wait for dark when it at least dies down a little. I am in two minds; it's like hell out there, but I also need to cross the lake! I decide to go. They watch me as I round the point. The big swells are immediate and steep. I paddle very hard but can see from the shoreline that I'm moving very slowly indeed. I choose to ignore this and I drive myself on. About 400 metres ahead of me and up on the treeless strip of shore sometimes covered by water, I see an unusual shape. I first think it is another fisherman's shelter but it is in a very exposed place. As I struggle towards it I begin to make it out. It's a wreck.

It actually looks like an old military landing craft. I watch it as I creep slowly past it and then something inside me begins to well up. It is a military landing craft! I begin to get angry. At first, it is just a sense of irritation. Then it is real anger. I swear. I don't know why I am angry – I just am. Is it all this military crap? Everything I look at is always, or seems always to be, interspersed by some

military image! I am mad. I use the anger. I harness its energy. I work into the waves and the spray. Up and down the rolling swells, water whipping off the bow and stinging my face, hitting my chest and slowly seeping into every part of me. I shout out my aggression – my anger. I roar like a caged lion. I let it surge into and through me and I channel it back into my effort. I bellow, 'Yaaaah!' at the top of my voice. It helps the release. I boil angrily onwards through the great heaving waters of Cahora Bassa. I feel the anger beginning to ease. It leaves me irritated, unsettled – as though something ugly has been inside me.

I paddle into a frozen forest – white, sun bleached trees protruding from the water as far as the eye can see. I am quite tired now and hang on to a stump for a few seconds. But it is too rough and even dangerous as the swell, though smaller here, thumps my kayak against the trunk with force. I let go and paddle and paddle. Ahead I see what looks like a point of land where I hope for some shelter. There, off to my right, a fishing shelter and soon – relief.

I climb out of my kayak and, taking my map, GPS and Lunch Bars, walk away from the water. Seated there, eating some food, I see a man in a *mokoro* making his way to the windy point. He is still in the

I boil angrily onwards through the great heaving waters of Cahora Bassa. I feel the anger beginning to ease. It leaves me irritated, unsettled – as though something ugly has been inside me.

sheltered lee of the ridge and I cannot believe that he is going out in this wind. I stand up to watch and wave. I see him look at me but he does not wave back. Mild irritation is suddenly there in me. I wave more purposefully and for longer. He looks at me – quite clearly he sees me – but he does not wave back. I get mad again. 'Hello,' I shout to the wind, sarcastically. '*Bom dia, sawubona*, how ya doin'?' All the time, I wave. He just looks expressionless and paddles. I swear and then sit back down. Shit, I'm irritated. Normally I would shrug and write it off to misunderstandings in cultural body language or hand signals. But I wouldn't be irritated. Now I am.

I munch on a Lunch Bar and I look at the frozen forest. 'I wonder if it's here – it could have been here,' I am thinking. In 1977 the Rhodesian SAS ran an operation called Cockleshell from Cahora Bassa. Hiding up by day on the lake – amongst the trees protruding from the waters – they mounted strikes and ambushes, retreating always to their canoes and the lake by day.

Is this it? Is this why I'm irritated? The wars touched me personally in Angola, Zambia, Namibia and Zimbabwe. I fought in all these places. But deep down, I guess, I wanted to end my journey in Mozambique in a state of peace. I never fought here. I wonder if that is why I am so mad. I was hoping for calm – peace – a place that would be free of all the angry and traumatic imagery of war. Yet it touches me still, this country that is so keen for a future of peace and prosperity. Just like me. Its memories and experiences linger on. It is a product of its memories and history just like us. Those memories and experiences cannot be obliterated – they are a part of what the place is. Just as it is the case with each of us. Good and bad, joy and tragedy are what makes us what we are. It's the dealing with it that matters.

So when I think about it – this was a part of my war – my history, whether I want it to be or not. I know it would have been our Reconnaissance regiments parachuting in here to train Renamo. I know so much of these men. I also know several of the men who served in Rhodesia's SAS. I know men who were in Mozambique with MK – who were supported by Frelimo, who were, by association, the enemy. But that was years ago. Damn! I just want to see a lake. I just want to see a fucking lake!

I paddle and slowly the wind begins to ease off. It's still strong but it's easier. As evening draws in it becomes calmer still. I watch the mountains on my left. Because of the change in perspective, 'Table Mountain' has now definitely transformed into the White Mountain from my home, '*Ntabamhlophe*'. I stop paddling and, using the ancient greeting, I acknowledge it, '*Sawubona mkaya*' (I see you, one from home). I say this slowly out loud. I acknowledge my roots. I acknowledge my connectedness to it all. The red sun sinks behind me. The sky shifts through its limitless colours. The waves lend a contrast to the calmness of the sky. The water breaks sharply up against the sandstone shore.

With the sun setting behind me and the near-full moon already high, a fish eagle makes its way into the east. She flies across the face of the moon and brings me peace. I feel love and happiness and I think of Annie. I look south and there, represented by the Southern Cross, the rest of my family is near. I feel good now – tired as though I have done battle – but good, at rest inside. Under the bright moon I paddle. An eerie light plays on the water. Sandstone faces begin to get ever steeper along the shore. After three hours I search for a place to land and, in a tiny bay, I make my camp.

I awake with the rising sun. I am high up on a platform carved in the sandstone by water and wind under a leafy tree. My bed is softened by fallen leaves and I enjoy the lazy start to the day. The wind is howling and my shoulder hurts. I decide to take the day, or at least the morning, to rest and catch up with writing and repairs. At around 12h30 or so I hear engines and, walking to the cliff edge, am surprised to see a motor boat with an adult and two boys in it. Then another rounds the corner. I wave and they wave back. One of the boats comes inshore to chat. The people tell me that there is a home not more than two or three kilometres from where I am, and that I would be most welcome. It's just what I need. The wind has been wearing me down and I can do with some company.

I quickly pack and paddle in the direction they indicated and soon see what they have directed me to. It is the home of Alan and Michelle Watt. They run their capenta fishing business from here, and have, over the past eight years, built themselves a lovely home. It rests on the edge of beautifully carved sandstone cliffs. The buffalo grass lawns are lush and green, the view spectacular over the lake, and the company excellent. They have friends visiting from Zimbabwe. After a great lunch a tent is erected for me and I happily settle in for the evening. Over supper we discuss Zimbabwe, as the visitors are farmers directly affected by the land repossession crisis there. We talk of subterfuge and blackmail, of threats to life and family, of murders carried out by well-known figures where the criminal charges have just 'gone away'.

I wake up to a heavy wind and the flapping of a piece of canvas in the tent I was given to sleep in. The water is rough with flecks of spray being driven off the tips of the swells. I groan inwardly. Alan is keen that I stay for a while and finds all manner of reasons to persuade me to do so – in the nicest possible way. He suggests waiting until the wind has died down a bit and I am easily persuaded. We take a drive through the countryside. It varies between mopane veld and montane and, broken by the sandstone bollards, it is very pretty indeed. I am distressed to see baobabs with huge slabs of bark cut out of them or, in other instances, completely ringbarked. I see one 800-year-old giant lying felled in the middle of what is being turned into a field for crops. Sadly, the soil here will in any case not support crops for more than perhaps one season, so the death of the giant is in vain.

After a wonderful lunch I bid everyone farewell and head off. The wind has died down, though it is still strong. But I am well rested now – and well fed! The going is good. Gradually through the afternoon the wind drops until, at sunset, it is almost completely calm. The water, like molten lead, lies magnificent under the fireball in the west. At the same time, the full moon rises in the east. Ibis, whistling duck and Egyptian geese, all making their way to roost, fly this way and that. I watch as the sun disappears below the horizon and I bid it farewell until the morrow. It is absolutely calm now. Not the faintest breeze. The bank of sand along the shore shines white in the moonlight. The mountains are dark; the jade of the water broken by the twisted boughs of trees that protrude from it.

I paddle on into the darkness and, at a point, listen while a standoff occurs between hippos and some people in a *mokoro*. The hippos grunt and snort – the people shout and call and beat their

paddles on their *mokoro*. Neither gives way for a while and then the *mokoro* changes direction and skirts the area of the hippo. I paddle until 22h00 then find a bay in which to make a camp. As I reach the shallows and my kayak touches ground, I startle a small crocodile which is lying at this exact spot and which somehow never saw me approach. There is a mad panicky diving scramble as he makes for deeper water. I can practically touch him as he goes. I have just been paddling through Eden once again and I marvel at how quickly it switches back and forth. My spirits are high. I am tired but I have done good distance and am deeply satisfied.

As anticipated, the wind begins to blow hard again in the early hours of the morning and by sunrise is once again lashing the waves. I choose not to push. It's better if I leave late and paddle into the night when it is likely to be calmer.

A lone fisherman, Domingo Sonto, paddles across the little sheltered bay to greet me. He is curious to see both my kayak and the crocodile skulls. We speak a mixture of Chilapalapa, Portuguese and English. He tells me that there are lots of crocodiles in this area for there are many fish. Alan warned me yesterday of a very large, excessively aggressive crocodile on the north shore. When I ask Domingo for the best route forward, he points to the north shore and also adds, 'Crocodile *mkulu*' (big). I nod and wonder whether I should take the longer route around the south shoreline or brave the crocodiles in the north.

I am also told that the one referred to has killed and eaten several people and has taken two fishermen off their *mekoro*. Alan told me this too. This is very unusual behaviour for a crocodile, as normally crocs do not distinguish between the boat and the people; they are seen as one unit and, therefore, not food. If this one has learnt that people in boats are food, it is very dangerous indeed, especially for me as I am so close to the water

I spend the night on a very steep, rocky and uncomfortable bank, so I get going very early in the morning. I have not paddled far when I see a cottage set high up above the water on an almost vertical drop. It's on an island and, as I paddle around it, I realise that it is, in fact, quite well developed and has a harbour as well. Alan has told me about his friend, whom everyone in the area calls Mawaya, and this is his spot. He, like Alan, runs a capenta fishing business, and when I pull into the harbour there are four or five capenta rigs pulled up side by side next to a launchway. Mawaya is not at home, but his manager, Steve, welcomes me and shows me around.

There are long drying platforms made out of shadecloth, on which thousands and thousands of fish from last night's catch are spread out. They glisten silver and blue in the morning light. They only need to dry for a day, so yesterday's catch is now being removed and put in bags. I glance over at my little kayak next to the enormous capenta rigs. It looks so incongruous. There is a small crowd of interested people around it, but it is the crocodile skulls that are most discussed. I notice that there are quite a number of Malawians working here, and later in the evening this is expressed in a game of soccer with Mozambique versus Malawi!

There are lots of smiles and laughter and the workers' morale is obviously high. It is good to see. Steve encourages me to stay here for the night, which I do, and I meet a most unlikely companion. I walk around the corner of his cottage and there, gambolling towards me, is a lion cub. He runs over to me and playfully attacks my ankles. His name is Mambo, which means 'chief', and he is an orphan that Mawaya is raising. I play with him for a while, but even at three months his claws are like razors and when he pounces during our play he goes for my back and bites into the back of my neck; astonishing instincts at play. It doesn't take long for me to retreat with all my scratches and cuts, but both of us have had fun. I hope he remembers me fondly if ever I bump into him when he is an adult!

I feel absolutely exhausted, though not having paddled very far in the morning and having had a rest at Alan's place two days before, I cannot understand why. I sleep through most of the afternoon. As night arrives, I am physically unsettled and my stomach is also unhappy. Perhaps I have eaten too much or too rich a food during the day and I'm just not used to it. But then I wasn't feeling entirely right yesterday either. I decide just to try and sleep off whatever it may be.

Early in the morning I wander about collecting seeds and feathers. Then I make up some special feathery gifts for Annie and Jess. After stashing them carefully away in my kayak, I bid everyone farewell – thanking Mawaya on the radio – and am gone.

I explore the bays and some of the islands, hoping that the wind will drop, but it's not to be. At 16h30 I cross a small bay and can see that I will be forced to cross a further lengthy stretch directly into the wind. The point I need to get to is directly across from me, so I will have to do it sooner or later. I decide to go, paddling into big swells and waves crested with white horses. Once the last of the evening light is gone, it is very dark. There is no moon for the first three-quarters of the trip. After a non-stop three hours and 45 minutes of heavy paddling, I reach land – according to my GPS a crossing of almost 11 kilometres. I make camp right there, on a little pebbly, sandy island which, in the morning I see, is just a few metres from the mainland.

Leaving the island I paddle north to locate the entrance to the upper part of Cahora Bassa Gorge. It's not at all easy to navigate here as there are so many islands, but I eventually find the gorge. From then on, navigation is no longer a problem as the valley walls are steep. I am pleased to be here. The crossing of the open water of Cahora Bassa has been very trying physically and psychologically, and now that I am in the gorge I know that the wall itself is within reach.

The Cahora Bassa Gorge above the dam wall is magnificent. Reminiscent of the lower reaches of Batoka Gorge below Victoria Falls, but with its own character. What looks like granite boulders balance precariously on cliff edges and great blocks of rock – having

The giant wall of Cahora Bassa.

fallen – have cut massive swathes down the slopes. The wind has disappeared completely and now I have the opposite problem. The heat is phenomenal and, with no ripple on the waves, the kayak sticks and is difficult to paddle. I sweat – a lot!

The gorge sides become almost vertical, and as I begin to paddle across to enter the gorge, breaking right, I hear the most angelic singing. It's a woman's voice, smooth and high, lilting in African rhyme. The beauty of the lone voice in this harsh and desolate place is exquisite and I sit quite still absorbing the moment to the full. She is quiet for a short while, so I begin to paddle again. Just then I see movement, which turns out to be a *mokoro*, hundreds of metres away from me, and she begins to sing again. She is in the *mokoro*, which looks minute under the enormous cliff that rises up above it. The sound is full and is carried by the gorge across the water like a great amplifier. I am deeply moved.

I know that off this gorge, somewhere up ahead, is another junction. The one I need to take breaks off at right angles to the left. It is narrow and I must be careful for I can easily miss it. It is early evening now and soon the gorge is in shadow. A motor boat is moored ahead of me and there are two men fishing. They hail me and we have a chat. Then they ask me whether I have come all the way through Zimbabwe on the river. They say, 'Oh, amazing! We know someone who saw you a few weeks ago near Chirundu. His name is Murray.'

I find out that these two men are farmers from Malawi and that Murray has just moved into their area to manage a neighbouring farm after leaving Zimbabwe. So poor Murray really did lose his farm, his entire investment, his implements and everything he owned. Now he is a manager for a farmer in Malawi. I am sad for him and for all the other refugees that may be even worse off than him. It is, however, beginning to get dark now. The fishermen wave goodbye and drive off, leaving me alone in this magnificent but now quite eerie gorge. I can hear the engine of their boat for a long time. But then it's totally silent except for the rhythmic stroke of my paddles.

Soon I have a decision to make: to try and find a spot to sleep – difficult here with the sides so steep – or to push on in the dark with pretty much no possibility of exit until I reach the wall. I examine the sides carefully then, decision made, I push on. After 30 minutes or so, with darkness drawing in strongly over me, I am lucky enough to hear and then see a large *mokoro* going in the opposite direction to me. There are eight people in it along with supplies of some kind. Four women sit up front and four men paddle. They are moving fast but even so, and through the language barrier, I am able to get some clarity as to where and how far away my turning is. Then once again I am totally alone in the darkness.

Then I hear the strangest singing-calling-talking mixture. There is silence, then someone – a man – shouts as if in command. Suddenly the same voice sounds like it is weeping and then, just as quickly, there is a change and it begins to sing. I approach slowly and carefully. It is good that I do, for suddenly the valley opens up to my left and I have found my turn-off. However, the man's strange monologue continues. And there he is – under an overhang partially hidden by brush at the base of the cliff, right at the gorge junction. He has a fire going so I can see him in the darkness.

He is all alone and clearly quite mad. He stands, arms raised, and shouts and giggles; then, as if suddenly wounded, whimpers, crouches and begins to cry. Everything in me wants somehow to comfort him, but I am also afraid. I can see he has been living here for some time. Prickles run up my neck as I begin to paddle again, for he shouts at me angrily, then once again begins to sing in a toneless, strange chant.

I can now see the lights on the top of the wall. I turn towards them and begin a nervous approach. This is one of Africa's biggest dams and I am coming at the top of the wall in pitch darkness with no exit on either side due to the steep, smooth cliffs. I slow down to a snail's pace as I get nearer, also concerned that security guards could well be a threat to me. Then, within about 250 metres of the wall itself, I find a spot where I can pull off.

There are other *mekoro* here and, I'm afraid, the village drunks. I have little possibility of escape but do my best. I find a spot still closer to the wall on a big boulder on which I think I can sleep. Closer inspection reveals that it is surrounded by the local latrine, but it will have to do.

The moon rises, peeping its head over the edge of the gorge. With the lights of the wall and hydro-electric plant in front, and the reflections on the water, backed up by the dark outline of the gorge ridge, it is really quite lovely. The crazy old man from the junction arrives in his *mokoro*. He really is quite lively now – talking loudly and constantly to himself and throwing his paddle into the *mokoro* – wild, loud songs over and over again. A few people from the edge shout at him to be quiet – but he is quite oblivious and carries on ranting in his own little world.

At around 01h00 a security guard approaches me with a torch and rifle in hand. He seems satisfied that I am no threat and goes away. But an hour later he is back, this time with a colonel. He is Portuguese, but speaks English. After carefully checking me and my canoe, and politely asking if I would not rather sleep near the guardhouse, he leaves, telling me he will be back in the morning. I am appreciative of his offer, but I will not leave my kayak alone here. It is an area with drunkards and louts stumbling about, and there's too much risk of theft.

He is all alone and clearly quite mad. He stands, arms raised, and shouts and giggles; then, as if suddenly wounded, whimpers, crouches and begins to cry.

Cahora Bassa to Tete

- Cahora Bassa Gorge
- The price of war and slavery
- Livingstone's blunder
- Fun with Immigration

Sunrise arrives in the Cahora Bassa Gorge. The sun peeps its head over the saddle-like ridge above the wall. The lights on the wall are still on and they, together with the pink sky, reflect on the absolutely still waters. Soon the first risers are washing at the water's edge and voices begin to call to one another. It is not long before I know what it is like to be on the actuality show 'Big Brother'. My rocky protrusion into the lake makes a perfect stage; the bank above, a gallery. The 15 or 20 people who sleep each night at this waterside harbour/market make themselves comfortable and watch the show. Every movement I make, every item I touch is registered with comment and discussion. 'Shower hour' gives them most satisfaction. I make my tea, eat my muesli, brush my teeth, all under the intense scrutiny of the small audience. Sometimes they are quite silent. At other times they comment and interpret

to one another. What is the item I touched? What is it for – how is it used? Little gasps of astonishment when my gas stove is fired up. Total silence when I write in my journal.

Soon they drift back off to their own spots but always keep an eye on me. When I decide to move my kayak, they are all on their feet again. Where is he going? What is he doing? Of course, there are resident experts who constantly inform latecomers, knowledgeably of course, about my journey, my craft and me.

Anxious to get going, I walk to the security point at the wall and ask permission to go through and look at the cataracts below. 'No,' a polite, but definite negative. I must wait for the colonel. But they tell me that the water is very dangerous. I'm sure it is – for it was here that people journeying up the river from the sea were forced to stop because of the cataracts. Indeed, that is exactly what Cahora Bassa in its original form, *Kebrabasa*, means – to 'stop work' or 'finish the service'. The Portuguese word *quebra* (pronounced kebra) means 'finish', while *basa* is common to many of the indigenous African languages of the area and means 'work'. In earlier times explorers

Captain Arnoldo Alfonso, second in command of Cahora Bassa security.

and, more specifically, slave traders would ply their way upstream in heavy canoes all the way from the sea. But at this spot they were met by enormous, insurmountable cataracts. Here they were forced to stop and carry their goods overland, hence the name Kebrabasa. It is also here that Livingstone's dream of navigating ships into the African interior met with disaster.

I am a little apprehensive because, if the sides of the gorge are as steep as those above the wall, portaging around Class 5 and 6 rapids will become impossible. I hope I now find someone who knows what the water down there looks like and I am impatient for the colonel to arrive.

Captain Arnoldo Alfonso, the second in command of Cahora Bassa MOSEG (Mozambique Security Group), arrives in place of the colonel. Very smart, very efficient. After gaining an understanding of the situation he gives some instructions for my *barco* to be watched and tells me to hop into his vehicle. I have told him I want to see the water below the wall, so that is where we are headed. A massive tunnel looms up ahead and into the very earth we go. For perhaps one and a half kilometres we descend, eventually emerging at the base of the wall, but still 30 or so metres from the water. I am hugely impressed. The scale of it is utterly enormous. Where the water pushes out after driving the turbines it moves with great force and purpose. It is not frivolous here – this water means business. The boils, swirls and whirls are terrifying. Downstream the water looks flattish from my vantage point but still the whirls and boils continue. It looks scary but I think I can run what I can see. The challenges are twofold. Firstly, there is nowhere to get down to the water from the wall and, secondly, once in the water there is no place to exit if I do run into serious cataracts or take a swim. The entry point will obviously determine a lot.

Back up the tunnel and into the town of Sengu, which lies some 10 or 12 kilometres from the wall. The road to get there winds its way up the steep sides of the gorge, passing some of the thickest concentrations of baobabs I have ever seen. The immigration officials find my papers in order, and away we go again.

We stop at MOSEG headquarters where Lieutenant Colonel Gracia Pinto, my visitor of last night, is in his office. He has authorised all this assistance and I am very grateful. We chat a little of times gone by. He originates from Angola and served in the Portuguese Special Forces. As a 'commando' he says – they used guerrilla tactics against the guerrillas – small teams, light weapons. He is amazed when I can relate to the areas he served in – Cazombo and Luena. He knew both well and lived in the eastern part of Angola. Sadness and a certain brief emotion – is it whimsical or nostalgic? – can be seen in his eyes. 'But,' he says, 'I was just a young lieutenant then.' It is as if he is talking of another person. I know that feeling well. It *is* another person he talks of, and even though he knows him well, he is quite different to the life and the person who now stands before me.

He checks, 'Is it not too dangerous in the water for you here? Is it alright to put your boat into that?' I laugh and say that I will be fine. There is danger and we both know it. He looks me in the eye, holds the side of my shoulder with one hand and, with the other, shakes my hand warmly in farewell. He says to be very careful of landmines and rather stick to tracks only. Captain Alfonso and I collect my kayak and several men and drive off towards the only spot that everyone says is possible to launch from. The road is circuitous and terrible. Eventually it is just a donkey track, and then that disappears too. We load the kayak onto our shoulders and carry it through the bush. I put landmines out of my mind; there is no point in stressing about that as well. The gradient is steep and it is difficult going. The kayak, loaded with all my equipment and food, is not light. We struggle and rest and sweat and struggle some more. We carry for several kilometres, sometimes down incredible gradients. At the water's edge we all drink long mouthfuls of the wonderful liquid. I quickly prepare – a few pictures, a wave, sincere thanks and away I go.

The water, however, immediately lets me know that it is no longer the flat, albeit wave-driven, lake of a few kilometres back. Boils lift me up and whirls spin me completely around before I have paddled 20 metres. The men on the bank watch intently. Remembering the woman at Sioma Falls, I do not give a last wave!

For the next several hours I am in non-stop combat with the water. I keep stopping and getting out to recce rapids that lie ahead. I run most and portage a few. It's not the big waves that worry me, it's the massive whirlpools and boils. I find it quite frightening, in fact, and have to work hard at giving myself complete positive focus. This is a stretch of the river I wouldn't mind walking. I find this quite interesting. The rapids are not massive – like in Batoka gorge. But to see what appears to be a small run of rapids that lures you in – only to be confronted by enormous whirlpools and boils – is for me even more threatening. At least in Batoka below Victoria Falls I knew what was coming. Here I deal with the completely unknown and a very different, predatory, lonely stretch of river.

But, even with all of this, it is beautiful. The steep, rugged slopes covered in baobab and lovely acacia look down at this jade-green, boiling river. The sky is tinged with pink and broken clouds filter the atmosphere. Tiger fish feed under granite slabs, polished by the water to look like burnished steel. Rock islands break up the river periodically, but it soon re-gathers itself into a single, surging mass of water.

I stop eventually after half running, half portaging a series of rapids and boils. There is a long beach here bracketed by shiny black volcanic rocks. The ridge line all around me is silhouetted and on its lip the trees stand stark and dry and beautiful. I drag my kayak well clear of the surges then quickly climb the rocks downstream to see my route for the morning. Within seconds of starting I am going to be a very busy boy. The water is big, but if I take it on the left it is runnable and I should also be able to avoid the whirls and boils by cutting at an angle as I come out of the waves.

The stress is telling here and I feel it. I joke with myself. 'You're getting old, sunshine, the water's getting to you!' I think of my analogy of the river representing a human life. If this section represents the first part of old age, then it's bang on track. Just as a person does in life – here, wiser because of earlier experiences – I have learnt to fear certain aspects of the river. I say to myself, 'No, respect is the word,' but that does not say enough. It is respect, fear, acknowledgement and admiration all rolled into one. I have felt the awesome power of this river. I have been in her hold. I fear her power.

Also, part of the analogy is that as we get older we find ourselves more alone. Here, I have a great sense of loneliness. The power of the water is unquestionable, and I confront it entirely alone. This part of God's garden is magnificent but hostile and needs to be handled with care.

Up well before the sun, I take a walk along the bank and up the ridges along the river. Montane trees, grass covered slopes, black polished rock and sandy beaches greet me as I go. I climb up to a deserted homestead which stands on the ridge overlooking my camp. Platform huts, so that the people can sleep in the cool breeze and well away from dangerous animals, still stand. It has been deserted for a season, so as soon as the rains start I'm sure the inhabitants will be back. I remain disturbed by the tree felling and noted yesterday how the young Captain Alfonso was too. Here though, it is not bad, but stretches of the banks yesterday looked like the slopes around Hiroshima after the bomb hit. Trees, all felled, lying where they had been dropped.

I take another look at my first rapid and prepare to leave. This was a good place to spend the night. I take note that the water has dropped about half a metre since I arrived last night and I adjust my planned route through the enormous surging water accordingly. This water fluctuation is due to the generators in the dam working at night to produce hydro-electricity for a hungry South Africa. During the day, they are either not running or are running at a lower output. This allows the dam to fill up again during the day and, of course, creates a lower flow in the river downstream.

Firstly, I paddle upstream against the current to warm up a little. Then I prepare myself, paddle hard, and go for my life. I am well into the rapid and doing well when I realise that there is a massive whirlpool coming up on my left that was not there an hour ago. Shit! I turn frantically in the big water and just pass it by on its right. The whirls and boils are big and terrifyingly powerful. Beyond the rapid they remain, and I am pushed around by the water like a twig in a torrent. I hit the next rapid and halfway down I am spun sideways in the middle of the waves. I paddle like mad but it keeps pushing me around. I take a rather undignified run down the last part of this one, backwards. The wave action at this point is not huge, thank goodness, but to rush by whirlpools and boils in reverse is a little disconcerting, to put it mildly. Exactly as it did in the rapid, it spins me again and, facing the way I should be now, I confront the very difficult washes and whirls.

Considering my own challenges, I think on other much more formidable characters who have passed this way before. In the early 1880s a man by the name of Monks decided to explore the Zambezi on his own. With practically no financial means, Monks left the South African diamond fields on foot, driving a pack donkey ahead of him.

He reached the Zambezi River around 40 kilometres downstream of the end of the Batoka Gorge. Near the confluence of the Gwaai River, Monks swapped his donkey for a dugout canoe and proceeded to descend the Zambezi, still on his own. He kept a meticulous map, which is now in the possession of the Royal Geographic Society, giving incredible details, especially of the numerous streams and tributaries entering the great river. This map covered the entire distance from the Gwaai River right down to Tete.

The great difficulties Monks must have experienced getting his dugout through the gorge at Kariba were never recorded in writing. Neither was his single-handed navigation of the awesome Cahora Bassa Gorge in which I now find myself. Each of these sites threw up rapids and cataracts akin to or worse than those below Victoria Falls. It was an incredible achievement, made all the more admirable for the humble manner in which he accomplished it.

Monks had single-handedly travelled over half the length of one of Africa's great rivers. Besides this, he also ascended the Shire River towards Lake Malawi and made several other incursions inland. I am deeply humbled by this. My own journey, challenging as it may be, pales in comparison to this great man's. It is not known how, or even where, Monks died. His last letter, written in 1887, indicated his intention to take some porters and goods from Tete, ascend the Luangwa River and establish a trading station in what is now northwest Zambia, on the shores of Lake Bangwelo. He was never heard from again.

I emerge from the rapids and the worst of the gorge at a spot where there are people. Not a lot though – just a few huts on the south bank and a few more on the other side. There are *mekoro* here, so clearly the water from here on cannot be a problem. I pull over and remove my helmet and life jacket. There were people on the bank when I headed in to the shore but they are gone now.

As I paddle further down the rapidly widening river I see this behaviour in the locals repeatedly. Mostly, they run first and then watch cautiously from a safer spot. In one instance, two women and several youngsters are netting fish with a type of throw net. They see me and stop – standing dead still. I turn slightly towards them, hoping for a picture of the netting. But they flee. Panic stricken, there are shrieks of fear. One woman grabs a little boy of about four by one arm. With him dangling there, crying, and her screaming, the others scrambling, splashing out of the shallows, there is pure terror in this moment for them. I sit dead still my hands held palms upwards and I call soothingly, 'It's all right, I'm sorry I frightened you.' One of them looks over at me and, seeing my posture, slows down and then stops. I decide laughter might work so I laugh, gently, trying to show the situation as funny. Others stop running too. I carefully take my paddle and give a stroke downstream to show them I will not be coming closer. All together, it works and a nervous giggle comes from the bank. They continue to watch me intently and silently. Then a few words, quick exchanges between each other, and the fear is replaced by relief. They laugh as well – just a little – but do not move closer. I wave a careful goodbye and paddle away.

All afternoon I get this reaction broken only two or three times by people who are willing to wave back at me and, in one case, where I could actually talk to someone. 'It's the war,' he tells me. 'That is why people are scared.' I want to know where he learnt English. 'Zimbabwe,' he tells me. 'I ran away from here when I was young because of the war – Frelimo and Renamo – big trouble here.' He tells me that the civilians all fled from this area at that time. As I paddle away I think about this. It is not only one conflict these people have had to endure.

Arab slavers raided these parts for nearly 600 years. The Portuguese followed in the 1500s. French demand for slaves on the plantations of Mauritius, Reunion and Rodriquez in the 1720s escalated the pace of this inhuman activity. The river was the highway to the interior and anyone living near to its banks was in severe danger indeed. When Livingstone came up this way in 1850, he witnessed the awful tragedy of slavery on this very stretch of river. Fredrick Courtney Selous

Page 163: Portaging the wall of Cahora Bassa.

Top and above: Terrifying swirls, boils and whirlpools below the dam wall.

The whirls and boils are big and terrifyingly powerful. Beyond the rapid they remain, and I am pushed around by the water like a twig in a torrent. I hit the next rapid and halfway down am spun sideways in the middle of the waves.

– a famous hunter and scout – personally witnessed it as late as 1877. Although internationally outlawed, the slave trade continued here in an organised manner well into the 1880s.

On top of all of this was the constant harassment of living under Portuguese colonial rule. Then, of course, came the struggle for independence and freedom. That was successfully achieved by 1974. Then the war in Rhodesia (as it was then called) started – so no respite for these people. The new Frelimo government supported Mugabe's freedom fighters, who were transported up this river into Cahora Bassa then across the lake to the frontier with Rhodesia. The craft I saw wrecked on the dam was a military landing craft, and that is what it was used for. When that war ended, the civil war between Frelimo and Renamo hotted up. The people here were yet again in the thick of it.

They see me coming quietly down the river – an unusual sight indeed – so they run. They run with over 500 years of conditioning built into their behaviour. The further downstream I go the more people seem willing to at least stand. Some will return a wave but mostly they just watch. I wonder how many of the little kids have ever seen a white man. Bearded and sunburnt, I'm afraid I am an unfortunate representative for Caucasians right now!

The people seem unperturbed by crocodiles for they wade in the water and act quite unconcerned. I wonder if perhaps crocodiles have been eradicated here. No sooner have I had that thought than I spot a 3.5-metre male crocodile.

Two fish eagles have nested in a baobab tree on a pretty island. I decide to approach and see if a photograph is a possibility. The baobab stands on the highest spot. It is surrounded by beautiful tree specimens and bush. Birds frolic here and I absorb the beauty of the spot. The reeds, a deep green against the jade of the water and the dry hills surrounding, are broken by little beaches. I pull up on one. Above the bank, just a few metres from the water, I find two graves. They are little graves – clearly those of children. One, in particular, is quite new and people have been here and placed little things on the grave. It would be flowers if there were any, but the land is harsh and so flowers are replaced with calabashes and prettily shaped branches. I wonder at the mother's loss. It is so sad to see. They were just little!

Brush above this spot tells me that the floodline is higher than the graves. In one season they will be gone. No trace; just once again the pretty island. Dust to dust. So many of us try to be immortalised – to be remembered after death. But all efforts are absolutely in vain. Where were our great, great, great grandfathers and grandmothers born and buried? Let's talk of their personalities, their beliefs and values. What did they contribute to society? Were they kind? How did they live their lives? It is all so fleeting. We have but this time here, now. What we give to the earth, to life, to each other, is what remains. Nothing else. I stand at the little graves so lovingly decorated by someone who loved these children dearly. In just one rainy season they will be gone. That is the way it is. The people here understand it.

I find a good spot to camp as the sun begins to set. Having set out my gear I go down to the water and I am in the middle of my evening bathing session when I see a man wading across in my direction. He gets to my bank, with me shaking my head at his disregard for crocodiles, and he too begins to bathe. The light is poor and he is relaxed – splashing about merrily and singing while he is at it. But as I emerge naked from the water he catches a glimpse of my lily-white bum, and he suddenly goes quiet. I walk about naked and he peers through the twilight in my direction. Then, realising that I am white, he grabs up his things and begins moving away from me. First he walks fast, and then he sprints – flat out – across a low sand dune, eventually disappearing around and behind a hillock. I chuckle to myself. With a beard hiding the white of my face and a deep suntan I guess in poor light I could be taken as a black guy. But it's that lily-white bum that does it!

I'm not far from where another dam is to be constructed. I pass survey points at a few spots and I am not sure of the exact site, but it is close by. It's called the Npandacua Project and construction will begin soon. That, of course, means that the gorge I passed through with its challenging washes, whirls and rapids will be flooded, never to be seen again. The same thing happened to the mighty cataracts which now lie under Cahora Bassa.

It was these cataracts that defeated Livingstone's plans to create a navigable highway into the interior. After his phenomenal work and expeditions, culminating in the 'discovery' for the West of what he named Victoria Falls, the total attention of the British Isles and the world was focused on him. Having personally travelled along the banks of most of the Zambezi as far as Katima Mulilo, he now declared that he was convinced that the Zambezi was navigable. If he could convince the English to react quickly, the river could potentially open up the African interior for Britain. He called it God's Highway, and developed such enthusiasm in Britain that funds were gathered and an expedition raised to return to sail up the mighty river. In 1858, the Zambezi expedition began their journey up the river. The boat provided by the Admiralty, the M.A. Robert, was painfully inadequate. They arrived in Tete in September. Then, after first going back to the coast, Livingstone pressed the expedition to leave for the interior. They did this in early November, leaving from Tete, and within five days entered the Cahora Bassa Gorge.

They progressed only three kilometres into the Gorge before they were forced to stop by the formidable current and the jagged rocks that barred their way. Going forward a short way on foot drove home the awful truth. The great boulders and torrent in the narrow gorge made further progress impossible. Livingstone was flabbergasted. Agreeing to retreat at this stage, he simply had to accept the evidence. He returned to Tete with the M.A. Robert and the expedition team, where he waited and brooded. The river was now almost at its lowest ebb. Early rains saw the water rise to half-flood levels and he was convinced that this would now make the river passable.

Taking a party upstream on foot for 40 kilometres, Livingstone's desperation must have been palpable, for nothing that they saw

It was these cataracts that defeated Livingstone's plans to create a navigable highway into the interior. After … the 'discovery' of what he named Victoria Falls, the total attention of the British Isles and the world was focused on him.

could change the terrifying nature of the rapids and river. Livingstone, however, succeeded in persuading his companion, Kirk, to accompany him in exploring further upstream. Eventually they came across the massive cataract called Morumbua and nothing now could change the obvious truth: the river was simply not navigable!

How could such a blunder have been made by so respected an explorer? It seems that on all his previous expeditions he had missed out the section of the river through Cahora, travelling at a distance from the river all the way from Zumbo to Tete. But even so, he must have heard reports of cataracts. Why did he not investigate? One possibility is that he had made a serious miscalculation in measuring the fall of the river and his flawed results led him to believe that it did not have a significant drop at all.

On all of his expeditions he calculated the altitude of the place he was at by measuring the temperature at which water boiled. He took measurements where he crossed the river above Cahora Bassa and did so again where the pathway he was on rejoined the river close to Tete. When he worked out the difference, his error added up to 186 metres! This clearly affected his understanding of the drop between the two places, making it far less than it actually was. He anticipated a fairly gentle slope to the river, even if fast-flowing. There are many other factors to the story, but for us this is sufficient. One of the most famous explorers in English history had erred so greatly that he felt totally disgraced.

He never fully recovered from this blow and when he eventually began the 1867 expedition to locate the sources of the Nile, it was not expected that he would be away long. But in 1871, after a long period with no sign of him, Henry Morton Stanley located him at Ujiji in Tanzania with the immortal words, 'Dr Livingstone, I presume?'

Nothing could convince him to return to England with Stanley, and he continued in his search for the fountains of the Nile. Depressed, ill, and still unnecessarily ashamed of his 1858 expedition, he died in 1873. His body, embalmed by his helpers, was carried to the coast and then transported to England, where he was buried as a hero in Westminster Abbey.

The night is very dark and I listen to the sounds around me as Livingstone must have done. There are no hippos right here, no lions or elephants, nor great herds of antelope. I hear frogs and wind and beetles. Every now and then a dog barks. It, too, is lovely. Different but still lovely. The stars above are set in the darkest of skies, the Milky Way a magnificent slash across the heavens. Scorpio lies boldly above; the Southern Cross is too low in the west for me to see. But I know it's there – just as my family is there.

Day 88. The old man stands a few metres from me, the paddle from his *mokoro* over his shoulder, and an adze held in his other hand. He watches. We have greeted, but now he just watches. There are just the two of us. He is not embarrassed by his curiosity. He does not see it as an intrusion. He is doing no harm. He is watching. It's so easy to become irritated by this. I, who have been raised on privacy and discretion, find this difficult. My impulse is to say, 'Go away please.'

But at sidewalk cafés or on actuality TV we, too, watch the ordinary behaviour of people. It is somehow fascinating. It's just that we do so 'discreetly'. The old man watches. I have smiled at him and now I simply ignore him. I go into my world – into myself to do what must be done. I don't allow this to become an intrusion or an irritation. But I remember – not long ago – when I may well have walked over to within a few paces of him and stood and stared at him too. Back then, I would have considered that a reflection of his own behaviour. But now I understand that it would not have been at all, because my behaviour would have been aggressive and confrontational. His is passive and gentle. His is just curious. I get on with my business and soon he wanders off on his. A polite farewell and a smile and he is gone.

A multi-storey building stands rather awkwardly overlooking the river, signposting my arrival in Tete. In an instant the river is full of people – washing clothes, washing themselves, and walking and riding bicycles along the shoreline. Then come the motorcycles and scooters and soon I can see vehicles and the dust trails they leave behind them as they go. The people in the water are quite uninhibited about their toiletries. The women cover their lower bodies and step out of their

panties. The men stand upright and soap away merrily without even a glance up at the multitudes around them.

I pull up close to the bank to ask for some directions to '*Immigracau*'. I am told to exit at 'the green building' and ask again there. Off I go. I have difficulty seeing this green building, but eventually I do. The building is white – and, granted, it does have a tiny green trim. It is the play and bathing spot for the youth of Tete. I am instantly surrounded by dozens of people. Some come sprinting across the shallows. Some are there, half-soaped up in the middle of their bath, but still they run over.

There are two real 'cool dudes' who appear to set the tone of what is going on. I stick my hand out and introduce myself. It takes the first one by surprise, but he recovers and says something half-intelligible in what he imagines to be English. I make a huge fuss of him: 'Wow! What great English you speak.' I point at my head and then at him, giving a thumbs-up to the crowd. 'Good guy, this.' They like it – they laugh – he pushes out his chest and I have a friend, guide, go-between, guard and 'translator'. I tell him what I need – Immigration, film, batteries. A few enquiries and off we go. A guard for the kayak appointed by my new friend – who takes his responsibility very seriously – sitting on the front end in total ownership.

Immigration closes at 15h00. It is 15h15. There is nothing I can do. I plead, I do everything possible. '*Não*, tomorrow, *senhor*.' This visa really has given me headaches. It also expires at the end of August,

just two days away. I have another ten or twelve days of paddling still to go. I must get the paperwork done, so I am forced to stay. I buy my few items and then we begin making our way back down to the kayak. What to do? Where to sleep? I tip my friends quietly, hop into my kayak and make a big scene of my farewell. I, in turn, get a swift offer of a 'quickie' from a nubile young lass who points downstream, indicates 'later' to me, and does some fairly explicit actions. I smile at her politely and wave goodbye.

They all watch as I paddle downstream towards the big road bridge. I go slowly now, talking to people as I go. I want as little interest as possible. There is a big island on my left – one that many of the youngsters were on when I first arrived. But on the downstream end there are thick reed banks and a large vegetable garden. Some fishermen's shelters seem to be the boundary for the people, because they do not pass these. I paddle around the point of the island – out of view for those I have just left – then paddle hard upstream on the opposite side. There is a man in a *mokoro*, but he is looking away from me as I turn quickly into the reeds. They are thick, but I'm soon dragging myself right in amongst them and become quite invisible to any passers-by. I sit in my kayak for a half hour or so – long enough to ensure that the last of the potential onlookers have lost interest. Then I pull myself further through the reeds until I hit the bank. It is no easy exercise but here I am in the middle of a river, in the middle of a city. What can I possibly do with my kayak? It is extremely vulnerable to theft;

if not the whole thing, then certainly its contents. I must sleep next to it – but where, in a city? My reed bank is my answer. I climb cautiously out into a mielie and tomato patch. I cover my kayak and, taking my writing materials and map, I crawl in amongst the stalks of maize. There I remain until it is on the dark end of twilight. Only then do I find a spot and get my sleeping gear out. Here I am, all clandestine again! Anyway, this time it is only because it is necessary, considering my situation.

Shortly after dark a nightclub turns up its music just across the waters from me. It gradually increases in volume and more and more people arrive. I can hear them all having a wonderful

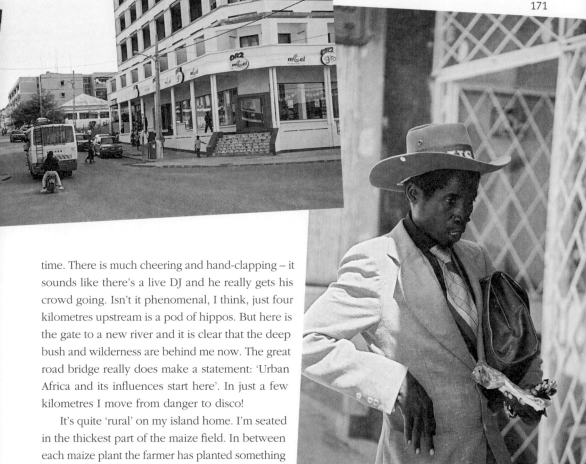

Above: A real character in Tete.

time. There is much cheering and hand-clapping – it sounds like there's a live DJ and he really gets his crowd going. Isn't it phenomenal, I think, just four kilometres upstream is a pod of hippos. But here is the gate to a new river and it is clear that the deep bush and wilderness are behind me now. The great road bridge really does make a statement: 'Urban Africa and its influences start here'. In just a few kilometres I move from danger to disco!

It's quite 'rural' on my island home. I'm seated in the thickest part of the maize field. In between each maize plant the farmer has planted something else. The land is rough and clod-strewn. Some of the crops require a mound – others a recess in the ground. It is not the most physically comfortable spot, and I don't wish to flatten the earth and damage any precious crops. On three sides of me lies water with the city lights reflecting up from it. The bridge to the east of me is an impressive structure. It too is lit up and the road is busy; lots of heavy traffic going to and from the north – Malawi and Northern Mozambique, even Tanzania. It is all actually quite attractive.

The heavy beat of the music – '*kwassa kwassa*' and periodic karaoke is loud and exciting. People's voices chant together between tracks and sometimes over the music itself. 'Mandoza, Mandoza!' they shout. South Africa is very present here.

Seated silently on my own in this tiny patch of green, I feel a little like the last of the Mohicans. Perhaps I am. I can cross over to that world and I do. I can live in it and do well, but my soul needs its nourishment too, and that it gets in the wilderness. But the wilderness is shrinking so fast. Even places that are called wilderness areas, I consider tamed. It stifles my spirit. The famous mountaineer, Reinhold Messner puts it well: 'Nature for man is truly manifest where

Opposite, bottom: By now I have lost a lot of weight.

danger, challenge and exposure have not been shut out.' I need to, at the very least, know that there are still true wilderness areas. I have seen much of this river now and I am afraid for it. I have a sense of dread, for with it gone, something in the human spirit will also die. In an entirely man-made and controlled world, man cannot retain the fullness of humanity, for the human spirit is free and needs rejuvenation and sustenance. This it gets in the wild. Even brief encounters with the natural world will do. But the natural world needs to still exist for this to be possible.

I deeply, sincerely appreciate the opportunity I have had to sweat and struggle on this great river. Because of that, I have seen so much beyond the visual. I have appreciated the simplest things and realised that, in their simplicity, they are the great things. I have watched the tiniest birds – not only the eagles. I have seen insects and lizards. I have watched a scorpion at work and seen spiders weave their webs. I have looked at blades of grass and pieces of stone and in them have seen so much. I have seen my very soul. And I have glimpsed the slow death of our world. I appreciate this time in God's garden more than my words can express.

Day 89. The mosquitoes are very bad here and it is not difficult to be up before dawn. I make some tea, eat, wash and carefully pack away everything into my kayak. When I return, I want to just hop in and leave. I may have lots of people around me again when I get back.

I am worried about my kayak and all my equipment, so I leave the spot early and walk a very circuitous route, doing some anti-tracking on the way. I walk in the shallow water for a while and then emerge barefoot. After a while I go across an area where tracks are not easy to see so I put on sandals to change the track – now I'm walking back towards my kayak wearing sandals, and slowly veer across to lead anyone following my tracks away from where it lies hidden. I get to a spot where I can wade across to the mainland and, as I start wading to find a shallow spot, a man in a *mokoro* draws up. 'Let's go,' he says and kindly ferries me across. The few women who are there at this hour watch for a while, making comments, but I do not linger. I hope they think I also hitched a ride from

the opposite river bank to get to the island.

I am at the Immigration office earlier than the 07h00 opening time, so I watch people as they pass by. Street cleaners are out at this time, sweeping the roads and picking up refuse. In a First-World environment this is not remarkable, but it certainly is in the developing world. It says a lot for the upward phase in which Mozambique appears to be. There is lots of building repair work and painting underway and workers are arriving at sites to commence the day.

At 07h00 the Immigration man arrives but says his colleague responsible for visas is not yet there – we chat while we wait. And we wait and wait.

Periodically through the day, however, I have opportunities to explore Tete. 'Come back at 10h00.' So I have an hour and off I go. 'Come back at 12h00.' This happens all day so I get a good feel for Tete. I see a man who, due to terrible deformation in his limbs, can only walk on his hands and knees. He gets from one place to another in a tricycle wheelchair with bicycle pedals set at chest height that he drives with his hands. He is employed as a gardener by the municipality, and I watch as he busies himself watering gardens, weeding and sweeping – all on his hands and knees. His actions have purpose and dignity.

I decide to walk down to the big suspension bridge. From there I will get a good view of the island and can try and check on my kayak at the same time that I explore the bridge surrounds. My island spot looks fine. There are many people on the island – but no one near my kayak. I hope it stays that way. The bridge is impressive. It can only handle one large truck at a time and when a truck crosses, the bridge moves underfoot. There are lots of pedestrians going both ways. I stand in the middle of the bridge for a while, just absorbing the magnitude of the river. It is flowing fairly fast here and it is wide.

On the south bank, just upstream of the bridge, is an old Portuguese fort. I walk around it to the entrance but it has no information on it and there are only a few people who have made their homes inside. The Portuguese truly were an amazing colonial power. They did not position their overseas possessions as colonies but rather as provinces of Portugal itself. They were the first European colonists in Africa, having been trading in Angola and Mozambique since 1505. They immediately went about ensuring that the local people were taught Portuguese and they took great pains with building architecture and style, ensuring it reflected the best of Portuguese culture. This is quite apparent along the river. Now, many years after the Portuguese left, after bloody, cruel wars and complete disruption of communities, Mozambique remains Portuguese. The sidewalk cafés, the language, the style of the people is all Portuguese and very clearly so. Yet the Portuguese themselves are long gone.

Exploring Tete.

I eventually have my passport returned to me at 15h45. My papers now in order, I make my way down towards my kayak, a very satisfied fellow. For a while there I had wondered if this was the end of the line, because the officials were quite strong on the fact that, because I had a multiple entry visa, I would need to leave the country and come back in before I could continue.

Tete to journey's end

- Lupata Gorge
- Mary Livingstone's grave
- Colonial ruins
- Taking stock
- The sea!

The river opens up dramatically after Tete. Lots of large reed-filled islands and, once again, hippos. I cannot see them but I hear them as I go. At last light I'm forced to pull out at a spot where there is a dwelling. It's a very simple mud and thatch hut. I walk over to get permission to camp in the owner's fields, but there are only little children there. They are a little afraid at first but my smile and waves settle them down. I point to where I will be camping and demonstrate sleep. They smile and nod but I don't know if they really understand. I decide that I will go later to talk to an adult as well.

Not long after, while I am settling in, the father of the homestead arrives to say hello. The children did get it right, even though the oldest was possibly only nine or 10. The father is very friendly – has a curious, somewhat disbelieving look at my kayak – and then waves goodbye.

About 20 minutes later he is back. This time he brings two mielies and a stick of sugarcane. He is also carrying a glowing ember from his fire. He offers this all to me and, through my protestations, quickly sets some dry reeds alight, throws on the mielies and gesticulates for me to enjoy them. Then he is gone. Once again I am deeply touched by the hospitality and kindness of the simple farmer folk. The mielies are delicious and make for a great supper.

Hippos are a bit of a plague tonight. The poor creatures have to eat but there are so many people along the banks now that they have great difficulty finding an exit point. A few keep coming back to where I am camped so I suppose I've messed up their routine completely. Anyway, I don't want them to get out here because I'm close to their runs and the water. With the noise the locals will make if the hippos are discovered on land, they will run straight for the water. If I'm in the way, which is likely, they'll run right over me. So I keep shining my torch at them to warn them off – sorry guys!

A *mokoro* comes by going upstream just before the sun rises. I see my host – the farmer – walk down to check on my kayak. All is well, but he stands there for a short while. He waves at me. He looks tired. He and the children have been busy protecting their crops all night. The busiest time for them is early in the evening when the hippos are looking for exit points. But all night they are vigilant and he sleeps in his *shamba* (vegetable garden).

By the time I'm ready to go, his children have cautiously come over to where I have been sleeping. I give each of the five something

Once again I am deeply touched by the hospitality and kindness of the simple farmer folk.

Rosetta is around eight years old, just a child, and her mother is dead. The handle of the hoe has been cut short so that she can work with it.

to nibble on. The oldest is probably 10. Two of them are sick. A little one of about three has a racking cough. Another is so weak he drags his feet as he walks. He is also pot-bellied, with slightly bulging eyes and is clearly very ill. 'Where is your mother?' I want to know. He tells me she is dead.

Rosetta, the little girl of probably around eight years old, has a hoe with her. The handle is cut short so that she is able to work with it. She is pretty and a little coy. She quietly begins to clear the field of weeds. My heart bleeds for them. They are so tiny. By dint of chance they are born here into poverty and hardship. They are born to good people but they are so poor. I want to heal the sick ones. I want to tell their father to take them to the doctor but I know there is no doctor here and he couldn't afford it even if there was one. I talk to them and smile and joke and touch their heads, ruffling their hair. But my heart bleeds. They are so little. I give them a packet of biscuits to give to their father. They are delighted. They stand on the bank and watch me go. They wave and they stand – the little group of five tiny children – for a long time. Life is hard for them. Very hard. You can see it in their eyes. They do not gambol and run. They do not play hopscotch or skip or draw. They hoe fields. They carry their smaller siblings on their backs and guard their crops from the hippos at night. My heart bleeds for them.

Of the 12 new penlight batteries I bought in Tete, six are completely dead and useless. The others, used two at a time in a torch, last for about 40 minutes each. They are not old. This is just awful quality. The poor people who can least afford it are simply the dumping ground for many manufacturers' sub-quality products. It makes me sick to the stomach and angry all at once.

The river flows strongly here so the paddling goes well. The countryside gets progressively more interesting and varied. There are channels which have created reed-covered islands. Sandbanks and montane trees, riverside bush and baobabs. There are gentle hills and enormous cliffs, big sandstone bluffs and sloping banks with fever trees. There are crocodiles and periodic pods of hippos and lots of birds. In all, this is a lovely stretch of river.

I stop for some lunch and I am discovered by a young man with a toddler in tow. He greets politely then sits down near me. I talk politely at first but actually want my own time now. I have paddled hard and I am tired and irritable. I cannot eat in front of him. I would consider that very bad manners, but I do not have enough to share with him. I am showing signs of malnourishment myself. I show him that I want to sleep, thinking that that would work, and ask him as politely as I can to leave. He understands and disappears back off into the bush. But then I hear him coming back. I am irritated. But then I see why he is back. Because I told him I was going to take a nap, he went and fetched a grass sleeping mat for me to lie on. I feel terrible; guilty for having allowed irritation to creep into my mind. I thank him most sincerely and he disappears again, leaving me alone.

I think about my own behaviour and I am found wanting. At every turn these people are hospitable and kind, always willing to share what little they have. I, on the other hand, want my privacy and rest where I can get it and I am, for perhaps very sensible reasons considering the nature of this expedition, unable to share. I would like to but I would not have enough food and supplies to complete the expedition if I kept on giving it away. I, too, am in a struggle to survive. My choice is logically correct but emotionally and ethically testing.

A second man, in an enormous hurry, runs along the opposite side of the channel calling to the man on my side as he goes. He leaps into his *mokoro* and races over to me. This is Domingo and he is very pleased to meet me. 'Never before in my life has a white man been here,' he tells me. I don't get to eat and I don't have a rest, but I know now that that is not as important as the human interaction has been.

As I paddle, I once again pass patches of deforested land; complete hillsides denuded of trees. It is disturbing – deeply disturbing. The people here are poor fishermen and farmers. They eke out an existence by cutting away patches or fields of trees on which to grow crops. They catch fish or, in some places, harvest and sell that which nature provides. They need fuel so they cut the trees. But I think about this now in the context of our planet and how to overcome these challenges.

The Myombo woodland that extends beyond the immediate riverine treeline on the banks of the Zambezi for most of its length is, in its own right, an extremely delicate ecosystem. Due to the relatively high rainfall, the soil is continually leached of nutrients. But because the trees grow fast, there is the generation of compost from the branches and leaves that fall, and from the animal dung of those creatures that feed off the trees. This allows for sufficient re-seeding and regrowth – a constant cycle that keeps the trees and animals in place and maintains a healthy ecosystem.

However, human populations, like these I see here, require land for their meagre crops and so clear the trees. Not surprisingly, the soil nutrients are sufficient for only one or, at best, two growing seasons, after which the farmer is forced to move away and begin again in a different place.

The treeless land that remains now holds no nutrients whatsoever, so if it recovers at all it takes many, many years. The most probable outcome is desertification. On and off along the banks I have seen exactly that.

I think about my own behaviour and I am found wanting. At every turn these people are hospitable and kind, always willing to share what little they have.

Deforestation, with complete hillsides stripped of trees.

The primary causes of the destruction of our planet, from my point of view, relate to only two things: poverty and greed. Poor people have no choice but to use that which is around them in order to feed their families and survive. Wealthy nations seek to exploit resources to make even better profits for shareholders. Long-term issues relating to the destruction of planetary resources are not a great consideration. There are, of course, responsible companies, but overall we are left wanting.

The solution to many of our planet's woes, from poverty to the ozone layer, lies in recognising our interdependence. The planet is one organism. We are responsible for the whole.

Day 91. The river here has a little of everything that has previously been a part of its experience further upstream. There are reedbanks and channels, reminiscent of those in Barotseland and up near the source. Periodically there is beautiful riverine bush and also the scars of deforestation. Just ahead I can see the start of Lupata Gorge, with its ridges and drops recalling the great gorges of Batoka, Kariba and Cahora Bassa. Every now and then – although it is unusual now – I pass a protruding rock outcrop which forms a strong eddy, a reminder of the powerful swirls and whirlpools of earlier times.

I am drawn to think of my earlier analogy of the river and life, for if I continue it here the river is definitely now in its cycle of old age. It is lovely, though not strikingly beautiful; powerful with purpose, yet not strong and dangerous as it was in its youth. It is calmer and slower than before. But it remains attractive, warm, friendly and special, and somehow wiser for it encourages thought – of self, of values, of history.

The gorge that rises around me is the last such barrier on the river before the coast. It is not as formidable as the previous ones. But the sides are steep and tree-covered, and pretty beaches adorn the inside loops of the river. I climb well up a steep slope, some ten metres above the water. Here, on a sandy bed, I stretch out my sleeping bag and spend a star-studded night. I watch the gorge long into the night, for the shadows cast by the valley slopes create a mixture of deep blacks against greys and other light shades, like a very old black and white photograph. I watch as the earth turns and the stars move over my head.

I leave my beautiful campsite in the Lupata Gorge in the knowledge that I'm commencing the final chapter. From here the hills will begin to disappear until there is only the meandering river on the floodplains. I enjoy the gorge thoroughly. There are high cliffs dropping off directly into the water. On the very lip of one is a baobab and in it sits a baboon. If he fell from his perch he would hit the water at least 40 metres below. He watches me curiously, comfortably perched in the fork of a branch. He is eating seeds and periodically drops the husks, which land in the water near me.

Slowly the range of hills falls away behind me and soon there are reed banks and channels. Reminiscent of the Barotse floodplains, the only difference here is that periodically it is possible to see a tree-lined bank off in the distance. Also, this is not as populated. The people here are always astonished to see me but are friendly. Once they realise I am no threat they are quick to wave and exchange some words. My problem is that the language is only Portuguese, but we still manage to communicate. Physical signs of the Portuguese here are most clearly seen in the remains of old forts along the water's edge. There was a big one at Tete, another halfway from there to Tambara and then one atop a hill in Tambara itself.

Even though these are Portuguese structures, I am well aware that they were not the first 'outsiders' to trade with Africa, or to make use of the river for access to the interior. Arab, Chinese and Sumatran (Indonesian) traders were already visiting this coast around the year 740. The Arabs established Sofala and other parts shortly after this date to facilitate an ever-growing trade with Africa. The Chinese had obviously established very good relations with African trading partners over the 600-odd years since their earliest visits, as in 1414 a present of a giraffe was sent to the Chinese Emperor. It was accompanied by African ambassadors, who were returned to Africa by a Chinese expedition in 1417. As much as 93% of the common vocabulary of the population of Madagascar is Indonesian. Trade with extremely distant countries had, therefore, been occurring years before the Portuguese – the first Europeans – arrived. Early Arab traders navigated a considerable distance up the Zambezi and established towns along its banks. One such town, called Seyouna by the Arabs, became known as Sena under the Portuguese. The same can be said of Tete. The Portuguese, however, claimed to have established these towns, but there is considerable evidence to show that they had already been in existence for at least 200 years under the Arabs before the Portuguese arrived.

The wind howls through the night, covering everything in a layer of sand. The sand gets into every fold of clothes and skin, into my eyes and ears. It seeps into my sleeping bag and embeds itself in my hair. I'm concerned about my kayak as the steep bank prevented my dragging it clear of the water. Although whipped by the waves, it is secure and I crawl back into my sand-filled bed.

Morning brings with it relative calm and soon I am packed and watching two men in a *mokoro* battle upstream. I think of all the many thousands of people in years gone by, particularly slaves, who did exactly what these two men are doing.

There are channels and long reed banks downstream from Tambara and I run alongside a pretty ridge line. Slowly emerging in the distance ahead I can see the hills marking the confluence with the Shire River. I'm in a narrow channel and search for dry land on which to camp. A big crocodile watches me then slithers into the green water. A few metres from where he lay, I find an abandoned fisherman's shelter and take possession for the night. It is partly standing – sufficient to block the wind – and the view of the stars through the remaining roof latticework is quaint. Mosquitoes, however, also like this spot

The wind howls through the night, covering everything in a layer of sand. The sand gets into every fold of clothes and skin, into my eyes and ears. It seeps into my sleeping bag and embeds itself in my hair.

Opposite: The water taxi.

Below: Another campsite.

and I am plagued all night. They are amazingly tenacious little things – finding their way inside my mosquito net somehow. It's also very hot. I don't have a good rest.

A man arrives, walking along the bank, on his way to his *shamba* in the morning. Soon joined by a second, they are full of questions and conversation. When I scrawl '92 *dias*' (92 days) in the sand, they are in absolute awe. They walk around and around my kayak pointing and exclaiming. I can't afford more time, so I begin my preparations for departure. They stand two metres from me now, as I write, and watch intently. It is not bad-mannered, just simple interest and curiosity and it is my

reaction that determines the mood. I am relaxed and so are they. They watch as I pack until every last item is in the kayak. As crocodiles are territorial, I look carefully at the water before I get in, then I move away fast.

Beyond the channels, the mountains on the northern Malawi side look stunning in their various shades of purple and grey. I marvel yet again at how the river can surprise me, for I felt confident that the flood plain would dominate everything right to the coast. Here, even though I am in a floodplain, the mountains give it a completely different feel. The river flows fairly fast and I cover good distance arriving at Sena as the sun is beginning to set around 17h00. Mutarara on the north bank is joined to Sena by a spectacular rail and road bridge called the Dona Ana Bridge. Built in 1934, it stretches 3.7 kilometres over 34 spans – the longest railway bridge in Africa. Several spans were dropped by the Rhodesian SAS back in the '70s, and it was not repaired until quite recently. I stop in at Mutarara at a quiet, old-style trading store and buy some provisions. The people here are all exceptionally friendly and polite and are in no way intrusive. I leave my kayak unattended when I go off to shop in total confidence. These are good rural people. The trading store also has a beer dispensing section. It is not very busy and, frankly, I'm quite glad to see that. Alcohol can wreak great havoc in areas such as these. I notice the bottle opener right away. It is made from a 14.5-mm Russian machine gun shell. I'm so glad these damned wars are all over now. May all the cartridges of the world be turned into bottle openers!

The young assistant in the shop is mulatto. Exceptionally attractive, she is the product of such a fascinating history on this river. What exotic blood courses through her veins? In these parts – once the Portuguese had wrestled control of the trade from the Arabs – some fascinating people and stories emerged. Much like the trekboers of the early South African Dutch settlements, or the mountain men of North America, the Portuguese spawned a group of men called *Sertanejos*. These were people who were beyond the control of the Portuguese administration, as they were in Mozambique as individuals. Many of them took local wives and completely immersed themselves in the ways of the tribal African people. Others married into the local communities but retained a certain degree of Portuguese culture. Many of them, over a number of years, came to control vast estates in this very area. Here before me stands this pretty girl who displays all the best qualities of all the strains of her genetic heritage.

I take shelter on an island. It's treeless and the sand is blasting across the beach. I have little choice, though, as darkness is upon me. I drag my kayak up onto the beach to create a windbreak. By tying a ground sheet over the kayak and creating a lean-to, I'm able to make myself a really comfortable home. As long as the wind blows the mosquitoes will not appear, but it will drop in the night and this is a perfect spot for mozzies. I enjoy the freedom from them while I can.

Now that I have only a few days to go my focus has shifted to 'getting there' – the very thing I have wanted to avoid. But reality says I need to have a specific pick-up time for Annie to work logistics around – so it's 'paddle, baby, paddle'.

The flow of the river has slowed down now and at an altitude of only 29 metres at tonight's camp it is likely to slow almost to a standstill as I progress even deeper into the delta. The going is really tough, made more difficult by the many channels and the headwind.

Even though I am physically and mentally struggling now, I still notice the beauty and the variety. The line of hills gradually beginning to emerge on the north bank masks the spot where the Shire River runs into the Zambezi. I paddle up to the confluence late in the afternoon and, pointing my kayak towards the Shire, I just drift for a while. This is a very historic place and I am quietened by the sense of all those who had gone before me. Firstly, it was a route used by Arab traders for almost 1 000 years. Then the Portuguese traders followed and finally Livingstone discovered it as a navigable route for the English-speaking world. Considering British designs on Africa at the time it was a very important discovery, because it gave motorised boats access up the Zambezi, along the Shire and into what is now called Lake Malawi.

But while all of this was underway still another issue was brought to the attention of the world. Although slavery had been outlawed by

I notice the bottle opener right away. It is made from a 14.5-mm Russian machine gun shell. I'm so glad these damned wars are all over now. May all the cartridges of the world be turned into bottle openers!

Opposite, top: Dona Ana Rail Bridge, Sena.
Opposite, middle and bottom: Mutarara Trading Store.

the Portuguese in 1836, the trade still flourished. The Zambezi and the Shire rivers made up a crucial part of this awful practice. In order to avoid British gunboats that patrolled the area of the Zambezi Delta, slavers took to travelling inland with their human cargo. Up the Shire, across Lake Malawi, and out of the unpatrolled parts of the Swahili coast for eventual trade in Brazil and the Mascarenes. But as pressure on the seas began to make trade in slaves off-shore more difficult, so another previously steady, but small market opened up. Many tribes from the interior, including the Kololo from Barotseland and the Matabele, were eager to buy slaves – especially women. It was, in fact, this trade in slaves that Livingstone stumbled upon, and it was his direct efforts that did such a lot to bring it to an end. Even so, the practice was still occurring into the 1880s.

By the time the sun is sinking low, so are my spirits. I have not got as far as I wished. I've paddled for what seems like a very, very long way only to move very little on the map. The crossings back and forth in the tangled channels and the slowing of the river are taking their toll. I try hard to re-adjust my mind and not to allow disappointment to weigh down my spirits, but it is very hard; the heat, fires, headwind and channels make for very, very tough going.

All day I have been disturbed by the fires. Reed burning is widespread here at this time of the year as people clear lands for planting. But the damage to the river banks and the erosion is very easy to see, with large chunks of the bank falling away into the water all around me as I go along, like great icebergs breaking from a glacier. Ash and bits of blackened grass rain down on me from the heavens. It is in my eyes and ears and I keep on swilling out my mouth to clear it of the taste and discomfort.

I'm forced by fading light to stop in an area that has been burnt. Picking my way through the blackened ground, I think of the hippos I saw today. They were a lot noisier than on previous days and I guess it's because they, too, are disturbed and hungry. I'm amazed that such large creatures can survive at all under such conditions.

Mosquitoes are becoming more and more of a problem – a combination of the time of the year and the area I'm now in. One of the first proper attempts that the Portuguese made to settle families in Mozambique started here in 1680. Seventy-eight men, women and children arrived and settled along the lower Zambezi, but almost all of them died of malaria or some other disease. A British expedition in 1823, led by a man called Owen, lost every one of its European members to malaria. Livingstone's wife, Mary, also succumbed to malaria in this area.

I take great care in preparing a place to sleep. No matter that it is ash-covered and filthy, I have decided that I will have a great night and spend time making sure that I'm as comfortable as possible. I carefully hook branches out of my way. I make a neat rail on which to dry my clothes, and as I create order, so my depression begins to lift and I enjoy a good meal and a cup of tea.

I start off with the hills on my left and move into the channels of the floodplain. Today, however, it's easier to follow a good flow and soon the hills are behind me. Everywhere the reed banks have been burnt or are burning, and for a while the smoke creates a pall that cuts out the sky. I stop for a break at a *mokoro*-maker's home. He is busy working and patching an existing *mokoro*. Alongside it is a brand new one, being constructed to match the first. It's massive – so large that he is able to sit sideways inside the *mokoro* and still wield an adze. The tree must have been huge, and I wonder where it came from.

A short distance away is the ruin of an early settler's home, so I walk over and take a look. This place is very old but must have been gracious in its day. It has big, high windows and a large entrance hall. In the thick wall of what was once the kitchen is a hive of bees and two owls. They are startled by my appearance and fly off but I get a good look at them. They are barn owls – such magnificent creatures. They leave me with treasure – four of their feathers – which I know Annie will love.

I bid the *mokoro*-makers farewell but it is not long before storm clouds are building and the wind picks up to gale force. Fortunately, the river is once again flowing quite strongly and the current helps me enormously, though a strong headwind negates some of this. The going is hard. The wind creates waves and a chop on the water and soon I am soaked. Fine black dust – ash from the fires – gets into my eyes and nose, sticking and clogging there because of my wet skin. It is very unpleasant. I wish it would just pour with rain. Further north it looks like it is raining but here there is none. Even so, I convince myself that it makes for a pleasant change from the channel-paddling through flat, fairly immobile water of yesterday and earlier today.

Soon there is once again beautiful forest on the sides of the river. The south bank, as I approach Chupanga, is very high. Chupanga is the place where Mary Livingstone died. I get there just in time to make camp and I do so under a massive wild fig tree in the garden of what was once the town water works, I think. There is a deep well, which, amazingly, has fish in it. I see them swimming around when I look in from above. Looking at the ruins of what was once a noisy, functional village makes me think about Africa, Zimbabwe, and empires in general.

Carving a giant dugout.

The farmhouses, or at least the remains of those I have seen along the river, were fully functional farming enterprises in 1974. The people who owned them were driven from the land and nothing replaced them. In Zimbabwe, farmers are being driven from the land. I hope that in 25 years' time those beautiful, functioning economic units don't look like these that I see in Mozambique now. I fear, however, that many of them will remain derelict.

The same thing has happened over and over throughout history. The Romans, the Greeks, the British – wherever there has been an empire with a colonial approach it has eventually succumbed to pressures and collapsed. Where it does, the local people, previously treated as underlings and never given appropriate education, are unable to continue. They probably also have no wish to continue the programs instituted by their former masters. In a way, whites in Africa fitted the 'empire' mould quite well. They never properly integrated into Africa. A strong 'them and us' attitude prevailed, just as occurred in previous empires. A separateness and an elitism has maintained itself for generations. As is the case with all such occupations, it eventually has to change.

By embracing Africa – like the *Sertanejos* – by becoming completely at ease and at one with Africa, everyone's security is guaranteed. As long as people sit on the fence, deciding whether to stay or go, the

By the time the sun is sinking low, so are my spirits ... I've paddled for what seems like a very, very long way only to move very little on the map.

risks will remain high. We need to commit to Africa and be African. Nothing then will be able to – or will want to – drive us from our shared continent.

Day 96. I am up and packed before the sun has risen, specifically to give myself time to explore Chupanga and try to locate Mary Livingstone's grave. Walking along the bank I soon find a pathway, little used, and I follow it towards the town. There are no signs of people except for a few tracks. I find the overgrown remains of an old road so I follow it towards the church steeple that now peeps up between the trees. A woman carrying an empty water container is walking down towards me. I smile and greet to reassure her, for I can see the momentary concern in her eyes. She is heavily pregnant, yet still she will collect water, lift it to her head, and carry it home.

Slowly I gain a view of the church. There is no roof on it but it remains a handsome structure. I walk towards what looks like a graveyard. It is all tangled in undergrowth but I find the ancient gate. It is locked, but two of the metal bars have been removed so I climb through. As I wander around, picking my way through the undergrowth, looking at all the gravestones and little crosses, I think about all the hopes and enthusiasms which lie buried here. Most of the tombstones are in Portuguese but there are some in English. Many of those buried here died of fever. Mary Moffat Livingstone's grave is marked by a tall metal tombstone on which there is an inscription. It is written in Portuguese but it is clear that this is where she lies. I wonder about the life she led. She was only 42 years old when she died on 27 April 1862. She had borne David Livingstone six children. Three of them died. She followed him on many perilous journeys. But her failing health prevented the final reunion with her husband from lasting for long. She died just three months after she was reunited with him, after not having seen him for four years. Out of 18 years of marriage, the two were together less than half that time. She died lonely and sadly, because at the end of her life she was an alcoholic. I say a prayer for her and then I turn and say one for all the souls who are represented by the little mounds and crosses.

I find a section where local people have begun to use the graveyard for their own dead. So here at last, spanning several hundred years, people from all different classes, races, cultures and language groups lie together in one place. It's quite ironic for I have no doubt that some of the people in this graveyard would never have believed that they would lie buried in such a place in such company. Bless them all.

The entire town of Chupanga is derelict and appears to be abandoned, yet there are signs that this is changing. Outside the church, little benches made from poles mark the spot where church services are still held under a lovely shady tree. I wonder where the people are. One building has doors fitted, and when I explore I find that it is in the process of rehabilitation. The floor has been redone, the walls patched, and it's nearly complete. Still another area is being cleaned up by a group of five men. This is good positive stuff for Mozambique, which is well on its way to recovery.

The river carries me out of a treeline into reed and then grass banks. Trees and reeds remain but trees in particular become less prolific. Tall coconut palms periodically grace the shoreline. Stately and, in most instances, solitary, they are by far the tallest of the palms. I pass *mekoro* moving upstream in the afternoon. They carry passengers and goods and are coming from the town of Marromeu.

Rounding a bend I see tall towers spewing smoke. There are warehouses and other buildings – a significant infrastructure. It's late so I begin to look for a place to stop. Ahead of me are four or five hippos. There's a *mokoro* on its way upstream and off on the north bank a group of five women are collecting water. The backdrop to this very African scene is an enormous sugar mill!

I am pleased for Mozambique, happy that they have managed to get investors' confidence to such a level that such developments are occurring even in very remote areas. I'm also a little sad for the river, for it immediately reduces its wilderness. But it is a good thing for the country and the people. I clamber up onto the bank.

As I am having my supper the hippos arrive to check if they can graze here where I am camped amongst the reeds. I shine my torch and talk to them but they are not immediately persuaded to leave. With just days before I get to the sea and after more than three months of handling such hazards, I'm not keen to be flattened by a hippo within sight of a sugar mill!

The stars through the leaves over my head are bright and clear, the atmosphere cleaned out after last night's rain. The wind is still and it's a good time to be quiet. Tomorrow I paddle what should be the final stretch to the sea. I'm excited and cautious at the same time. I must not let my guard down until it is definitely over.

I think about what I have achieved in this time.

A certain inner peace. I know who I am and what I am made of. I am comfortable with myself. I have sought and found a greater clarity of spirit. God is great.

I have understood so much more clearly the darkness which lies within. That in wanting people to be as wounded, crushed and hurt as I had been through their actions I, too, was in darkness. That my anger was as evil as the evil I had suffered. The ugliness, hypocrisy, lack of integrity, glibness and callousness that I so abominated in them, was also a reflection of myself. In a way, I was them. These people that I so despised – so close to me in family ties – were my shadow. That rather than repel and fight, I had to embrace with all my very soul. For in so doing, the darkness in us all is obliterated by the light.

Opposite, top: There is no roof on the church in Chupanga, but it remains a handsome structure.

This page, top and middle: If only these buildings could talk.

This page, bottom: I begin seeing dhows now that have come upstream from the sea. It is very exciting.

I have thought about my family. I love my children very, very much. I love Rory very much and want that to be clear to him now as well. I love Annie. I understand the free spirit inside myself better now and it is no longer caged.

I have rested my mind (a bit) and worked my body hard. It feels good and I want it to stay that way.

I have given myself order and focus and I have achieved.

I have understood that it is not important that people know about one's achievements. It is nice when they do, but the greatest acknowledgement needs to be from oneself. I allow myself to accept that I have done well.

I have understood the journeys others have gone on while I have paddled the river: Annie's journey, Jess, James and Rory's journeys. The journeys of our close family, of our friends, many of whom I didn't realise were the friends they clearly are.

I have paddled, rowed, swum or walked all the way from the source of the Zambezi, and tomorrow, God willing, I will paddle into the sea. No one else has ever done this.

I have had the chance to feel utterly exhausted and totally self-reliant. To feel depression and elation. Anger and peace. I thank God for this journey – it has been quite long!

Day 98. Excited and very keen to get started on the final leg, I am ready to go at sunrise. It is a magnificent morning, the air still and the water helping with a good current. There appears to be a sign of tidal activity here and, if that is the case, then the wash is probably the tide. I pass a few *mekoro* and a tug and barge going upstream. An enormous flock of open-billed storks, interspersed with a few sacred ibises and reed cormorants, stands almost motionless on a mud bank. I decide to get out and explore but it is like quick-sand and I quickly withdraw. This is definitely a tidal area.

Soon I am at a spot that I believe is just around the point from the little harbour of Chinde. I decide to stop and wait here, because Annie should be arriving in a small charter plane at 14h00 and it is only 11h00 now. I want to share the arrival with her. I watch the water and, by 13h30, can see that the tide has turned and is now flowing into the river. Cautious lest it becomes too strong a wash, I decide to

call and see if Annie is still in the air. She answers, sounding distraught. She is still on the ground in Johannesburg! The weather has not permitted them to leave. I try to cheer her up but we decide that I should paddle at least to the harbour – short of the ocean itself. That must be shared. Annie will try again tomorrow and, weather permitting, should be here just after two in the afternoon.

I am disappointed, of course, but refuse to let this set me back. I start to paddle immediately as the incoming tide is clearly very strong already. The going gets tougher as I go. By the time I reach the bend in the river making the entry to the final lagoon leading to the sea, the water is pushing back upstream at an incredible rate. I am paddling now as hard as I can and am only inching forwards. It is like a very strong river and, if I hesitate for a moment, it kicks the nose sideways and washes me back upstream very far indeed.

Up ahead of me I see something protruding from the water. It's not too long before I realise it is the mast of an old river steamer. Then, partially hidden by the mangroves, I see another wreck. This one is sufficiently visible to allow me to see what it is. These are the sad remains of an empire's dreams. Starting in 1878, the British established a fleet of paddle steamers on the Zambezi. These ran cargo up and down the Zambezi, using the Shire River to access Lake Malawi and Nyasaland (Malawi). The British leased Chinde from the Portuguese between 1892 and 1922. In that year a huge tornado struck Chinde, devastating the little settlement and wrecking no fewer than 10 ships. These are the remains of two of them.

I paddle under incredibly difficult conditions now. Tiring, I try holding on to a mangrove tree for a break, but the wash takes the canoe sideways immediately and I am forced to continue. My arms and shoulders are burning – the muscles screaming for relief. I force myself to ignore it and push myself harder. Slowly, slowly I creep forward and then, brief relief, as an outcrop of mangroves blocks the tidal flow a little. Here, for about 20 metres, I can paddle more easily, though to do so means I stay stationary. I use it to catch my breath.

Then around the barrier I go and into what I can now see is the final stretch. Up ahead of me is a gathering of little vessels. These are wrecks, and rusted machinery lies everywhere. I pull into a little cove, to the enormous relief of my body. A small crowd immediately gathers and I give my customary greeting and explanation. Fortunately, one of the men who arrives can speak some English. I find out that the airstrip is a 30-minute walk from here and that there is no 'hotel'. The pilot and Annie will be camping with me, I'm afraid. I am very tired.

I walk in to the village to try and arrange various things for Annie's arrival tomorrow. Not very successfully, though. I also try to find a spot to camp where there will not be lots and lots of people. This, too, proves to be impossible, so I make myself as comfortable as I can right next to my kayak, accept the curious crowd as a feature of my environment, and watch the goings-on as the evening progresses.

My walk has shown me that the first breakers of the ocean lie a few kilometres away so that is what I will cover tomorrow when Annie arrives.

Then around the barrier I go and into what I can now see is the final stretch. Up ahead of me is a gathering of little vessels. These are wrecks, and rusted machinery lies everywhere.

Below: The sad remains of a British paddle steamer.

I am very tired, and now have the challenge of finding water for my cooking and washing. I decide to erect a shelter first and do so under the watchful eye of my onlookers. I chat to them, telling them everything I am doing and what everything is for. I know they only partially understand, but it is the gesture that counts and they seem to enjoy it. Much chatter accompanies my comments.

Eventually I need to rest, so I ask the English speaker to ask them if they wouldn't mind leaving now as I would like to relax. I do so politely and, just as politely, they leave. Not five minutes later two people arrive bearing a container of drinking water for me. As always, I am deeply grateful.

At about 01h00, a vessel arrives – dhow-like in its construction. It has a large load of sacks. They busily unload it, peering through the darkness in my direction. I watch them for a while. I sleep well, hoping, of course, that the morning brings with it clear weather and an aeroplane.

Day 99. The sailors are back early – clearing out and then repairing their vessels. One of the group comes over to me and I realise that we saw each other two days back near Luavo. Back then I had a quick but good chat with them. They were under sail going upstream but battling the river current so they passed by quite slowly at the time. Now they are pleased to see me and, I think, are quite proud to show the others that they know me

I pack up slowly – what a luxury – and then paddle with the outgoing tide towards the sea. This afternoon when I am with Annie the tide will be coming in again and, after yesterday's experience, I don't want too far to travel with her. I walk and paddle until I find a spot under a grove of coconut palms. I decide that if we are going to spend the night this will be as good a place as I can find. I am afraid that we will have lots of company but there is little I can do about that. I eventually make contact with a German aid organisation doctor. She is a Mozambican by the name of Sonja, and she is very happy to help me. I arrange to hire a tractor and trailer to collect Annie and the pilot, return us all to the aircraft – probably tomorrow – and allow me to leave my kayak at her premises until we can collect it. What a scoop!

I collect my kayak, drag it to the camping spot, and am surrounded by a large crowd of kids. They are just curious but it does become trying after a while. I hope that by just sitting quietly they will eventually get bored and drift off. However, when they see Annie, I'm afraid it will be like a magnet, so I hope she is prepared for the multitudes.

I have waited longer than expected so, using what is almost the last of my battery power, I call. Annie is only in Pietersburg! South Africa! It is 14h30, the weather is not good, and they have been unable to fly any further. I definitely won't see her today. What a disappointment. What makes it even worse, is that I have now established contact with Chris, who is transporting my kayak back to SA. He is upstream in Marromeu now. I must get my kayak onto the ferry tomorrow morning at 06h00. It will be three days before another ferry will run. Chris cannot wait in Marromeu that long, and one cannot get to Chinde in a vehicle. I am forced to make some logistical decisions that I don't like but I now have no choice. I must paddle out into the ocean now. The timing is bad. The tide is well on its way in again and running fast, like a train. The wind is blowing hard and I will be battling directly into it. The river is not giving herself up without a struggle! But this is my chance and I must use it. I quickly take all the equipment I won't need out of the boat. Then, with assistance from the multitudes, I put into the waves.

I paddle hard, making good headway in the lighter craft, but still the going is tough. But my excitement is rising now and I am feeling good. I am bitterly disappointed that I cannot share this moment with Annie, but I have decided that I will not empty the water I collected from the source into the ocean now. That I will share with her, come hell or high water!

The mangroves begin to disappear behind me. I move slowly against the wash out into the very centre of this massive river mouth. A tug towing a barge appears on my left and travels towards the south. Now I really am excited. Over on my left I can see breakers rolling up against the northern point. In the water ahead I see what looks like a line in the water. On the river side the water is somehow smoother. Then there is a distinct foamy line in the waves with odd bits of reed and brush floating at this point. On the other side of the line the water is choppy and broken. Clearly this is where the two great forces push against one another for the last time: the river and now the sea. The pressure of the currents from both is creating this visible rip. I paddle onto it and, with real excitement, through it. Then, here I am. Is this the ocean? Where does the river end and the ocean begin? I paddle directly out to sea. The swells get even bigger and then, at a point where it can no longer be debated, I stop and turn sideways. Looking north and south, the bluffs are now west of me. The river mouth is difficult to distinguish against the landfall that merges into itself. The sun is low on the horizon and I am sitting in my kayak in the Indian Ocean. I say a little prayer of thanks. I think of Annie and, in my mind and heart, will her to share this moment with me. But such is the nature of a solo – one is alone no matter whether one is close to death or experiencing the greatest beauty or joy.

The river mouth is difficult to distinguish against the landfall that merges into itself. The sun is low on the horizon and I am sitting in my kayak in the Indian Ocean. I say a little prayer of thanks.

I look at this mass of water that surrounds me now and I think of the incredible privilege I have been given. I look back towards the river mouth and I watch the water. It flows into the sea and gradually evaporates into the atmosphere. Then it rains and replenishes the earth, refilling the great underground water resources. It bubbles up out of the ground in some places, and one of those is near a place called Kaleen Hill in northwest Zambia, where a mighty river called the Zambezi is born.

I sit in my kayak with the ocean and breathe deeply. Then I turn back towards the mouth and begin paddling west. I have paddled the mighty Zambezi, and after 99 days my journey is done.

Postscript

Two days later Annie arrived after an epic journey of her own. We walked as far along the point as we could and then quietly knelt down next to the water. Each of us carried our little containers filled with water, which we had so carefully collected at the source. Now with tears welling in our eyes we poured our treasure out together. The water from her container spilled free and entwined with that from mine before striking the salty water of the ocean. In an instant it was gone – a part of the great surging mass of river and sea – once again a part of the cycle of life. We held each other for a long time.

My Annie arriving at Chinde!

A RECORD OF CANOE OR SIMILAR CRAFT EXPEDITIONS DESCENDING THE ZAMBEZI

Never before this expedition has the Zambezi River been descended in its entirety from source to sea.

Only a few really long boat trips have been made on the Zambezi. David Livingstone made several trips in dugouts and steam launches in the late 1850s and early 1860s. All of these covered the stretch between Tete in Mozambique and the sea.

His longest voyage was undertaken between October and November of 1860. On this one he travelled with his brother Charles and Dr John Kirk in dugouts, starting not far downstream of the confluence of the Sebungwe River and the Zambezi. They had an accident in the Kebrabasa rapids, lost their dugouts and almost their lives, and were forced to walk the rest of the way to Tete.

Sometime in the early 1880s Mr F. Monks (known in the colonies as Mr F. Foster) in an absolutely epic voyage travelled alone in a dugout canoe from a point 32 kilometres downstream of the confluence with the Gwaai River (In present-day Zimbabwe) to Quelimane on the Mozambique coast.

In 1903 Harold de Laresoe entered the river some 40 kilometres below the Gwaai. His expedition, consisting of himself and 11 companions, intended to navigate the middle and lower sections of the Zambezi. He was aware that this had not been achieved before and that even renowned explorers such as Livingstone and Gibbons had failed to achieve this. But he, like Livingstone before him, believed that the river could be made navigable almost throughout the distance from the Gwaai River to the coast.

They travelled in two boats – a six-metre steel craft that could be dismantled and carried, and a small wooden boat for rough usage. Other than portaging the sections at Kariba, they successfully descended the river, reaching Chinde on the coast on 7 October 1903 after two months on the river.

More recently other expeditions have followed. Three of these involved canoes.

The first trip – 4 July 1968 to 24 August – was made by three Rhodesian policemen. In the report of their trip it is noted:

Despite many claims to the contrary, our research revealed that this was the first time anyone had travelled by canoe from Kariba to the Indian Ocean. Others have made similar journeys in different types of craft, but they have either started at Chirundu or finished at Marromeu.

The policemen paddled in a modified Canadian-type canoe and had a police escort in a motor boat on the Rhodesian leg due to the security situation.

The second canoe trip from Kariba to the sea was made in August/September 1970 by Malcolm Cambell, Vic Naude and Chris Hamilton.

The third voyage made from Kariba to the ocean in recent times was undertaken by Steve Edwards in 1971. This was the first time that anyone had paddled this section in a canoe, solo. Steve had entered the Zambezi via the Umfuli and the Sanyati Rivers in Rhodesia, accompanied initially by others. However, from Kariba (7 June) he found himself alone, arriving at Chinde on 19 September.

Due to wars and the security problems in Rhodesia and Mozambique, the lower part of the river was not accessible until the early 1990s. After this, however, the war back in Angola increased to a fever pitch, making access to the upper reaches of the river impossible.

In 1998 Paul Templar led an expedition in an attempt to become the first to ever descend the mighty Zambezi by canoe. Sadly, the Angolan stretch was impossible to access due to the war and so their expedition started at Chavuma in Zambia. What makes this expedition so incredible is that Paul paddled with only one arm – the other having been lost in a hippo attack above Victoria Falls just two years earlier.

My expedition was therefore the first in history to start at the source of the Zambezi and to travel the entire length. I was unsupported – with no land party following my progress, unsponsored and, other than three days in Batoka Gorge where I travelled by raft with three others to help me portage the raft, entirely solo.

Abbreviations

ANC	African National Congress – former South African anti-apartheid liberation movement and current ruling party
DRC	Democratic Republic of Congo
FAA	Armed Forces of Angola – official Angolan military created through the integration of MPLA and Unita
Fapla	People's Armed Forces for the Liberation of Angola – originally the armed wing of the MPLA movement, later becoming the country's official armed forces until integration with Unita
Frelimo	Front for the Liberation of Mozambique – former Mozambican liberation movement and current ruling party
GPS	Global positioning system – a portable electronic device using satellite communication to plot bearings and positions
MDC	Movement for Democratic Change – Zimbabwean opposition party
MK	Umkhonto we Sizwe – former military wing of the ANC
MPLA	Popular Movement for the Liberation of Angola – Angolan political party that has ruled the country since 1975
NCO	Non-commissioned officer
Renamo	Mozambican National Resistance – former rebel movement opposing Frelimo, now a political party
SAS	Special Air Service – Rhodesian Special Forces unit
Swapo	South West African People's Organisation – former Namibian liberation movement and current ruling party
Unita	National Union for the Total Independence of Angola – Angolan opposition party, formerly a rebel movement opposing the MPLA
Zanla	Zimbabwe African National Liberation Army – armed wing of Zanu during the struggle against white rule
Zanu	Zimbabwe African National Union – former liberation movement and current Zimbabwean ruling party (now called Zanu-PF)
Zipra	Zimbabwe People's Revolutionary Army – armed wing of the political movement Zapu (Zimbabwe African People's Union) during the struggle against white rule

REFERENCES

David Livingstone – The Dark Interior, Oliver Ransford (John Murray Publishing, 1978)

Livingstone's River – A History of the Zambezi Expedition 1858–1664, George Martelli
(Chatto and Windus, 1970)

Management of River Basins and Dams – The Zambezi River Basin, M. J. Tumbare (editor)
(AA Balkema, 2000)

Narrative of an Expedition to the Zambesi and its tributaries, David and Charles Livingstone
(Nonsuch Publishing, 2005)

Wilderness called Kariba, The. The Wildlife and Natural History of Lake Kariba, Dale Kenmuir
(Mardon Printers, 1978)

Zambezi – Journey of a River, Michael Main (Southern Book Publishers, 1998)

Zambezi Odyssey – A Record of Adventure on a Great River, S. J. Edwards, (TV Bulpin, 1974)

First published in 2007 by Struik Publishers
(a division of New Holland Publishing (South Africa) (Pty) Ltd)

New Holland Publishing is a member of Johnnic Commmunications Ltd

Garfield House
86–88 Edgware Road
W2 2EA London
United Kingdom
www.newhollandpublishers.com

Cornelis Struik House
80 McKenzie Street
Cape Town 8001
South Africa
www.struik.co.za

14 Aquatic Drive
Frenchs Forest
NSW 2086
Australia

218 Lake Road
Northcote
Auckland
New Zealand

Copyright © 2007 in published edition: Struik Publishers
Copyright © 2007 in text and photographs: Mike Boon
Copyright © 2007 in maps: Struik Publishers

ISBN 978 1 77007 484 2
1 3 5 7 9 10 8 6 4 2

Publishing managers: Dominique le Roux and Felicity Nyikadzino Berold
Managing editor: Lesley Hay-Whitton
Project co-ordinator: Samantha Menezes-Fick
Designer and cartographer: Daniele Michelini, Hirt & Carter Cape (Pty) Ltd
Editor: Russel Brownlee
Proofreaders: Anthea de Villiers and Jacqueline de Vos

Reproduction by Hirt & Carter Cape (Pty) Ltd
Printed and bound by Tien Wah Press (Pte) Ltd

All rights reserved. No part of this publication may be reproduced, stored in a retrieval system
or transmitted, in any form or by any means, electronic, mechanical, photocopying or otherwise,
without the prior written permission of the publishers and copyright holders.

Democratic Republic of Congo

11° 30 South
(Near death experience)

● Kalene Hill

● Mwinilunga

● Luena

● Cazombo

● Caripande

Chavuma ● — *Chinyingi suspension bridge and pont*
● Zambezi

Angola

● Lukulu

Zambia

Mu

Lusaka ◉

Zamb

Chirundu ● Va

● Senanga

LAKE
KARIBA

● Karib

● Sioma Falls

● Mutemwa Lodge

Fothergills ▶

● Sesheke

Katima Mulilo ●

● Schuckmansburg

● Binga

Kazungula ●

Victoria
Falls

Botswana

Batoka Gorge

Zim

Namibia

DAY	DATE	PLACE
1	2 June	Source of the Zambezi
2	3 June	The journey begins
7	7 June	Waterfall
8	9 June	The Narrows and the near death experience
12	13 June	Capture at Cazombo
13	14 June	Flown to Luena by military
18	18 June	Back in Cazombo
21	22 June	Border crossing from Angola to Zambia
23	23 June	Chavuma Falls and Andy
27	27 June	Lukulu
28	28 June	Mirimba musicians camp
33	4 July	Senanga
35	6 July	Sioma Falls
38	9 July	Mutemwa camp
46	17 Ju